Poverty and Disability

The Disability and
Inclusive Development Series

Poverty and Disability

**Edited by Tanya Barron
and Jabulani Manombe Ncube**

Leonard Cheshire Disability

The Leonard Cheshire Disability
and Inclusive Development Centre

Leonard Cheshire Disability
66 South Lambeth Road
London SW8 1RL
United Kingdom
www.LCDisability.org/international

Notes on the Editors

Tanya Barron is the International Director of Leonard Cheshire Disability. She is a Senior Associate Member of St Antony's, Oxford and has worked in disability and development since 1986. She was the Chair of the UNICEF NGO Committee in Geneva for five years. Tanya serves on the board of the Global Partnership for Disability and Development, a World Bank Initiative.

Jabulani Manombe Ncube has been active in disability and development for 31 years in a variety of roles in his native southern Africa, East Africa and outside the continent, including consultancy work over the past 17 years. He holds a Masters from the University of East Anglia in Norwich, UK. He also led the international programme work while at Action on Disability and Development (ADD, UK).

Notes on the Contributors

Javed Abidi is a noted disability rights activist. With a degree in journalism from the US, he returned home to pursue a career in India only to face discrimination because of his disability. He has previously worked at the Rajiv Gandhi Foundation, where he headed the disability unit. In 1994, he founded the Disability Rights Group to work specifically on cross-disability issues, in particular the drafting and passing of the Disability Act 1995. Javed was instrumental in setting up the National Centre for Promotion of Employment for Disabled People (NCPEDP) in 1996 and has been its Director since 1997.

Rosangela Berman-Bieler is a Brazilian journalist, publisher and disability rights advocate who has served as an expert to the United Nations on disability issues, representing Latin America. Founder of the Independent Living Movement in Brazil, she is also a founding member and former president of the Brazilian Organization of Persons with Physical Disabilities (ONEDEF), Honorary President of the Center for Independent Living of Rio de Janeiro (CVIRJ), and

founder Director of the Inter-American Institute on Disability (IID).
Rosangela was previously Rehabilitation International Deputy
Vice President for Latin America and is the editor of numerous publica-
tions on disability.

Peter Coleridge has focused on the inclusion of disabled people in
development programmes in the Middle East, Asia and Africa,
working for NGOs, the UN and as a freelance consultant. He is the
author of the book *Disability, Liberation and Development*, as well
as other books and articles arguing for the inclusion of disabled people
in mainstream development.

Maria Kett, PhD, is Assistant Director of the Leonard Cheshire
Disability and Inclusive Development Centre, based at University
College London. Maria leads the research team at the centre working
in the field of disability and international development, particularly
in disaster and conflict-affected countries. She has a special interest
in disability-related issues in situations of disasters and conflicts.
Maria is Chair of the IDDC Task Group on Conflict and Emergencies
and honorary lecturer at the Centre for International Health and
Development (CIHD), UCL.

Enzo Martinelli has 20 years' experience working in international
development in Italy and the UK. His expertise includes microenterprise
development, disability issues and human rights promotion. Enzo
has worked as ACRA's Regional Manager and for PLAN International
UK as Programme Funding Manager for child-focused programmes
worldwide. He previously worked for Leonard Cheshire Disability
as International Resource Development Manager and chaired the IDDC
Livelihoods Task Group. He currently serves as Director of Fundraising
at Panos International.

Charlotte McClain-Nhlapo originally trained as a human rights
lawyer. She has worked on child protection for UNICEF and
represented the National Human Rights Institutions at the UN during
the development of a Convention for People with Disabilities.
She has been appointed twice to the South African Human Rights

Commission. Charlotte currently works at the World Bank in Washington, DC as Senior Operations Specialist. She has written widely on human rights issues, serves on a number of community boards and is committed to social justice.

Roy Mersland has extensive international management, consulting, and research experience within the field of microfinance in more than 20 countries in Latin America, Asia, Africa, and Europe. He organises his own consulting practice (www.microfinance.no) and holds a research position at the University of Agder in Norway. His research and consulting topics cover corporate governance in MFIs, self-help microfinance systems and microfinance in relation to persons with disabilities. Roy has recently assisted the Norwegian Association of the Disabled in their efforts to increase microfinance outreach to persons with disabilities.

Daniel Mont, PhD, is a senior economist with the Disability and Development Team of the World Bank, working on issues of disability measurement and inclusive economic development. Previously, Daniel worked at the US Congressional Office and as an assistant professor in the policy analysis and management department at Cornell University. Amongst his current projects he is working on developing indicators for monitoring the implementation of the UN Convention on the Rights of Persons with Disabilities.

Bev Moodie is a social entrepreneur (Ashoka Fellow), personal and business development consultant, facilitator and author, who for the past 19 years has helped thousands of people from all walks of life tap into their own inherent entrepreneurial potential and start their own successful enterprises, quickly and easily. She has worked in many countries and diverse environments including corporate, community development, disability and government.

Bob Ransom is Executive Director of the Ethiopian Center for Disability and Development (ECDD) in Addis Ababa, an NGO that promotes inclusive development. He has spent most of his professional life working in African countries, promoting the development of vocational training and employment opportunities for youth and adults with disabilities. Bob served the International Labour Organization (ILO) of the UN for 20 years and has also served as Director of African Programs and International Programs for Goodwill Industries of America, the largest employer of persons with disabilities in North America.

Roger C. Riddell has been actively involved in development for more than 30 years, including 15 years as a research fellow at the Overseas Development Institute in London and 5 years as International Director of Christian Aid. He has worked for developing country governments, the private sector and NGOs, and with leading bilateral and multilateral aid agencies and international institutions. Roger is the author of two previous books on foreign aid, including *Foreign Aid Reconsidered*.

Balakrishna Venkatesh is a freelance consultant and trainer in disability and development issues. His work has taken him all over the world as trainer, consultant and trustee, attending conferences and workshops and co-facilitating courses. His experience as a development worker with ADD led him to establish ADD India in 1989. Balakrishna is currently working to promote the implementation of the United Nations Convention on the Rights of People with Disabilities at the village level.

List of Abbreviations and Acronyms

AAA	Accra Agenda for Action
ADA	Americans with Disabilities Act
ADD	Action on Disability and Development
AIDS	Acquired Immune Deficiency Syndrome
AMFIU	Association of Microfinance Institutions of Uganda
APPT	Alleviating Poverty through Peer Training (Cambodia)
ASCA	Accumulating Savings and Credit Association
AusAID	Australian Agency for International Development
CBM	Christian Blind Mission
CBO	Community-Based Organisation
CBR	Community-Based Rehabilitation
CBRP	Community Based Rehabilitation Programme
CBSE	Central Board of Secondary Education (India)
CBVR	Community-Based Vocational Rehabilitation
CCT	Conditional Cash Transfer
CGAP	Consultative Group to Assist the Poor
CHS	Community on Human Security
CIDA	Canadian International Development Agency
CII	Confederation of Indian Industry
CoA	Council of Architecture (India)
CPA	Comprehensive Peace Agreement
CRPD	Convention on the Rights of Persons with Disabilities (also known as UNCRPD)
CPA	Comprehensive Peace Agreement (Sudan)
CSO	Civil Society Organisation
DAC	Development Assistance Committee
DEWD	Developing Entrepreneurship among Women with Disabilities (Ethiopia)
DFID	Department for International Development, UK
DPO	Disabled People's Organisation
DRG	Disabled Rights Group (India)
EBT	Enterprise-Based Training
EFPD	Ethiopian Federation of Persons with Disabilities
EU	European Union

EVI	Extremely Vulnerable Individual
FICCI	Federation of Indian Chambers of Commerce and Industry
GNI	Gross National Income
GPDD	Global Partnership for Disability and Development
HIV	Human Immunodeficiency Virus
ICRC	International Committee of the Red Cross and Red Crescent
IDBI	Industrial Development Bank of India
IDDC	International Disability and Development Consortium
IDMC	Internal Displacement Monitoring Centre
IDP	Internally Displaced Person
IEP	Individualised Education Plan
IL	International Law
ILO	International Labour Organization
INGO	International Non-Governmental Organisation
JEM	Justice and Equality Movement (Sudan)
JICA	Japanese International Cooperation Agency
LAC	Latin America and the Caribbean
LCD	Leonard Cheshire Disability
LTTE	Liberation Tigers of the Tamil Eelam
MDG	Millennium Development Goal
MDTFs	Multidonor Trust Funds
MFI	Microfinance Institution
MSI	Muscular Skeletal Impairment
NCD	Non-Communicable Disease
NCPD	National Centre for Persons with Disabilities (Trinidad)
NCPEDP	National Centre for Promotion of Employment for Disabled People, India
NDSA	National Disability Survey in Afghanistan
NEC	National Examination Council (Trinidad)
NGO	Non-Governmental Organisation
NID	National Institute of Design (India)
NUDIPU	National Union of Disabled People of Uganda
OAS	Organization of the American States

OCHA	UN Office for the Coordination of Humanitarian Affairs
ODA	Official Development Assistance
OECD	Organisation for Economic Co-operation and Development
PATH	Programme of Advancement through Health and Education (Jamaica)
PRSP	Poverty Reduction Strategy Paper
RGF	Rajiv Gandhi Foundation, India
ROSCA	Rotating Savings and Credit Association
SACCO	Savings and Credit Cooperative
SARPV	Social Assistance and Rehabilitation of the Physically Vulnerable in Bangladesh
SCR	Success Case Replication
SEDA	Small Enterprise Development Agency, South Africa
SHGs	Self-Help Groups
SIDA	Swedish International Development Agency
SLA	Sri Lankan Army
SLA/M	Sudan Liberation Army/Movement
SLUDI	Sierra Leone Union of Disability Issues
STD	Sexually Transmitted Disease
SWAp	Sector Wide Approach
TDVA	Tigray Disabled Veterans Association
TVET	Technical and Vocational Education and Training
UD	Universal Design
UGC	University Grants Commission (India)
UK	United Kingdom
UN	United Nations
UNAB	Ugandan National Association of the Blind
UNCRPD	United Nations Convention on the Rights of Persons with Disabilities (also known as CRPD)
UNCTAD	United Nations Conference on Trade and Development
UNDP	United Nations Development Programme
UNESCAP	United Nations Economic and Social Commission for Asia and the Pacific

UNESCO	United Nations Educational, Scientific and Cultural Organisation
UNFPA	United Nations Population Fund
UNHCR	United Nations High Commissioner for Refugees
UNICEF	United Nations Children's Fund
USA	United States of America
USAID	United States Agency for International Development
VO	Village Organisation
WHO	World Health Organization
YIP	Young India Project
YSFDP	Yemen Social Fund for Development Project

Contents

Chapter 5: Community Approaches to Livelihood Development: Self-help Groups in India

Peter Coleridge and Balakrishna Venkatesh

Chapter 6: Microfinance for People with Disabilities

Enzo Martinelli and Roy Mersland

Foreword

Worldwide, poverty is the single most pressing issue for millions of people with disabilities. While the United Nations estimates that 10 per cent of the world's population lives with a disability, the World Bank estimates that one in five of the world's poorest people are disabled or live in a household with a disabled member. Not only are persons with disabilities therefore twice as likely to live in poverty, but they will often also be among the poorest of the poor. Go into any impoverished urban slum area or walk into any poor rural village and ask the people who live there 'who is the poorest person in your community' – you will more than likely be directed to the door of a disabled person.

Despite these clear links, we are only beginning to understand how poverty and disability interact. It is an area that continues to be inadequately understood and significantly under-researched. Without an accurate understanding of the links between poverty and disability, our capacity to know when, where and how to intervene to break these links will be significantly limited.

Such poverty is all the more problematic because, as is clearly noted in the following chapters, research increasingly shows that poverty and disability are not inevitably linked. Most often, it is not people's disabilities that block their ability to support themselves and their families adequately. Rather, it is the stigma, discrimination and lack of knowledge or awareness about disability in the surrounding environment that limits their abilities and talents. Access to education and employment, an accessible physical environment and changes in legal, social and cultural norms to ensure social inclusion mean that persons with disabilities can be full, participating members of the surrounding community. Such findings are coming from a small but growing body of work on disability and poverty that has begun to broaden our understanding of what can be done – of what works.

Until quite recently most of the research on disability and poverty has taken place 'in house' among disability researchers and advocates. Comparable research on disability, poverty and development within the ranks of the international development community has been significantly less common. In fact, there has been a serious lack of extended conversations between the two groups that has hindered the inclusion of disability issues within larger theoretical constructs and major data collection efforts in international development. However, the fact that so many disabled people in low- and middle-income countries face grinding poverty should come as little surprise to international development experts. The risk factors for living with a disability in much of the world today are virtually identical to those risk factors for living in poverty that are so familiar to those working in international development circles: social marginalisation, lack of access to education and employment, limited political clout and the restricted right to self-determination.

Things are beginning to change. Growing attention to disability has been fostered by the UN Convention on the Rights of Persons with Disabilities (UNCRPD). Coming into force in May 2008, the UNCRPD approaches disability, access and poverty from a rights perspective, broadly confirming that people with disabilities have the same claim to full participation in society as every other citizen. Certainly the UNCRPD has also brought a number of international development organisations and experts to the table, with global disability advocates making a clear and coherent case for why inclusion of disability is a human right.

A small but growing body of data on poverty and disability is now becoming both clear and compelling – more than 90 per cent of disabled children still do not attend school; the health and well-being of persons with disabilities are still significantly less than those of their non-disabled peers; and they have far less access to clean water, adequate housing, enough food, equal work or equal pay. Unless persons with disabilities are included in general international development programmes and policies, none of the Millennium Development Goals will be met, and no society will be able to significantly reduce poverty.

For these reasons, international development experts are taking note. Increasingly UN agencies, governments and civil society are asking for facts and figures regarding disabled populations and requesting evidence of 'best practices' for effectively reaching disabled persons – through both disability-specific and general programmes. Agencies and governments are also demanding new standards in programme monitoring and evaluation. As a number of chapters in this volume will attest, this new forum holds great promise, but also brings with it great responsibility to ensure that that the work done meets the requirements of this new and expanded global audience. As increasing collaboration develops between groups in disability and those in international development, new theoretical constructs must also be developed.

Also, as will be discussed throughout this volume, disability issues must be set in a wider matrix of current theoretical thinking and practice in development economics, social justice, political science and human rights.

From the outset, international development efforts must be undertaken with full inclusion of and consultation with disabled people's organisations (DPOs) – groups that are run for and by persons with disabilities. The slogan *Nothing About Us Without Us* is nowhere more important than in international development circles, where organisations that often work at national, regional and global levels need to ensure that groups representing disabled persons are part of the dialogue at all stages.

Because all of the issues cited above are raised in the ensuing chapters, this book represents a substantial contribution to the literature. It provides a valuable summary of much of what we know and, even more importantly, clearly identifies areas that need further exploration and pinpoints important 'next steps' that need to be addressed. The information, observations and thoughtful analysis of many of the authors raise as many questions as they answer and, in sum, provide an insightful overview of current work and a potential road map for future work.

Nora Ellen Groce, PhD
Leonard Cheshire Chair

Director, Leonard Cheshire Centre
for Disability and Inclusive Development
University College London

Full inclusion is the UNCRPD's aim
Photo: Jenny Matthews/Leonard Cheshire Disability

Chapter 1

Introduction

Tanya Barron and Jabulani Manombe Ncube

The purpose of this book

The purpose of this book is to promote change; to help move policy and practice towards real inclusion and participation of disabled people.

This is the second book in the *Disability and Inclusive Development* series. In the introduction to our first book, *Disability and Inclusive Development* (Barron and Amerena, 2007), the editors expressed frustration with the pace of change, and the persisting absence of the meaningful participation of disabled people in development programmes. Since that publication we have seen the introduction and coming into force of the UN Convention on the Rights of People with Disabilities (UNCRPD). This is an extraordinary treaty, which was motivated by, and to a great extent built through, the efforts and participation of people with disabilities. Full implementation will require a genuine paradigm shift of attitudes, policy and practice, and it is therefore accepted that the UNCRPD is not only ambitious but also to some extent aspirational.

Progress is also evident in that more of the governmental development cooperation agencies now specifically identify people with disabilities as a target group for development assistance. However, it is still usually the case that disability issues are relegated to small non-governmental organisation (NGO) budget lines. Governments and the bigger NGOs are still unable or unwilling to mainstream disability effectively or put in targeted budgets to achieve inclusion through a twin-track approach. Despite a clear consensus on the importance of 'beneficiary' participation in development, it is still rare for disabled people to be fully involved in programme design or implementation.

There are also signs of some progress in finding ways to render the Millennium Development Goals (MDGs) somewhat more inclusive. Given that the original MDGs were drafted without any specific reference to disabled people, this can be seen as a positive move.

Disability and Inclusive Development is a call to action. We will only achieve inclusive development when disabled people represent themselves at all levels. Disability issues must be included in global and local development goals and processes to improve the quality of life of some of the world's most disempowered people.

Poverty and Disability explores the interaction between poverty and disability in low- and middle-income countries. It looks at their impact on lives, economies and societies and how this, in turn, affects policy and practice. This volume forms the second of a series of books on the subject of disability and inclusive development, which will provide important, relevant and well-researched discussions on a range of related topics.

This book is for you if you:

- are an international development policy maker, planner, implementer or practitioner

- work at international, national, regional or community level

- work for government, a civil society organisation or an international development organisation

- are a trainer in international development or the disability sector

- are a trainee or student in international development or the disability sector. You represent the new generation of practitioners and we hope the drawing together here of current thinking on inclusive development issues will be particularly relevant to you.

Disability

Some contextual background and definitions may be useful to set the scene for the chapters that follow regarding the understanding of the term disability. The World Health Organization (WHO) uses the International Classification of Functioning definition:

> Disability is a generic term that includes impairments in body functions and structures, activity limitation and participation restrictions. It indicates the negative aspects of the interaction between an individual (with a 'health condition') and his context (environmental and personal factors). (WHO, 2006)

Impairments are *'problems in body function or structure such as deviation or loss'* (WHO, 2006). Impairments therefore refer to physical, sensory and mental problems, including illness and lack of emotional well-being.

Most definitions of disability capture the fact that bodily impairment leads to disability, which is a social construct or a result of society's reaction to the person with impairment. Thus the United Nations Economic and Social Commission for Asia and the Pacific (UNESCAP, 2005) states: *'many [disabled people] are so excluded and alienated from their own society that they are no longer treated as respected 'citizens' of their own society'.*

For summaries of the main models concerned with disability, such as the medical model and the social model, and discussions on mainstreaming, please see the introduction to the first book in this series, *Disability and Inclusive Development.*

Poverty

There is no one generally agreed definition of poverty, and indeed there are models that offer very different understandings of the concept – those of absolute and relative poverty.

An attempt to define absolute poverty was made with the Copenhagen Declaration of the World Summit for Social Development in 1995:

> Absolute poverty is a condition characterised by severe deprivation of basic human needs, including food, safe drinking water, sanitation facilities, health, shelter, education and information. It depends not only on income, but also on access to social services.

Amartya Sen argues that 'there is an irreducible absolutist core in the idea of poverty. If there is starvation and hunger then, no matter what the relative picture looks like – there clearly is poverty' (Sen,1983). The World Bank uses a widely accepted fixed measure of extreme poverty as a purchasing power of less than US$1 a day.

Probably the most quoted voice for the relative approach to poverty is that of Peter Townsend. He defines poverty as 'the absence or inadequacy of those diets, amenities, standards, services and activities which are common or customary in society'. In most countries a familiar relative measure of household poverty is through a defined national minimum basket of goods, and a similarly comparative measure of income is used by the European Union, which defines poverty as an income of 50 per cent of mean income.

It can be argued that living on half the mean national income will consign an individual to poverty, as they will not be able to participate in the normal activities of the society, and thus they will suffer measurable deprivation. But if some countries are so affluent that even at half of mean income an individual cannot be said objectively to suffer from a deprivation of diet, water, sanitation, health, education or other services, then the relative approach to poverty could be argued to be a measure of inequality, rather than of poverty itself.

A separate difficulty with many of the national measures of poverty, both absolute and relative, is that they relate to households, and are not dis-aggregated for the individuals within the household. This is particularly serious when trying to understand the poverty of disabled people, as a family may have the resources to provide every opportunity for good outcomes, but a disabled family member may nevertheless still not enjoy those outcomes.

Whether poverty is seen as something that can be defined absolutely, or understood to be relative, absolute measures can be useful in focusing attention on a measurable target, and they appear to promise a route to reducing or even removing poverty. Surely if we know what poverty is, we can more easily do something about it. In an attempt to make real gains in the battle against extreme poverty, development partners have essentially agreed to use US$1 a day as a key measure of poverty. However imperfect, having a measure of this kind allows us to focus resources on getting people out of income poverty, and allows us to measure outcomes and success.

The MDGs use specific income as an absolute measure, but that is only one of the eight development goals. The MDGs suggest that poverty is complex and multifaceted, and that to eradicate poverty and achieve our development goals we will also need to see improvements in education, health, maternal mortality and so on. Two challenges for the MDGs (apart from the rather obvious one that they look unlikely to be reached) are, first, that they make no mention at all of disabled people and second, that the multidimensional approach leaves the question of how best to have an impact on poverty as unresolved as ever. Should we assume that increasing income will result in improvements in health and education, or should we increase resources in education and health in the expectation that this will result in better earning capacity and income?

In addition, focusing on incoming resources, whether absolute or relative, may not tell us as much about poverty as we expect. Amartya Sen cautions us against being so focused on inputs (income and other resources that are a means to an end) that we fail to measure what really matters – the outcomes for poor people. Recognising the need to look to the outcomes that bring about well-being has brought about a much broader view of poverty, a human development perspective, where self-esteem, dignity, the fulfilment of creativity and opportunities all matter very much.

From around the 1980s, thinking on poverty started to have to share space with new discussions on social exclusion. Social inclusion theory proposes social cohesion (or solidarity) as a common good, and analyses poverty as multidimensional. The dimensions enabled us to see measures of consumption as being equally important to income, and brought dimensions of social, political and cultural exclusion into the frame. Although social exclusion theory can coexist with absolute measures of poverty, it is a more natural bed-fellow with the relative perspective. This is partly because it argues that cash or income poverty may not, in itself, result in social exclusion or overall poverty. Each individual or household may have mitigating or protective factors that provide resilience, making the impact of income poverty relative to the other circumstances of each individual.

As social inclusion theory developed, participation (social as well as economic) became an important and accepted part of discussions on poverty. This recognition, that social exclusion and lack of participation were central to many people's experience of poverty, opened up the path to understanding that the active participation of marginalised people was vital to the process of inclusion, and that people's subjective experiences of exclusion and poverty were not just legitimate but essential things to measure.

The development of thinking on poverty has thus moved from a position where people were mostly concerned with economic factors, primarily income, to a view that services such as health and education should figure in the overall picture, to a perspective that includes the extent to which a person is empowered to be able to participate freely in all that their society and community has to offer.

Some, in particular Piachaud, have proposed that the reason it is so difficult to define poverty is that it is essentially a moral issue. Very few people today would suggest that inequality in itself is wrong, but when an individual's inequality leaves them deprived of basic needs and causes them to suffer, most societies concur that it is wrong to do nothing if it is possible to reduce or eradicate that suffering. The ethical foundations for the desire to eradicate poverty have different sources, from religious beliefs to the utilitarian rationale that it is better to maximise productivity and minimise potential social unrest in society. But whatever the motivation, as Professor David Piachaud (1981) notes, the term poverty carries with it '... an implication and moral imperative that something should be done about it'.

A society's moral rights and wrongs are usually structured into legal entitlements and protections, and many development organisations have positioned themselves as rights-based organisations. This can mean using legal and human rights mechanisms to achieve development outcomes, but in many cases it simply means working to realise the same access to rights, entitlements and opportunities for all members of a society.

The chapters in this book do not, by and large, talk much about extreme poverty; they are more about being poor. We are familiar with media images and words that portray people who are starving, destitute and experiencing extreme poverty. But there is also another poverty that reduces individual lives to a daily struggle for basic needs, excluded from the benefits of education, work and participation in society.

Even when a disabled person lives in a household that does not consider itself to be poor, they may have little or no education compared to their siblings. They may be unemployed whereas their non-disabled siblings are employed. They may not suffer material deprivation, but have no personal disposable income. They may feel frustrated and greatly discriminated against, but not obviously cash poor. It is a complicated business.

This less than extreme poverty keeps individuals deprived and at the margins of their societies, and disabled people find themselves disproportionately consigned to these margins.

Poverty and disability

The perspectives shared in this section are informed by a lifelong involvement with organisations of disabled people.[1] The understanding and insights gained about the subject of disability and poverty are informed by the struggles of disabled people to organise in their groups around issues they have defined as being most important to them. Among these is the need for awareness of disability issues as being essentially concerned with human rights, along with the need to ensure that disabled people are in the forefront of efforts to articulate for themselves the sort of changes they require in order to support their enjoyment of life on an equal basis with non-disabled people.

The denial of the human rights of disabled people has in recent times been vindicated by the coming into force in May 2008 of the UNCRPD. The UNCRPD does not create new human rights but seeks to extend the enjoyment of all human rights to disabled people.

Ignorance, fear of impairment and negative attitudes about disabled people mean that they are marginalised and excluded from opportunities for human development. In Tanzania, survey data showed that households with a member who has a disability have a mean consumption of less than 60 per cent of the average and include 20 per cent more members than average (Elwan, 1999a).

An important cause of poverty among disabled people is their exclusion from accessing education on an equal basis with non-disabled persons. Such exclusion often results from negative attitudes concerning their perceived human worth. These attitudes exist in families and they influence the kind of decisions made about the welfare of disabled members of households. For example, a Namibian study into the living conditions of disabled people (Sintef, Oslo/University of Namibia, 2003) found that attendance in school of disabled members of households is lower than that of non-disabled members, indicating that disabled persons are being denied access to the right to education. Schools are also rarely adapted sufficiently to the needs of disabled children and students. The same study showed, importantly, that twice as many disabled members of households had never attended school, compared to non-disabled members. Hoogeveen's (2005) research in Uganda also shows that children living in households with disabled family members are less likely to attend school.

Social as well as economic inclusion defeats poverty
Photo: Gideon Mendel/Leonard Cheshire Disability

Growing up with little education and skills means that life for the affected disabled individual is a struggle to secure and maintain a meaningful livelihood, while surviving ever-present disabling attitudes. A recent World Bank study in India found that disability is a stronger correlate of non-enrolment in school than either gender or class. It also found the employment rate of people with disabilities is 60 per cent lower than that of the general population (World Bank, 2007).

The relatively weak position of some disabled members of households (such as persons with intellectual disabilities or children) makes it difficult for them to decide independently on the use of their resources, such as employment income or disability grants. This relative incapacity pushes the concerned individuals deeper into poverty.

In Croatia, two thirds of people with disabilities live with their families and most view their financial situation as being very unfavourable (UNDP, 2006).

Poverty in households with one or more disabled members, along with discrimination against disabled girls, often leads to decisions to keep these girls away from school. In later life, such decisions render girls vulnerable to sexual exploitation, poor employment prospects and other hardships.

> Working as a consultant has brought about a situation of unique privilege and trust while working closely with organisations and groups of disabled people from diverse settings and countries. It has allowed me to sit in and listen to discussions about what life is like for them, during which they have described in vivid terms such problems as their deprivation from educational opportunities, the impact of limited skills in seeking and holding down jobs, limited access to livelihood activities and unavailability of assistive devices and aids, among others. That, against this background, disabled people have over the last three decades managed to organise and build their own organisations in many parts of Africa and other developing countries constitutes one of the success stories of social movements (Ncube, 2005).

It is recognised that 20 per cent of the world's poorest people are disabled (Elwan, 1999b). In this respect, the self-organisation of disabled people is important to ensure that their voice is included in efforts to address the poverty they face through national and international cooperation efforts.

Putting inclusive development into practice: the chapters

When we planned the text we aimed to inform, provoke debate and increase understanding of the range of interacting issues that operate in this complex area. More than this we wanted to provide practical ideas for improving inclusive practice in development without being prescriptive. The book includes authors who are people with disabilities and non-disabled people, women and men, academics and practitioners, and writers from Africa, Asia, South America, North America and Europe.

The chapters all discuss aspects of poverty and disability, and the contributors have interpreted the commissioning guidelines in ways that are meaningful for them and the sectors in which they operate. The result is ten chapters that are individual, with differing perspectives. There are, however, two common threads. The first is that whether the authors are discussing income, consumption, access to services, rights or social solidarity and inclusion, there is an underlying consensus that poverty is multifaceted, and that although access to resources is of enormous importance, the experience of poverty stretches far beyond being cash poor. The second is that each chapter proposes, however discretely, that the goal of development is social justice. Although the terminology and the way social justice might be achieved for disabled people differ for each topic, there is a united call for empowerment as a right.

This book, then, links the aspirational to the practical; it taps into what motivates development and disability workers at all levels and offers ideas on how to begin to translate guiding principles into effective action. Not everyone will agree with what they find in this book, but we hope it provokes critical reflection and renewed urgency in each reader's contribution to the inclusion of disabled people in development.

Poverty, Disability and Aid: International Development Cooperation

Roger C. Riddell

The theme of this chapter is poverty, disability and aid – or international development cooperation, as aid is frequently and more formally referred to today. Increasingly over the last decades, the purpose of providing aid has narrowed to focus ever more sharply on reducing the numbers of people living in extreme poverty. The purpose of this chapter is to look closely at the relationship between aid, poverty and disability, examining the ways in which aid has contributed to the reduction in poverty of people with disabilities living in extreme poverty or vulnerable to it, especially in poor, low-income countries.

The chapter is divided into three parts: a summary, a section on aid and poverty, which provides an overview of the contribution that aid makes to poverty reduction and a third section that looks specifically at the issues of aid, poverty and disability. This discussion helps us to understand better which of the problems faced by poor people with disabilities are likely to be resolved by providing more and better aid, and which are likely to require us to address issues outside the more narrow relationship between aid, disability and poverty.

The last subsection sketches the way that the important non-governmental (NGO) sector, including disabled people's organisations (DPOs), have approached disability and poverty issues, discusses the different ways they have used aid funds and summarises what we know – and still do not know – about the impact of their different activities.

The chapter ends with four sets of recommendations for improving the role, contribution and impact that aid could have in addressing the problems of poverty for those with disabilities.

Mainstreaming and Inclusive Development

Charlotte McClain-Nhlapo

Simply prohibiting disability discrimination through legal redress is not sufficient to achieve equality in practice, as has been acknowledged by many development workers, governments and policy makers. Furthermore, implementing and enforcing policy that seeks to mainstream people with disabilities is not enough to tackle the multifaceted and deep-rooted patterns of inequality experienced by these people. Policies that mainstream disability into generic publically funded development initiatives need to complement the rights of people with disabilities, as contained in the United Nations Convention on the Rights of Persons with Disabilities (CRPD), with wider measures designed to promote and advance equality. This chapter explores some of the ways in which this mainstreaming can be advanced and explores approaches that should be considered in addressing the needs of people with disabilities.

Lifelong Learning in Education, Training and Skills Development

Bob Ransom

This chapter outlines the components of lifelong learning that people with disabilities in developing countries can use to escape from poverty and dependence. These are competencies and qualifications. After discussing the various types of skill that people need to make a livelihood, the author shows that they can be acquired in non-formal ways at home and in the community, and in formal technical and vocational education and training institutions. The next section analyses the advantages and disadvantages of different institutions in training people with disabilities for a livelihood. The author then sketches a number of success stories: a skills transfer programme in Cambodia, a programme in Ethiopia that trains very poor women with disabilities in business skills, a community-based vocational rehabilitation programme in Nigeria and on-the-job training in a large company in Brazil. The last section focuses in detail on the National Centre for Persons with Disabilities in Trinidad and Tobago. The author concludes by emphasising that people with disabilities can learn skills in numerous ways to reach their full potential, earn a livelihood and contribute to their family and community. The key to this is to ensure equality of opportunity at every level while making adaptations according to needs.

Community Approaches to Livelihood Development: Self-help Groups in India

Peter Coleridge and Balakrishna Venkatesh

Poverty is not simply the lack of income; it is a denial of the fundamental freedom and opportunity to develop as a human being. The elimination of poverty lies, in large measure, in the creation of a just society in which all citizens have equal opportunity to develop their full potential.

Global trends show both increasing support for and increasing obstacles to the creation of just societies. On the one hand international and national legislation outlaw discrimination and governments proclaim the values of equal opportunity, including equal opportunity for disabled people. On the other hand it is primarily economics, not human values, that drives much of global development and there is often little interest from those who have economic power in sharing it on an equitable basis. Poor people all over the world, from landless peasants in Brazil to *dalits* and women in India, have learned that if equality is to become a reality it is they who must take the initiative through mobilising themselves for both political and economic power.

Disabled people are in the same position and have made the same discovery. In many parts of the world they have found that the most effective way to do this is through the formation of self-help groups (SHGs). SHGs open the doors of possibility to both individual and community development in the fullest sense.

This chapter takes the view that the development of livelihood goes well beyond the ability to earn an income. It involves creating opportunities to develop one's full potential as a human being and the ability to contribute to the development of one's community and society.

Microfinance for People with Disabilities

Enzo Martinelli and Roy Mersland

Microfinance is considered an important tool in reaching the United Nations' Millennium Development Goals. Nevertheless, few people with disabilities have access to microfinance.

The chapter, first, provides the reader with basic knowledge about microfinance and how this is relevant for people with disabilities. Second, it outlines the main mechanisms leading to exclusion from services and identifies strategies to improve the current situation. The overall objective is to give the readers a background to understand better how microfinance can be used as a tool to reduce poverty for one of the most marginalised social groups and to provide important knowledge useful in advocacy and project efforts.

Aside from a few authors, the academic literature on microfinance and disability published in peer-reviewed journals is virtually non-existent. Thankfully, some reports do provide guidelines, conceptual frameworks, basic knowledge and, when available, some statistics. The authors therefore want to make the case for information dissemination and awareness creation among the microfinance providers as well as among disabled people's organisations, the academic community and disabled people in general.

Self-employment for People with Disabilities

Bev Moodie

The focus of this chapter is on self-employment for people with disabilities, arguing that if they are properly encouraged and supported and given the right tools, people with disabilities can and should become self-employed. The author starts by discussing the context in South Africa. She then offers some case studies of people who have succeeded in becoming self-employed as well as some who have not. In the next section she draws a number of lessons that can be learnt from the case studies. The following section is devoted to an examination of strategies by which people with a disability can become self-employed. She starts by discussing Die Werkswinkel (The Workshop) in Knysna, Cape Province, outlining ways in which people can transform themselves from being workers to contractors and independent businesspeople. She then considers different kinds of skills and resources that they need to succeed. In her conclusion she points to the overall benefits that self-employment can bring to the community and to people with disability themselves, including increased earnings, greater self-confidence and self-esteem, wider social relationships and inclusion in the community.

Waged employment

Javed Abidi

The *Concise Oxford Dictionary* defines 'waged employment' as 'regular paid employment'. The objective of this chapter is to understand why disabled people don't find employment, as in a regular job, and also, perhaps, what can be done to change that situation.

When the author was asked to write this chapter, he felt privileged but cautioned the editors that being a disabled activist, the narrative would have to cover his own story and that of his country. He believes that, by and large, the issues are the same across the world: disability, prejudice, stereotypes, self-created barriers, insensitivity, poor leadership, lack of unity amongst disabled people themselves and many others. If the issues are the same, then the remedy will also be similar. It requires the adoption of a rights-based approach and then sticking to it. We have to question the basics. The status quo has to be changed.

Social Protection and Disability

Daniel Mont

This chapter asks whether people with disabilities are afforded the same protection against poverty as non-disabled people. Starting with a discussion of the concept of social protection, the author outlines different kinds of social protection measures. He goes on to discuss when and how social protection measures should specifically target people with disabilities, and then in the next section discusses how general social protection programmes can be made more inclusive. As an example, he discusses how disability can be incorporated into conditional cash-transfer programmes. The chapter concludes with a set of policy recommendations.

Disability and Poverty in Post-conflict Countries

Maria Kett

There is an ever-expanding literature on the causes of conflict – of which poverty, and its resulting inequalities, are seen to be primary factors. There is also a growing awareness that poor environments – and poor people – are disproportionately affected by such disasters and emergencies. Furthermore, research now indicates that poverty alone is not the only factor in determining how people fare in times of conflict.

Violent conflict results in a loss of resources, infrastructure and essential skills and personnel. Social structures and networks are destroyed and there is an increased lack of security. Health systems are also destroyed, and take years to regenerate. The effects of conflict and ensuing poverty are reflected in health indicators such as maternal and child mortality rates, nutrition, infectious diseases (including HIV/AIDS) and mental health problems. Mitigation of conflict encompasses protection from violence, reduction in weapons circulation, empowerment of people through economic securities and universal access to basic education and healthcare.

Conflict and emergencies therefore drain resources and perpetuate poverty, yet poverty itself is a driving force for war and conflict, and often develops due to scarce or valuable resources or unequal opportunities (perceived or real).

Inclusive Development: Paving the Way as We Walk

Rosangela Berman-Bieler

This chapter proposes that disability is an experience that we all undergo at one time or another during the course of our life. After discussing the relationship between disability, poverty and exclusion, the author presents an inclusive concept of development. At the core of this is an understanding of the relationship between impairment and the social and economic environment that is responsible for disability. The first section describes how demographic changes impact on the issue. This is followed by a sketch of the steps needed to initiate inclusive design and to implement policies and changes to the built environment. The next section describes the research and data collection needed for improving the quality of life of people with disability, after which the author explains why planning for all is possible and how an inclusive approach to disability will enhance the lives and security of all. This is followed by articulation of the author's vision that an inclusive approach to disability will enhance general human experience and reduce poverty.

Conclusion

Disabled peoples' experience of poverty makes it clear that it is a situation that is complex and multilayered, one that can (and often does) change over time. The view that poverty and disability are inextricably linked is not always borne out by the experience of people with disabilities and, indeed, seems overly deterministic and passive. It is, however, also evident that for most people an impairment creates enormous barriers to participating in the social and economic life of their community, and has a disproportionate negative impact on an individual's life chances.

The Make Poverty History campaign and the global development ambitions of the MDGs have been historically extraordinary efforts that have mobilised enormous human and financial resources. But the 650 million disabled people of the world, who are statistically far more likely to live in poverty than their non-disabled peers, have been largely left out.

The hope and promise of the UNCRPD is that development will become inclusive, and that disabled people will enjoy their rights to realise their potential and live their lives free from poverty. How and when will this happen? Without the political mobilisation of disabled people, change is likely to be slow. The reality of the world is that economic power generally equals political power in the north and the south. Those that hold economic power rarely take action to contribute to the empowerment of marginalised people unless there is an incentive. This places a disparate, disempowered group like disabled people at an enormous disadvantage.

Change will require two essential driving factors. The first is the mobilisation of disabled people: the momentum of disabled people focused on finding their voice, articulating their rights and needs and truly participating in decision-making processes. Peter Coleridge, in his book 'Disability, Liberation and Development', writes:

> ... the truth is the oppressor is not likely to change behaviour unless the oppressed person makes the first move ... If [disabled people] refuse to see themselves as victims, if they claim their own dignity, see themselves as positive and able to contribute, they will be seen as positive and able to contribute. This is not at all the same as saying that disabled people should be quiet, stop complaining, and settle for some kind of half life. Absolutely not ... In the words of Rachel Hurst of Disabled Peoples' International: 'Social change initially comes from us, from disabled people. It has to.' (Coleridge, 1993)

The second necessary driving force will be the mobilisation of resources. Progress on social inclusion will only be achieved hand in hand with appropriate levels of funding in the development process. We should shine the spotlight on examples of weak political will for social justice, where there is no evidence of budgetary or financial provision to implement inclusion.

Our aim is to generate action. The exclusion of disabled people from social, economic, political and community life is perpetuated by ignorance and poverty and is exacerbated by conflict. Without change at all levels, disabled people will continue to be largely excluded from the development process. Without their active participation in decision making, development efforts will not be relevant. This disempowerment leads to loss for both the individual and the community, where each would benefit from unlocking the potential of disabled people. Whether you agree or disagree with the contents of this book, we hope it motivates you to evaluate the sector you work in and stimulates action to increase the rate of progress towards inclusive development.

Notes

1. Some of this section has been published in World View, *Disability Now* (Ncube, 2007).

References

Barron, T. and Amareena, P. (eds.) 2007. *Disability and Inclusive Development*. London: Leonard Cheshire International.

Coleridge, P. 1993. *Disability, Liberation and Development*. Oxford: Oxfam.

Elwan, A. 1999a. Poverty and disability. A survey of the literature. *Social Protection Discussion Paper Series*, 9932. Washington, DC: World Bank.

Elwan, A. 1999b. *Poverty and Disability; a background paper for the World Development Report*. Washington, DC: World Bank.

Hoogeveen, J. 2005. Measuring welfare for small but vulnerable groups: Poverty and disability in Uganda. *Journal of African Economies*, 14(4).

Ncube, J. M. 2005. *Understanding myself, and my role in the world: meetings in the classroom to learn rebellion*. Unpublished essay, University of East Anglia, Norwich.

Ncube, J. M. 2007. Poverty has a life-long impact on many disabled people in Africa, especially women. In World View, *Disability Now*, January 2007.

Piachaud, D. 1981. Peter Townsend and the Holy Grail. *New Society*, 10, September.

Sen, A. K. 1983. Poor, relatively speaking. *Oxford Economic Papers*, 35, 135–169.

Sintef, Oslo/University of Namibia, 2003. *Living Conditions among People with Disabilities in Namibia. A National, Representative Study*. April 2003, STF78 A034503 Report. Windhoek, Namibia: University of Namibia / Oslo, Norway: SINTEF Unimed.

UNDP 2006. *Survey: Quality of life and risk of social exclusion in Croatia (Social Welfare Service Providers). The right to live in a community: social inclusion and people with disabilities.* Brussels: EU. Available online at http://ec.europa.eu/employment_social/soc-prot/soc-incl/joint_rep_en.htm [Accessed 18 March 2010].

UNESCAP 2005. *The strategic approaches to disability inclusive development.* Regional Workshop on Comprehensive National Plan of Action on Disability,19–21 October 2005, Bangkok, BMF. Available online at http://www.worldenable.net/bmf2005/basicdoc3.htm [Accessed 1 July 2010].

WHO 2006. 13th Session of the Executive Committee. Agenda item 4.7.

World Bank 2007. *People with Disabilities in India: From Commitments to Outcomes.* Human Development Unit, South Asia Region.

Accessibility is crucial for aid to reach the poorest
Photo: Pietro Cenini/Panos Pictures

Chapter 2

Poverty, Disability and Aid: International Development Cooperation

Roger C. Riddell

Summary

The theme of this chapter is poverty, disability and aid – or international development cooperation, as aid is frequently and more formally referred to today. Increasingly over the last decades, the purpose of providing aid has narrowed to focus ever more sharply on reducing the numbers of people living in extreme poverty. The purpose of this chapter is to look closely at the relationship between aid, poverty and disability, examining the ways in which aid has contributed to the reduction in poverty of people with disabilities living in extreme poverty or vulnerable to it, especially in poor, low-income countries.

The chapter is divided into three parts. After this summary, a section on aid and poverty provides an overview of the contribution that aid makes to poverty reduction. It looks – all too briefly – at the types of aid provided and what we know, and still do not know, about aid's impact on poverty. It highlights a series of problems that continue to impede and limit the overall impact that aid has on poverty reduction, and cautions against having too optimistic a view of what aid could do. At best aid can help to make a difference to the lives of poor people but, on its own, aid is unlikely to be *the* solution to poverty. This discussion helps us to understand better which of the problems faced by poor people with disabilities are likely to be resolved by providing more and better aid, and which are likely to require us to address issues outside the more narrow relationship between aid, disability and poverty.

Against this backdrop, the third section looks specifically at the issues of aid, poverty and disability. It starts with a discussion of key concepts and what we know about poverty and disability, noting that, in common with the aggregate data on poverty discussed in the second section, our detailed knowledge is severely limited by major gaps in the data. This is followed by a discussion of the total amounts of aid channelled into initiatives to help poor people with disabilities, providing a brief critique of the way such data are gathered. It then discusses the approach to disability and poverty by leading official aid agencies, and what we know about the contribution and impact that official government aid has had on poor people with disabilities. It discusses both the impact of discrete projects and the objectives and impact of new approaches to aid giving, commonly referred to as the 'new aid modalities'. The final subsection sketches the way that the important non-governmental (NGO) sector, including disabled people's organisations (DPOs), have approached disability and poverty issues, discusses the different ways they have used aid funds and summarises what we know – and still do not know – about the impact of their different activities.

The final conclusions and recommendations draw together and summarise the main problems with aid and highlight which problems seem to lie outside the aid, poverty and disability world and which can be traced to the wider world of aid. It ends with four sets of recommendations for improving the role, contribution and impact that aid could have in addressing the problems of poverty for those living with disabilities.

A dominant theme running through the wider literature on disability is that disabled people have been ignored, left out, forgotten, under-valued and marginalised by the wider society, their inability to gain access to and share equitably in society's benefits being due in part to their marginalisation in the decisions and processes of building and shaping that society. Two of the main conclusions of this chapter are, first, that this broad picture of discrimination and marginalisation facing people with disabilities has been mirrored in the way that the aid system, and aid agencies in the system, have treated the issue of disability and, second, that far-reaching changes need to be made to the aid system if there are to be substantial improvements in addressing the poverty that so many people with disabilities experience.

It might be argued that this judgement is unduly harsh, and that it ignores, in particular, the changes that have been taking place across the aid world, as most aid agencies recast their approach to disability and give priority to the issue. It is true that in recent years a succession of leading agencies have introduced new policies on disability and, though the evidence remains largely anecdotal, the aid allocated to disability initiatives would appear to have increased, providing tangible, immediate and more systematic gains for growing numbers of people with disabilities than in the past. However, significant gaps remain between the rhetoric of giving more priority to the issue of disability, including the policies articulated and accepted by a growing number of aid agencies, to mainstream disability more centrally into their work and what is actually happening on the ground. Today, in practice, the reality is that disability remains a marginal issue for almost all official aid agencies as well as for the large generalist NGOs. This provides the context for the final discussion, which outlines a number of specific measures that need to be taken if the relationship between aid, poverty and disability is to contribute more effectively to substantial, more extensive and long-lasting outcomes that will benefit far more disabled people living in and vulnerable to extreme poverty in poor countries.

Aid

From its early beginning around the time of World War I to its more formal origin after World War II, the modern aid system has grown and expanded over the past six decades to become an important and permanent part of contemporary international relations. Today, all countries of the world are either aid donors or aid recipients and a small number, such as India and China, are both. This is the world of official aid – aid provided predominantly by the governments of the richer countries of the world to assist the poorer and poorest countries of the world. Indeed, official development assistance (ODA) is defined as the flow of concessional funds by official agencies to developing countries provided to promote the development and welfare of developing countries.[1] In recent years, especially since the 2000 Millennium Summit, official aid has been increasingly focused even more narrowly on poverty and its role in helping to achieve the Millennium Development Goals (MDGs), the first of which is to eradicate extreme poverty and hunger.[2] In the year 2005 total ODA first exceeded US$100 billion. However, in early 2010 it was estimated that total ODA in 2010 would be only US$107 billion (in fixed, 2004, prices), US$21 billion less than the amount promised at the Gleneagles and Millennium 5+ Summits in 2005.[3]

The aid world, however, extends beyond the relationship between official donors and recipient governments. Indeed, aid was provided by NGOs and church-based agencies, such as Norwegian Church Aid, Oxfam and CARE, before it was provided by most governments of rich countries. Today, hundreds of thousands of NGOs and civil society organisations (CSOs) across the globe both give and receive aid, the biggest ones with budgets in excess of US$100 million. More recently, aid has been channelled to poor countries by new philanthropic organisations, such as the Bill and Melinda Gates and William J. Clinton Foundations, joining other older ones such as the Rockefeller and Ford Foundations. The earliest aid from NGOs was emergency assistance provided particularly to civilians caught up in war, though after World War II the focus switched to poor countries, and especially to poor and hungry people. Today, while emergency aid remains important, most aid from NGOs, CSOs and philanthropic organisations comprises development aid, which is focused, even more sharply than official aid, on poverty, poor countries and poor people.

As the numbers of emergencies and disasters have risen in recent years, humanitarian aid has become increasingly important: in the 30 years to 2005 there was a 17-fold increase in emergency aid while total ODA only rose two and a half times (in real terms). However, in spite of this expansion, most aid is still provided for development and not for emergencies and, today, humanitarian aid probably accounts for less than 15 per cent of all aid. Information on the amounts of emergency and development aid provided by these non-state donors is not systematically gathered, but it is estimated that the total amounts used are in excess of US$20 billion a year.[4]

Aid and poverty

Historically, aid has been provided for a variety of different reasons and to achieve a range of purposes. Saving lives and addressing extreme poverty have always been at the central focus of aid given by NGOs. However, for donor governments these motives have usually also been mixed with others, with short-term political and strategic, as well as commercial, interests all influencing decisions about how much aid to give, to whom and for how long. After the Cold War ended there were great hopes that motives of national self-interest and short-term political gains would become far less influential in the decisions states made about the allocation of their aid funds. However, these high expectations have not been met. To this day, national self-interest continues to influence donor decisions of whom to aid. For example, in 2008 only just over 40 per cent of all official aid was channelled to the 63 poorest countries of the world, in which well over 90 per cent of the world's poorest people live (Riddell, 2008, pp. 103–5).

What role can aid play in addressing problems of poverty and in reducing the numbers of people living in extreme poverty? The answer is still debated and remains unsettled. Over time, different donors have answered this question in very different ways. In some periods aid was provided directly to poor people and poor communities to help address their core immediate needs of health, housing and education, to expand their access to credit or to raise their levels of agricultural production. In others it was provided to help reduce poverty indirectly by trying to stimulate growth, enhance wealth creation and expand jobs, for instance, by helping to address skill shortages, strengthen institutions, enhance good governance or expand the country's basic infrastructure. Since 2001 the international commitment to the MDGs has influenced the way in which many donors provide aid. However, this has not settled the question of whether aid for poverty reduction should be provided directly or indirectly, and most donors continue to provide aid in different forms. What is more, aid giving still continues to be characterised by high levels of volatility and unpredictability, with the amounts provided to a country often varying by 10–15 per cent or more from year to year.

To some extent, deciding how aid might best contribute to poverty reduction has been informed by impact studies of what aid has achieved. But the information provided by aid impact studies has been far less robust than one might expect for three main reasons. First, it is only in recent decades that donors have begun to approach aid impact assessment systematically and currently only a small proportion of aid is subject to rigorous assessment. Second, aid impact studies are still dominated by assessments of discrete aid projects, which have tended to focus on the relationship between aid and immediate outputs – such as whether the basic medicines, anti-retroviral drugs or bed-nets supplied with aid money have been distributed or whether more school-aged pupils are in school, whether teachers have been trained, clinics constructed or roads built. They have told us far less than we would like to know about the impact these discrete interventions have had on the lives of those assisted. Third, there have been very few studies that have been successfully able to assess the causal relationship between all aid provided by all donors to a country and the lives and prospects of those living in poverty. This is both because donors are still far more concerned with the impact of their aid and because of the paucity of information and especially the quantitative data available, especially in poor countries, that is able to measure change in key poverty variables.[5] For instance, according to the UN, for over 65 countries (mostly the poorest) there are no data on the numbers of people living in poverty; for almost 100 countries there are no data that record changes in poverty over time and for 115 countries no data are collected to monitor changes in child malnutrition (as recorded by weight), a key indicator of poverty (UNDP, 2005, p. 336).

The aggregate impact of aid on poverty reduction is also constrained by a range of key impediments at both the recipient and donor end. At the recipient end the core challenge in aiding the poor is that most of the poorest people live in the poorest countries, where the prospects for aid to work well are amongst the least encouraging. In broad terms, the evidence suggests that aid is effective when it is provided in countries committed to, and capable of, using aid funds efficiently and effectively, with transparent systems and where those making decisions and spending the money are accountable to their own citizens. Yet, the poorest countries – those that really need aid – tend also to be characterised by a combination of severe shortages of skills, weak institutions, inadequate legal and regulatory systems, underdeveloped markets vulnerable to manipulation by powerful interest groups, limited press freedom and a civil society and parliamentary system that are unable to monitor public spending and call politicians to account: precisely the mix of factors that are likely to undermine and reduce the impact of aid.

Additionally, the impact of aid on poverty is also critically linked to the way in which donors provide aid. A fundamental problem here is that what is commonly termed the official aid system is not really a system at all. The official aid provided for each recipient country comprises, in essence, the cumulative outcome of individual decisions made by every donor about how much aid each will give, the form in which it will be given and the time period over which it will be given. As the number of donors has increased, so have the systemic problems arising from this way of giving aid. One problem is the sheer number of official donors with whom each recipient has to interact. Today there are more than 200 official donor agencies. In 1990 no single aid recipient country had to interact with more than 40 individual donors, whereas today, at least 30 recipient countries do.[6] Another set of problems concerns the lack of harmony between donors concerning the different ways they choose to give aid, the different reporting requirements they impose on recipients and the lack of alignment between recipient country development policies and donor conditions and practices. It was only in March 2005, in what became known as the Paris Declaration, that donors formally acknowledged the importance of these systemic problems and agreed to take action to address them, explicitly acknowledging that for aid to be effective in poverty alleviation it needs to be provided in ways that assist countries to achieve their development polices and strategies, with recipients (not donors) taking the lead in coordinating the aid provided.[7] Three years later in Accra, at a meeting to assess the progress achieved, all agreed that progress had been too slow and that considerable gaps remained between the commitments of donors to address these systemic problems and what has been achieved.[8]

Is enough aid provided? This is a crucial question for the relationship between aid and poverty, especially since, as discussed above, there continues to be a significant mismatch between the allocation of aid and aid needs. The most widely known measure of sufficiency is the ratio of overall ODA to gross national income (GNI). For many decades, the target ratio has been set at 0.7 per cent. This target has never been reached. In 2007 the ratio for the 21 leading Development Assistance Committee (DAC) donors was 0.28 per cent – less than half the target level – and the leading donors have pledged to increase their aid to reach an ODA/GNI ratio of 0.46 per cent by the year 2010. However, this target is not going to be met. Early 2010 projections from the OECD suggest that the ratio will be close to 0.33 per cent (see note 3). When it was created, the 0.7 per cent ratio was based on a rough-and-ready assessment of aid needs, so today it provides an extremely crude indicator of aggregate aid needs (see Riddell, 2008, p. 427, n 4). However, extrapolations of more recent studies of aid needs at the country level reinforce the view that there remains a significant gap between the amount of official aid currently provided and the amount needed – even if most aid were to be channelled to the countries where most of the poorest people live.[9] On this basis, most informed commentators would concur with the view that aid could make a far greater difference to poverty reduction if more of it were provided, and that one of the reasons for the persistence of extreme poverty is the yawning gap between the amount of aid needed and the amount of official aid provided.[10]

Aid matters for poverty reduction, but is aid the answer? Is it either the sole or the crucial factor in the elimination of extreme poverty? The view that seems to be conveyed by those campaigning for more aid is that it is, while there is a related and widely shared public perception that if only more aid were provided then this would ensure that the MDGs are achieved. The reality, however, is different. There is a wealth of evidence to show that countries have developed and reduced, if not eliminated, extreme poverty without, or with very little, development aid and that countries in receipt of significant amounts of aid over prolonged periods have experienced no marked improvement in the incidence of poverty. What this suggests is that an array of factors other than aid can have a bearing on growth, development, wealth creation and poverty reduction. Consequently, it is often factors other than aid that make a crucial difference to aid-recipient countries and to the numbers of people living in poverty. This is not surprising as ODA accounts for less than one per cent of the GNI of all developing countries, only five per cent of the GNI of sub-Saharan African countries, and less than ten per cent of the GNI of the world's 50 poorest countries (UNDP, 2007, pp. 292–3). However, it is equally important not to swing the argument completely the other way and suggest that aid is irrelevant to poverty reduction. The evidence, as discussed above, suggests that aid has been effective in helping to meet the immediate needs or to fulfil the basic human rights of significant numbers of poor people, both directly and indirectly. Aid works best when provided in sufficient amounts, under the control of a recipient committed and able to use it well, and when donor country policies are consistent with and supportive of the poverty-focused objectives that underlie their aid giving.

It is against this brief summary of the wider discussion of the relationship between aid and poverty and what donors are doing that the rest of this chapter discusses the relationship between aid, poverty and disability.

Aid, poverty and disability

We live not only in a world of sharp inequalities, but in one of growing inequalities.[11] Neither wealth nor poverty is evenly distributed and extreme poverty affects particular groups of people disproportionately. If aid is to be used to help address and reduce extreme poverty then it is important to identify the main groups of people who are poor, understand the nature and causes of their poverty, and why and how aid might be used to assist them – ideally, to help them escape permanently from poverty.

In this section we discuss the relationship between aid, poverty and disability. We focus in particular on the way in which aid agencies have understood and analysed the problems of disability, the policies they have adopted to address the problems of disabled people living in extreme poverty and the impact these policies have had and are having. We examine the way that aid funds have (and have not) been used to assist disabled people who are living in extreme poverty.[12] We review the evidence of the impact of aid projects and programme that have aimed either directly or indirectly to assist disabled people, and discuss the implications arising from the new approaches of aid giving on the ways that aid has traditionally been provided to help address the problems of disabled people living in extreme poverty.

Poverty and disability in poor countries: concepts, data and data gaps and the findings from recent research

Disabled people constitute the world's largest minority, and some 80 per cent of disabled people live in developing countries. The poorest people of the world include a large number of disabled people and the incidence of poverty tends to be far higher among disabled people than across the population at large, as discussed recently by Amartya Sen (2009, pp. 255–60). The most widely quoted statistics suggest that about ten per cent of the world's population or 650 million people live with a disability, but that 20 per cent of the world's poorest people are disabled.[13]

At one level, these figures are helpful inasmuch as they show that disability is an important issue for aid agencies, one of whose main concerns is the reduction of poverty, suggesting that poverty reduction projects and policies supported with aid funds need to ensure that they include poor disabled people. However, there are two main difficulties with this sort of presentation of data on disability and extreme poverty.

The first is that, as yet, we do not have a very accurate picture of the numbers of disabled people living in poverty. The aggregate figures quoted are little more than very crude guesstimates; the fact that the same numbers are repeatedly quoted year after year is itself an indicator of their inaccuracy (see Eide and Loeb, 2005). The second problem is that drawing up and presenting crude raw data that focus simply on the estimated total number of people with disabilities and in poverty, without providing the contextual analysis of why so many (and almost certainly a disproportionately high number of) disabled people are poor, risks applying inappropriate and ineffective approaches to reducing the numbers of very poor people with a disability. This is because a key reason for extreme poverty among those with disabilities can be traced to the way that society has traditionally treated disabled people – characterised by discriminatory practices and by approaches that have not been based on principles and processes of inclusion.

This brings us to one of the central issues in this discussion of the role of aid in helping to reduce the poverty of those with a disability: precisely how one approaches and defines disability. Defining disability is far from easy, not least because disabled people comprise a heterogeneous group of people with a range of impairments and functional capabilities (Guernsey et al., 2007, p. 7).

In broad terms aid agencies have historically approached the issue of disability through the medical model of disability (Barron and Amerena, 2007, p. 9). Here, disability is viewed predominantly as an issue affecting individuals; one that focuses on the physical or mental state or attributes of particular individuals characterised by quite easily identified impairments, who need to be looked after by the fit and able. Perceived thus, it is fairly easy to identify and hence to count the numbers of people who are disabled.

Viewed from this perspective, the purpose of aid is seen predominantly in terms of trying to improve the lives of individuals with different disabilities by helping them to live better with their impairments. Here the issue of aid effectiveness tends to focus on discussions of who to help, balancing the (higher) unit costs of assisting fewer people with more severe disabilities versus the (lower) unit cost of assisting more people who are less severely disabled, in which cost effectiveness is widely assumed to favour the establishment and maintenance of institutions and facilities set up to cater exclusively for those with different sorts of disabilities, such as the deaf or the blind. Using aid in this manner not only separates disabled people even more from the wider society but reinforces the notion that they are different and need to be treated differently; at the extreme, this approach confirms the prejudice that people with disabilities are abnormal and so should be excluded from the mainstream.

In sharp contrast to the medical model, the social model provides an understanding of disability drawn from a holistic and inclusive view of society in which all human rights apply equally to all citizens, including people with disabilities. Against this backdrop, disability is viewed as the outcome of an interaction between any impairment (physical, mental, intellectual or sensory) and obstacles. The obstacles include not only physical barriers, but also prevailing attitudes and discriminatory practices and prejudices that prevent or limit the participation in society of those with disabilities. Hence, disability is viewed as a multifaceted concept in which society, through its failure to champion people with disabilities and practise inclusiveness, contributes to disability as much as the impairment itself does. Social attitudes have an impact that is likely to extend well beyond individuals to different groups of people with disabilities and to their families as well.

In recent years the social approach to disability has occupied a more central position in the discourse about disability. For example, it informed and helped shape the basis for the World Health Organization's (WHO) International Classification of functioning, disability and health, endorsed by member states in 2001 (see WHO, n.d.) and underpinned the UN's Convention on the Rights of Persons with Disabilities (UNCRPD), which was adopted by the General Assembly in December 2006 and came into force in May, 2008.[14]

While this growing consensus on what constitutes disability is a welcome advance, not least because of its close alignment to the rights-based approach to poverty and development that the UN and key aid agencies have championed for almost two decades,[15] it raises some new and different questions for the discourse about aid, poverty and development that has been shaped for so long by the medical model. In the first place, as a recent study puts it,

> although it should be possible to estimate the size of the various disability populations, determine their needs and develop appropriate and cost-effective strategies to meet those needs … this is yet to be accomplished … largely because disability is a complex inter-connected bio-medical, social and environmental phenomenon [that] *is yet to be fully analysed and understood* (Metts, 2004, p. 2, emphasis added).

In spite of a range of important initiatives to try to address both significant data and conceptual gaps, this comment still holds true.[16] This has profound implications for those providing aid in order to help reduce the numbers of disabled people living in extreme poverty. Because we do not know a) precisely who is disabled, b) what relative importance ought to be given to different people with different disabilities and c) how they might best be assisted, it is not easy to know precisely how to deploy aid funds and whether they should be focused on directly assisting people or channelled to address the wider systemic factors that contribute to disabilities.[17] However, what we do know is that the social model of disability has significantly expanded the numbers of people with disabilities who are now recognised.[18]

To try to bridge the data and conceptual gaps in our knowledge of the incidence and the extent of poverty among those with disabilities, in-depth case studies of particular developing and poor countries have been undertaken. One such initiative has been to construct a database on living conditions among people with disabilities in specific southern African countries, using the evidence gathered as a basis of comparison with the wider population. Another has been the more rapid, but informative, country case studies undertaken as part of the UK-based disability knowledge and research programme.[19] India, Zambia, Malawi, Namibia, South Africa, Nigeria, Rwanda and Cambodia are among the countries closely studied in this programme.

These studies have not as yet been able to provide detailed and complete data on the numbers of disabled people living in poverty. This is hardly surprising because in most of the poorest countries accurate data on the overall numbers of people living in extreme poverty is not readily available. However, they have provided broadly consistent and complementary data across different countries, which contribute to our still partial knowledge about the nature and extent of poverty among those who are living with a disability compared with those who are not. Box 2.1 summarises some of the findings that are emerging from contemporary research and studies. These need to be read against the backdrop of the considered opinion of two respected scholars working in the field that 'the relationship between poverty and disability has not been well established in the literature' (Braithwaite and Mont, 2008, p. 18).

Box 2.1 Poverty and disability in poor countries: a summary of recent research findings

Crude historical data suggest that the proportion of people with a disability in the industrialised world is far higher than in poor countries. However, recent case study material suggests that the differences are far less, and that the numbers of people with a disability in poor countries are significantly higher than earlier studies suggested.

Proportionately more people with a disability than the general population are likely to be living in extreme poverty, not least because of the higher proportion of disabled people who are unable to gain access to formal education and the linked, far higher rate of unemployment among disabled people than in the wider population. Estimates from Asia and the Pacific suggest that less than five per cent of *disabled* children have access to any education and training, and usually more than half of disabled people in poor countries are unemployed. What is particularly worrying is that in a period of greater consciousness of disability issues, some country case studies (for example, India) record rising rates of unemployment for disabled people (O'Keefe, 2007, p. xiii). According to one source, disabled people comprise between 15 and 20 per cent of the poor in developing countries (Elwan, 1999, p. 15).

Women and minorities are also disproportionately poor. Yet when disability is added to these attributes, both the extent and depth of their poverty are likely to be higher still.

As poor people are likely to have fewer assets, disabled poor people and their families are also likely to account for a higher proportion of those facing the prospect of long-term poverty and a lower proportion of those vulnerable to short-term bouts of poverty (Lwanga-Ntale, 2003).

Additionally, the poor living standards, vulnerability to disease, marginalisation and isolation of those living in extreme poverty in turn increase the risk that such people may acquire a range of different physical and psychological impairments. The WHO judges that about half of disabilities in poor countries are preventable and are directly linked to poverty (DFID, 2000, p. 3).

Studies suggest that people with disabilities acquire HIV/AIDS at rates up to three times higher than those of non-disabled people because of their higher risk of physical abuse, isolation and poverty and their access to services and information (World Bank, 2007, p. 11).

Conflict is a major cause of permanent disability; a significant proportion of countries experiencing conflict are among the poorest countries.

The influences of these factors, in turn, mean that poverty for disabled people is more likely to spread and affect their families than is generally true for the wider population of poor people. It is judged, for example, that a quarter of the population of the Asia–Pacific region are impacted by disability. In some countries people with particular and severe impairments and their families frequently face social prejudice, isolation and, at the extreme, ostracism, based on the belief that the full range of human rights do not and should not apply to them.

In sum, country case studies tend to confirm the working hypothesis in the literature (Yeo and Moore, 2003) that, on the one hand, disability is a cause of poverty (in India, it is assessed as being the biggest cause [Thomas, 2005a, p. 4]) and, on the other, that poverty is a cause of disability, suggesting that those with a disability present a risk of being doubly vulnerable.

Finally, the studies confirm the findings of the wider literature on poverty (see, for instance, Narayan, 2000) that analyses of disability by poor people with a disability and from organisations representing such people provide fresh and different insights and understanding of the problems of disability. These insights are vital to obtaining a holistic picture that both enriches and deepens our understanding of the problems of poverty and disability.

Source: The points made here are drawn particularly from Braithwaite and Mont (2008), DFID (2000), Eide and Loeb (2005), Elwan (1999), Loeb *et al.* (2008), Lwanga-Ntale (2003), O'Keefe (2007), Thomas (2005a, 2005b, 2005c), World Bank (2004, 2007) and Yeo and Moore (2003), as well as from a range of other donor studies cited at the end of Box 2.2.

Against this backdrop, the next section focuses on the aid provided by official agencies and tries to answer the following question: what contribution has aid made to disabled people who are poor, especially those living in the poorest countries?

Official aid, poverty and disability

An overview: how much official aid goes to disability projects and programmes?

In considering the contribution that official aid makes to poverty and disability, the initial question is: how much aid has been provided by donor governments to help address the problems of poor people with disabilities? The answer could help us understand the priority that aid agencies have given to the issue of disability. The short answer is that we do not know: the following paragraphs help to explain why.

For more than 40 years, official aid statistics have been gathered by the DAC of the Organisation for Economic Co-operation and Development (OECD). Besides focusing on the total aid provided by official donors and the countries to which it has been provided, aid statistics have also classified aid by the different purposes for which it has been given. However, to this day, the OECD/DAC aid statistics do not provide a separate category for aid projects or programmes for people with disabilities and they have never attempted to capture aggregate data on aid for disability or required donors to provide them with such information. The term disabled is referred to, but just once, where it is mentioned with ten other groups all lumped together under the heading social/welfare services.[20]

As there is no global donor-wide institutional obligation for official donors to report on the aid they channel into disability initiatives, very few individual agencies provide such data in their (often more comprehensive) aid statistics. For instance, the UK's Department for International Development (DFID) annual publication *Statistics on International Development* (DFID, 2008) provides no data on UK official aid used for disability projects and programmes. However, the World

Bank has tried to capture the share of resources (grants and loans) it has allocated to disability interventions and judges that between 2002 and 2006, four per cent of all World Bank projects by number and five per cent of new volumes of lending were to projects with a disability component (US$4.9 billion), comprising six per cent of all economic and sector work (World Bank, 2007, p. 2). Similarly, it is estimated that from 1991 to 2003 Finland allocated about five per cent of its official aid to disability-specific initiatives (STAKES, 2003, p. 8). Given Finland's long history of giving priority to disability issues and the lead of the World Bank among multilateral donors in trying to mainstream disability issues into its overall programme portfolio, the share of total ODA going to disability interventions is likely to be far lower than the amounts provided by these two donors, suggesting that considerably less than five per cent of all ODA is currently used for disability projects and programmes.

If we compare this figure with the World Bank's estimate, that upwards of 15 per cent of the poorest people in poor countries have disabilities and that specifically targeted initiatives are needed to address this poverty (see Box 2.1), then disability does not appear to constitute a priority for official ODA. Indeed, the absence of key data and the low priority given to disability issues in overall aid flows supports the view that historically disability has been largely invisible to aid agencies. The way that most agencies approach poverty has not included an explicit focus on the issue of disability, nor any systematic proactive engagement with disabled people. For most of the past 40 years of aid, when the medical or welfare approach to disability provided the dominant mind-set, the lack of data on aid given to disabled people is especially worrying.

As the social model of disability has increasingly become the preferred way to engage with the issues of disability for many official aid agencies, as described below, the absence of statistics explicitly capturing the amount of aid channelled to projects and programmes for the disabled is more understandable. This approach points to the need for aid agencies to approach poverty and disability, at least in part, as a cross-cutting issue that needs to be mainstreamed across the whole portfolio of aid interventions, just like gender and the environment. Against this backdrop, it is therefore particularly worrying that the current OECD/DAC aid classification, which was most recently revised in 2007 after the General Assembly had adopted the CRPD, continues to require official donors to collect aid data on disability based on the older medical/welfare view of disability. This is done only in relation to aid used to fund projects and programmes exclusively for disabled people. In contrast, the revised codes include a question that attempts to capture at least part of the official aid funds allocated for gender work, while the environment is highlighted as a cross-cutting/multisectoral issue.[21] It thus appears that for the OECD/DAC, disability continues to be a marginal issue.

Recent changes in official development assistance and disability

For the past 40 years the dominant approach of official aid agencies to the problems of disability and poverty has been to channel aid funds directly into discrete projects targeted at specific groups of disabled people or to fund NGOs to undertake similar sorts of work. For some countries, indirect funding through NGOs has been of major significance: in the case of Finland, as much as 70 per cent of official aid for disability projects has been used to support NGO activities (STAKES, 2003, p. 10). In recent years, however, official agencies have been making changes to these traditional approaches, influenced in part by the wider discourse on development cooperation that has led to changes in emphasis and priorities in aid giving.

The first of these changes has been the growing and sharper focus given by aid agencies to issues of poverty, and the concern shown by many official donors for the forging of sharper direct links between aid and poverty reduction. It is against this background that the development of the MDGs mentioned above should be seen. They have led to some agencies targeting their aid to the achievement of specific poverty goals. The second change, in part linked to these aid-MDG initiatives, has been the development of new or different ways of giving aid – often referred to as the new aid modalities. In recent years this has involved shifting attention away from the focus on discrete stand-alone aid projects to providing and packaging aid to support broader development and poverty-reducing policies and activities. In the past (for this is not a particularly new approach), this was termed programme aid. Today, programme aid is channelled to different sectors (such as education and health), through different sector-support programmes, one form of which is through sector-wide approaches, or SWAps, where aid funds are provided to a given sector within the framework of an overall sectoral strategy. Programme aid is also being provided to levels higher than discrete sectors, notably central governments, to boost aggregate spending through what is termed budget support.[22]

It is against these changes that donors approach the issue of disability (and hence the sub-issue of disability and poverty) through the social model perspective described above. Donor attention to and growing awareness of this markedly different approach to the issue of disability can be traced back to the adoption of the UN Standard Rules on the Equalisation of Opportunities for Persons with Disabilities in 1993.[23] However, the impact on the official donor understanding of, and especially its policy on disability was, initially, quite limited. Indeed, during the 1990s only one donor agency, the United States Agency for International Development (USAID), introduced (in 1997) new policy guidance specifically for work on disability, the *USAID Disability Policy Paper*, reflecting a more inclusive approach to the issue. However, in 1996, Finland's policy document, *Decision-in-principle*, had incorp-orated the issue of disability formally into Finnish development cooperation and since then Finland has continued to give priority to disability as a cross-cutting theme in its overall approach to poverty, as confirmed in its *Towards a Sustainable and Just World Community, Government Decision in Principle 2007* (see Kokkala, 2006, pp. 15–17; Ministry for Foreign Affairs of Finland, 2007).

However, changes in other agencies then began to happen quite quickly. From 2000 onwards a growing number of major official aid agencies set about drawing up their own new policies on disability, all characterised by the shift in emphasis to the more inclusive social model within which the issue of disability was viewed. Box 2.2 provides examples on these on an agency-by-agency basis. By 2006 at least half of the main OECD donors had adopted a specific new policy on aid and disability. A number of agencies began to use the term 'mainstreaming' to describe the way they sought to ensure that decisions about all their aid projects and programmes would be informed by their actual or potential impact on people with disabilities, minimally to ensure that these would do them no harm.[24] Most agencies have used the term 'twin-track approach' to encapsulate how they approach the issue of disability. One track involves continued direct support targeted at particular groups of people with disabilities; the other is aimed at addressing the range of systemic problems that underlie, cause, contribute to or perpetuate the poverty of those with disabilities. In both cases these new approaches dovetail neatly with the wider changes to official aid giving that were taking place, linked to the MDG initiatives and the new aid modalities mentioned above.

Box 2. 2 New official donor policies on, and approaches to, aid and disability

The World Bank cites its 2001 social protection strategy as a turning point in its approach to disability. Its policy and subsequent approaches are summarised in Braithwaite *et al.* (2008). The Bank (www.worldbank.org) was instrumental in setting up the Global Partnership for Disability and Development (GPDD), an alliance of official agencies including UN agencies, NGOs and DPOs established with financial support from official donor countries including Norway, Finland and Italy for a multi-donor trust fund aimed at accelerating the inclusion of people with disabilities and their families in development policies and practices.

For its part, the UK produced its issues paper, *Disability, Poverty and Development* a year earlier (DFID, 2000), its policy paper, *Reducing Poverty by Tackling Social Exclusion*, in 2005 and its *Working on Disability in Country Programmes*, in 2007.

For the Nordic donors the November 2000 conference on Disability and Development Cooperation provided the basis and catalyst for a series of new policies and approaches, all emphasising the human rights dimension of their approach to disability and its inclusion in international development cooperation initiatives. Norway produced its own policy, *The Inclusion of Disability in Norwegian Development Cooperation* in 2002, Denmark, *The Inclusion of Disability Aspects in Danish Development Cooperation*, in 2004 and Sweden, the SIDA position paper, *Children and Adults with Disabilities* in 2005.

Beyond the Nordics a new European-wide approach to disability, *Guidance Note on Disability and Development for EU Delegations and Services*, was published in 2005, while Germany's *Disability and Development: A Contribution to Promoting the Interests of Persons with Disabilities in German Development Cooperation* policy paper was published in 2006.

At the end of 2008 Australia produced its *Development for All: Towards a Disability-inclusive Australian Aid Program 2009–14*.

Source: Braithwaite *et al.* (2008); Commonwealth of Australia (2008); Danish International Development Agency (2004); DFID (2000, 2005, 2007), EU (2005); Federal Ministry for Economic Cooperation and Development (2006); Norwegian Agency for Development (NORAD, 2002); Swedish International Development Cooperation Agency (SIDA) (2005).

These changes need, in turn, to be placed alongside discussions that took place to develop and agree a stand-alone CRPD, promoted by Australia, among other leading donor countries. While the CRPD does not contain any new rights or any substantial new insights into the rights of disabled persons beyond those contained in other UN documents, it is particularly important to the issue of aid and disability because it contains a unique and specific Article (32) focused exclusively on the issue of international cooperation. While not specifying precisely how aid funds should be used, this Article (together with some others) provides pointers to guide official donor approaches. For details of Article 32 and references to other articles relevant to international cooperation, see Box 2.3.[25]

Box 2.3 Key articles in the CRPD directly relevant to aid and international development cooperation

Article 32

1. State Parties recognise the importance of international cooperation and its promotion, in support of national efforts for the realisation of the purpose and objectives of the present Convention, and will undertake appropriate and effective measures in this regard, between and among States and, as appropriate, in partnership with relevant international and regional organisations and civil society, in particular organisations of persons with disabilities. Such measures could include, inter alia:

a) ensuring that international cooperation, including international development programmes, is inclusive of and accessible to persons with disabilities;

b) facilitating and supporting capacity-building, including through the exchange and sharing of information, experiences, training programmes and best practices;

c) facilitating cooperation in research and access to scientific and technical knowledge;

d) providing, as appropriate, technical and economic assistance, including by facilitating access to and sharing of accessible and assistive technologies, and through the transfer of technologies.

Article 4

2. With regard to economic, social and cultural rights, each State Party undertakes to take measures to the maximum of its available resources and, where needed, within the framework of international cooperation, with a view to achieving progressively the full realisation of these rights, without prejudice to those obligations contained in the present Convention that are immediately applicable according to international law.

Article 37

2. In its relationship with States Parties, the Committee shall give due consideration to ways and means of enhancing national capacities for the implementation of the present Convention, including through international cooperation.

Source: UN Enable (2006)

By early 2010, a total of 145 countries were signatories to the Convention, including all 22 members of the OECD/DAC . The USA only signed after the election of President Obama in July 2009. However, by July 2010, 87 countries had ratified the Convention, a marked improvement on the 41 that had ratified it by the end of 2008. However, among the major OECD donors, the European Union, Finland, Ireland, Luxembourg, Norway and the United States had not ratified the Convention. They account for over a third of all ODA.[26]

Official aid, disability and poverty: an assessment of impact

In this section we shift our focus from what donor agencies have said about how they address the problems of poverty and disability to what has happened in practice: what has been the impact of the aid that official donors have provided and what impact have their policies had on the poverty of people with disabilities and their prospects for becoming permanently free from extreme poverty?

These are critical questions, but space does not permit more than a brief overview of the evidence. Additionally, the review of evidence is severely hampered by the paucity of robust and systematic evidence of impact. For instance, although we have discussed above some crude estimates of the total (and very low) aggregate amount of official aid channelled to projects and programmes for disabled people, we have no data at all on either the total number of acutely poor disabled people who are directly or indirectly in receipt of aid funds, or even the total number of disabled people, whether they are poor or not.

The impact of discrete projects and programmes

With support from the Canadian International Development Agency (CIDA), the OECD/DAC hosts a website containing comprehensive data on the evaluations undertaken of all official aid projects and programmes from the mid-1970s to the present day. This contains details of many thousands of evaluations. However, the database contains only 50 evaluations of official aid projects and programmes that make any mention of the words *disability, disabled* or *disabilities* and of these only 14 are evaluations of projects and programmes specifically or primarily focusing on disabled people, and only two of these have been published in the last eight years. Almost all of these turn out to comprise the funding of NGOs and NGO projects by official aid donors, which is discussed in the next subsection. Only one evaluation, *Label Us Able: Proactive Evaluation of Finnish Development Cooperation in Disability Issues* (STAKES, 2003), even begins to attempt to assess disability within the wider framework that a mainstreaming approach would require. Additionally, and in common with other official evaluations, the small number of evaluations that have been carried out suffer from the following weaknesses.[27]

– They tend to focus predominantly on reporting the link between aid inputs and outputs (numbers of people assisted, whether those assisted received the aid provided, such as glasses for the partially sighted and hearing aids for the deaf) and not on outcomes (most notably, the impact of aid on the lives and well-being of those in receipt of aid).

- Relatedly, because of poor baseline and monitoring data, the evaluations are largely unable to assess the causal relationship between the aid provided and the lives and livelihood of those assisted.

- There is a lack of in-depth data on the overall impact of aid provided at the sectoral level on the lives of disabled people, whether they are poor or not, and there is no reliable and detailed data and information on the overall impact of all aid to particular recipient countries on disabled people.

This does not mean that we have no information on the impact of official aid and aid policies on disabled people and disabled people who are poor. Rather, it means that we have no comprehensive and accurate data to enable us to form an overall view of the impact of such aid interventions. This is due in part to the failure of individual agencies and aid agencies as a whole to give priority to such assessments of impact. For instance, DFID introduced its policy on disability and poverty in the year 2000, but it was only in 2008 that the organisation started commissioning evaluations to assess the impact of its policies. Likewise, while the OECD/DAC has working groups and commissioned studies on the cross-cutting issues of gender and the environment, it has no formal group for disability issues and has commissioned no study of the issues surrounding efforts to mainstream disability.

What we have are a small number of one-off studies that examine – sometimes specifically, more often indirectly – the impact of disability aid interventions or policies. While some of these provide a rich source of information, we are not able to say how representative they are of the broader picture. This is important because, as with the wider literature on aid impact, individual studies contain a mixed bag of results. Some show important and tangible gains for disabled people, some suggest there have been few, if any, major improvements and some are unable to draw robust conclusions. Additionally, consistent with the wider literature, agencies that are themselves involved in projects tend understandably to place in the public domain evidence, or anecdotal stories, of successes, and to give less prominence or remain completely silent about their failures, so that the available literature emanating from the agencies tends to be positively biased.

Box 2.4 provides an illustration of the sorts of disability projects funded by official aid agencies. It shows a rich range of different initiatives and varying claims of successes and failures, strengths and some weaknesses. However, the evidence we currently have is extremely limited. Hence, there is an urgent need to increase the quality and the number of studies that rigorously assess the impact of these sorts of official aid interventions.

Box 2.4 Official aid disability projects and some examples of impact

A number of official donors have used their influence successfully to lean on recipient governments to initiate or expand activities to ensure they include people with disabilities.

Examples from DFID include the following: supporting the Government of Vietnam's primary education for disadvantaged children programme, which makes a special provision for disabled children, including teacher training and making schools accessible; funding a study in Zimbabwe on the scope of disability to provide an overview of the current situation of disabled people in that country, to map channels of support for work on disability and to identify strategies to facilitate greater involvement of disabled people in poverty reduction policies.

In Cambodia, Indonesia, Mongolia and Vietnam the World Bank has helped to build administrative capacity and to develop an inclusive management information system. In Cambodia it has helped in the development of socially inclusive materials.

In Benin, Denmark has piloted an education sector programme (2004–5) that aims to include 200 children with disabilities in public schools. This includes procuring assistive devices and campaigns for schools and parents aimed to ensure that each child with a disability gets a tutor. The pilot is to be followed up with funds to co-finance a national policy for persons with disabilities, with a special focus on access to education.

From 1997 Denmark funded a range of initiatives aimed at preventing disability in India through three major health projects to eradicate leprosy (1986–2003), control blindness (1977–2003) and immunise against polio (1996–2003). Since 1977 early detection and health education have been integral parts of these activities, while rehabilitation was included as a smaller component of the polio eradication project. All three projects succeeded in bringing down the prevalence of the targeted diseases and providing models for interventions but the sustainable integration of the prevention activities into the overall health system has at times been complicated. By 2005 all three projects had been handed over to the Indian health authorities.

In Vietnam, Germany has set up an International Society for Prosthetics and Orthotics, run training courses and worked with the Ministry of Health and advised the Social Affairs Ministry in expanding its orthopaedic service structures. A complementary microfinancing scheme provides physically disabled men and women with loans to create sustainable livelihoods.

In Ghana, Germany has supported the establishment of integration classes at regular schools for children and young people with intellectual or learning disablities. In addition, inclusive models are being developed to integrate these children and young people into their families' productive setting after they leave school so that they can contribute to the family income and help secure their own livelihoods. A further focus of the project involves advising partners in the field of special education and upgrading teaching staff.

In Mali, a USAID initiative called the trickle-up programme managed to more than double the number of disabled entrepreneurs participating in its micro-enterprise programme, as well as to encourage numerous civil society organisations to develop relationships with DPOs and people with disabilities.

In Vietnam, USAID has been supporting disability rights and reforms for more than ten years. It has recently funded support for the establishment of the National Coordinating Committee on Disability. Representatives from 15 line ministries as well as people with disabilities sit on this committee to make recommendations to policy makers and other government officials. This support has led to the passage of national construction standards for accessibility and the US mission has worked very closely with other donors to ensure that newly planned mass transportation systems will be accessible to persons with disabilities.

USAID funds support activities to ensure the inclusion of people with disabilities in political processes and elections. In Ghana, USAID has supported a tactile balloting effort through which a new ballot was designed for people with visual impairments. In the 2004 national elections 18,000 visually impaired people were trained to use the new ballot without assistance. This training marked the first time that people with visual impairments were able to vote independently in Ghana.

Source: Reports and policy statements from different official aid agencies: Danish International Development Agency (2004); DFID (2000); Federal Ministry for Economic Cooperation and Development (2006); Guernsey *et al.* (2007); Nilsson and Qutteina (2005); O'Keefe (2007); STAKES (2003); USAID (2003, 2005) and World Bank, Disability and Development Team (2004).

The new aid modalities

Moving beyond the consideration of discrete aid projects aimed to assist those with disabilities, we need to ask the following questions. What has been the impact of the new aid modalities on disabled people? What have been the effects and impact of the new policies on disability on the way that official agencies approach disability issues? Has the mainstreaming of disability occurred, and if so, to what effect? Like the data and information we have for judging the impact of discrete projects, information on these questions is poor and patchy, so that answers to them are necessarily also limited, drawing in part on anecdotal evidence. However, it provides a more consistent and uniform picture, with two recurring themes.

The first is that the new aid modalities appear to have made little significant difference to people with disabilities, because of the complete or almost complete absence of the issue of disability in the ways they have been both constructed and implemented. For instance, the word disability is entirely absent from the text of the MDGs, implicitly suggesting that general strategies to reach the MDGs will trickle down and impact positively upon people with disabilities, whereas the evidence strongly suggests that specific policies, including the direct targeting of the disabled poor, are needed (see, for example, Shepherd et al., 2008). Likewise, the template produced by the donor community under the leadership of the World Bank for developing recipient-led development and poverty reduction strategies, termed poverty reduction strategy papers (PRSPs), not only failed to include disability as a central or cross-cutting issue, but often failed to mention the issue of disability at all. According to a 2002 study by the ILO, only 2 out of 31 of the earliest PRSPs dealt with disability adequately (see ILO, 2002; STAKES, 2003, p. 69).[28] While changes have occurred in more recent years and references to disability in PRSPs are now more commonplace (see, for instance, World Bank, 2004), even recent and revised policies have been criticised for failing to give sufficient clear attention to disability issues and their integration into broader policies (see, for instance,

Miller and Ziegler, 2006, pp. 24, 35). What is more, no study has yet been undertaken to assess the difference made to the lives and living standards of poor disabled people as a result of the policies and activities surrounding PRSPs.

Next, what impact have the new sector-wide approaches and budget support had on poor disabled people? The picture is not encouraging. In the first place, and mirroring the experiences with the PRSPs, there is little evidence of these new, more all-encompassing ways of giving aid that actively incorporates and mainstreams disability. Second, and relatedly, the assessments that have been made of the impact of these new instruments have mostly either completely ignored the issue of disability or treated it extremely cursorily. For instance, there has been one major multidonor assessment of the impact of budget support aid, which was published in 2006. However, neither the long synthesis study – extending to over 300 pages of text – nor the methods and approach paper make even one mention of the word disability (see Lister, 2006; IDA, 2007). Likewise, a major joint-donor cross-country study of official aid to basic education, which included more than ten country case studies, also failed even to comment on how this new way of providing aid impacted on people with disabilities (Freeman and Foure, 2003). Two early studies, on the impact of education SWAps undertaken by UNESCO's International Institute for Educational Planning in Namibia and Zambia, likewise provided no analysis of the impact of SWAps on disabled people (see West, 2003; Eilor, 2004). The absence of references to disability also apply to the early studies of health SWAps. For instance, a 2003 mapping exercise of health SWAps in 11 aid recipient countries did not consider it sufficiently important to ask any questions about SWAps and disability (Jeffreys and Walford, 2003). A 2007 review of health SWAps in six African countries also failed to mention their impact on disabled people, though it did comment on the difficulties of drawing firm conclusions about the overall contribution of these SWAps to poverty reduction, suggesting that discerning its impact on different groups of poor people would be even more challenging (Walford, 2007). This sort of conclusion is reinforced by the views of donors engaged in SWAps in particular countries. For instance, a study in Nepal reported that donors there did not believe that SWAps were well enough designed to be able to look specifically at ways of targeting the most excluded groups (SDD and OPM, 2008, p. 17).

Notwithstanding this overall critical assessment, there is some evidence, though not much, which paints a more positive picture of the impact of the new aid modalities on the issue of disability. For instance, the 2006 evaluation of Finnish development cooperation from the disability perspective contains a rare assessment of the Zambia educational SWAp, the basic education sub-sector investment programmes from the viewpoint of disability, with Finland, Denmark and Ireland actively involved in components related to inclusive education. The evaluators highlight key tangible changes in policy and decisions made by the government that favour disabled people, attributing this, in part, to the long-term engagement of donors, notably Finland, with disability issues in education, and noting that their engagement also influences other donors involved in the SWAp.

> Overall the finnish experiences in sector-wide support in education, including special education, are positive. The results are the fruits of long-term commitments and capacity-building in the field (STAKES, 2003, p. 39).

However, in common with other studies, this evaluation failed even to ask the most crucial questions: what effect have these policies had on the proportion of poor disabled people in school and finishing school, and what impact have these (positive policy) changes had on the lives and economic well-being of poor disabled people?

However, these seemingly rare positive assessments of particular initiatives need to be placed alongside a dominant criticism of agencies' wider efforts at mainstreaming. The dominant conclusion of assessments has been the consistent failure of agencies effectively to mainstream disability into the rhythm of their wider work, notwithstanding the rhetoric of mainstreaming contained in so many of their recent policy statements.

The best longitudinal evidence we have of progress made comes from the USA. Since the new policy was introduced in 1997, by early 2010 five studies had been undertaken to assess the implementation of USAID's disability policy, the most recent of which was published in December 2008. Although these report progress over time, most notably in relation to the awareness of disability issues among agency staff and (in the 2008 report) undertaking far more activities that include disabled people (USAID, 2008, p. vii), the constant theme is that far more can and needs to be done, especially to ensure the inclusion of people with disabilities in official aid programmes. The third (2003) report, for instance, notes that many USAID missions still do not make the link between disability and their current strategy, not least because of a still limited understanding of the policy (USAID, 2003, pp. 8, 13). The 2005 report continued to echo these findings, commenting that although

> ... we are better than we were, we are not as good as we should be: much work remains ... [to] systematically include people with disabilities in our development efforts, ...
>
> not least because
>
> ... most missions do not have a disability plan, notwithstanding the publication and distribution to all missions of a manual on including disabilities in international development programmes (USAID, 2005, pp. vii, viii, 9).

The gap between donor policy statements and donor practice has been confirmed in a number of more recent studies, including those focusing on issues in which donors have been more aggressively engaged in promoting and mainstreaming, such as gender. For example, a recent international study of donor compliance with their gender, rights and equity approaches concluded that

... while there has been progress in attention to human rights, gender and equity issues at the policy level, the extent of implementation and monitoring of these commitments is less advanced and has not been given the sustained attention by partner governments and donors. This is where efforts should now be focused, and this presents a series of challenges for achieving better outcomes (SDD and OPM, 2008, p. v).

More widely, the Australian policy on disability, *Development for All*, provides a useful summary of the problems and weaknesses still faced by official donors who have introduced new policies on disability, listing the following factors to explain why translating disability-inclusive policy into practice has been 'slow and challenging' (Commonwealth of Australia, 2008, pp. 35–6):[29]

- there is relatively little review and documentation of the impact of bilateral programmes on disability and development, and there is limited information on lessons learned and best practice approaches

- disability is not explicit in the MDGs

- there is a lack of broad institutional support (in and across aid agencies) for incorporating disability in what staff do, and this goes some way towards explaining why policies are often resisted

- staff may be resistant due to a lack of understanding, a lack of confidence, a lack of skills, workload pressure and prejudice

- there is a lack of resources for programming initiatives and monitoring progress

- there is a lack of accountability mechanisms for monitoring progress.

Yet this negative assessment needs, in turn, to be placed alongside some other recent evidence that points to changes that have been occurring in donor practices, suggesting that some donors at least are beginning to address in a more substantial way some of the systemic problems of the continued invisibility of disability in the new aid modalities and the widespread failure to embed mainstreaming effectively into the ongoing work of agencies. This is illustrated, for example, in the education sector, where in the last few years official donors have begun to commission in-depth research that is attempting to discover both why the issue of disability has not been addressed in mainstream research and what donors need to do to change their practices (see, for example, Savolainen et al., 2006). Examples of these include the DFID-funded study on disability, poverty and education being undertaken by the Research Consortium on Educational Outcomes and Poverty and the five-year research on education and exclusion undertaken by the Consortium on Research on Educational Access, Transitions and Equity, which includes specific studies on the exclusion of people with disabilities.[30] DFID is also embarking upon research across the agency, but particularly with key decision makers to try to understand precisely why their policies on social inclusion that include disability in practice have produced such minimal institutional change in traditional ways of working.

However, it remains to be seen whether this new wave of initiatives and the serious and holistic way, for example, that Australia seems to be approaching the implementation of its new policy on disability (in mid-2009, it set up a Reference Group to provide strategic guidance to the government on implementing its policy) will result in the substantial changes in donor practices that are still needed. It is not merely one element of the twin-track approach that still seems not to be working. For all the new policies enunciated by official donors and for all the research they have commissioned, the reality today is that most poor people with disabilities are still excluded from and remain untouched by the aid activities funded, directly or indirectly, by official donor agencies.[31]

Disability, poverty and NGOs

Introduction and overview

In this section we shift our attention from official aid to focus on the activities of NGOs engaged in disability work, especially in poor countries. Its main purpose is to provide a broad, albeit brief, overview of the relationship between aid and aid funds provided to support the work of these agencies on disability and poverty, with a particular focus on their impact. We start, however, with a brief outline of the sector, drawing attention to its complexity and to the range of activities undertaken.

The engagement of NGOs and faith-based groups in issues of disability in poor countries goes back a long way. Indeed, it pre-dates the involvement of official aid agencies by many decades. This early work was predominantly undertaken within the framework of the medical and charity model, where assistance was provided first to individuals with disabilities and then, increasingly, to groups of similarly disabled people, often in institutions set up with the funds from charitable aid donations. To this day considerable amounts of aid money are used to fund such activities, though there is still no reliable overall statistical database available to show how aggregate aid funds are allocated to different end users. In the early days little attention was given to providing any rigorous assessment of the impact of these activities, especially their effect on living standards and opportunities open to people with disabilities, the cost-effectiveness of the aid provided, its sustainability and the extent to which those who most needed assistance were in fact those who received it. The emphasis was on helping, and if the aid reached those who needed it and achieved its short-term immediate objectives, that was predominantly considered good enough.

After World War II changes began to take place, accelerating from the 1970s onwards. One change was the creation of a growing number of NGOs, such as the UK-based Leonard Cheshire Disability, specialising in issues of disability and then the extension of their work from the industrialised donor countries to poor countries. Another change was the establishment of new agencies such as Sightsavers

International in the 1950s, whose work was focused exclusively in poor countries. A further change was that as more generalist NGOs grew and expanded their work, some, such as Oxfam, began to support projects and programmes explicitly for people with disabilities. A fourth change that began in a small way in the late 1970s but that became particularly important from the early 1990s onwards was the funding of disability programmes of NGOs by official aid agencies. In Scandinavian countries official aid has always constituted a significant share of the total income of NGOs undertaking activities in developing countries (commonly much higher than 50 per cent). What was different for NGOs engaged in disability activities was that in some countries they were allocated a disproportionately higher share of total funds earmarked for disability work. In Finland, for example, NGOs working on disability issues have received up to 70 per cent of all the funds the government has earmarked for disability activities (STAKES, 2003, p. 10). However, and notwithstanding the steady rise in income from official aid sources, the total amount of official aid channelled to NGOs working on disability issues in poor countries has continued to be lower than the amounts needed, in part because of the changing ambitions of a growing number of agencies.

A different sort of change began to be evident from the 1980s. From this time onwards an increasing number of NGOs and faith-based organisations working in poor countries began to alter their approach, extending their activities well beyond assistance to targeted groups of poor people, with resulting changes in the way in which their aid funds were spent. Underlying this change was an analysis of under-development that attributed the causes of poverty to issues beyond the specific poor communities to whom aid funds were directed in the form of discrete projects and programmes. These included the power structures and political processes at the village level, through to international institutions, systems and structures and the operation of markets that either excluded poor people and poor countries or that were assessed as functioning in ways that operated to their disadvantage. This analysis stimulated agencies to begin and then rapidly expand the range of their work to undertake advocacy, campaigning, lobbying and informational activities, which highlighted the nature and importance of these impediments and then sought to address them. As these changes took root, most agencies continued their grassroots project work – though some abandoned their direct project work entirely – while others, such as the UK-based agency War on Want, were created exclusively to focus on these systemic and structural issues. This way of approaching development and poverty eradication was given an added boost by the human rights movement and the linked expansion of what became known as the rights-based approach to development, and by the growing importance of international and cross-border influences on development in the world of increased globalisation. This in turn helped to highlight the need to address cross-cutting themes such as gender and, more recently, the environment, if poverty-reduction efforts were to reach all people and produce sustainable and lasting results.

These wider developments in turn influenced the way that NGOs engaging in disability issues perceived their role and the range of activities they undertook. However, though linked, changes among NGOs working in the disability field were also profoundly influenced by the changing discourse taking place internally and specific analyses in relation to disability, which have been highlighted in the subsection above. One consequence of this was that far more attention began to be given to the role and importance of people with disabilities and the organisations that they were beginning to establish – the DPOs. It is now widely recognised that DPOs contribute in unique ways to developing a deeper and different understanding of the nature and causes of disability, and hence raise different questions about the ways in which aid funds might be used to assist in poverty reduction. In the UK a key purpose of Action for Disability and Development (ADD), set up in 1985, was to support and strengthen DPOs.

The consequence of these different influences has been to create an approach to poverty reduction and the use of aid funds by NGOs working on poverty and disability issues that comprises a range of many different types of activities, including the following:

Humanitarian aid can inadvertently exclude disabled people
Photo: William Daniels/Panos Pictures

- project work directed at assisting specific groups of disabled people *in loco*, by addressing their needs, promoting the fulfilment of human rights and, where relevant, increasing access

- advocacy, lobbying, campaigning and informational work aimed at increasing the profile of disability, changing laws, policies, institutions, structures and processes that continue to exclude, marginalise and discriminate and undertaking work to place disability issues in the mainstream

- research work, including activities aimed at deepening and developing understandings of the nature, causes and extent of disability in poor countries

- capacity-building activities aimed at strengthening and increasing the engagement and influence, or 'voice',[32] of disabled people in poor countries

- networking, solidarity and fund-raising work.

Many NGOs working on disability issues undertake a wide range of these activities, yet a significant number continue to work exclusively on discrete projects for specific groups of people with disabilities. However, more specialised agencies have grown up focusing on one or a more narrow range of activities and the mainstreaming perspective is now dominant in the discourse about disability issues led by NGOs involved in disability issues and DPOs.

How much aid do the NGOs working on disability and the poor receive and spend, and is it sufficient? How many poor disabled people directly benefit from the discrete aid projects aimed directly to assist them, and what share of the total number of number of poor disabled people do these activities reach? What share of total funds used comes from official donors and what proportion from private donations? To what extent do official donors influence the nature and direction of the work that NGOs working in the area do by the funding decisions they make, and what influence do these agencies have in determining such aid allocations?

These are all important questions. They are asked because of the growing importance that NGOs, including DPOs, now have in the overall aid, poverty and disability system. However, these questions are not easy to answer, either for NGOs working in the field of disability and poverty or for those working in the wider world of poverty and development.[33] This is because, historically and in common with the wider world of NGOs, NGOs working in the disability and poverty fields have seen themselves primarily as independent agents and not as integral to and part of an overall system that they have a particular interest in understanding and analysing.

In recent years some agencies have grouped themselves together into federations or consortia, such as the International Development and Disability Consortium (IDDC, n.d.) However, there is no body equivalent to the OECD/DAC for official aid agencies whose aims include gathering aggregate data and statistics on their activities and trying to harmonise and align cross-agency activities. As a result, no agency is responsible for the collection of aggregate and systematic data on the overall and combined contribution of NGOs working in the poverty and disability field. We do not have accurate information upon which to provide reliable answers to our earlier questions. Indeed, it is difficult even to estimate the total amount of official aid received by NGOs because the OECD/DAC does not compile such data, and even its published aggregate statistics on total funds given to all NGOs are known to be inaccurate as the largest donor, the USA, still does not submit figures to the OECD on this item (Riddell, 2008, p. 418, *n 34*). The time may soon come when either leading DPOs and agencies working on disability or the general public, or both, believe these gaps in our knowledge are sufficiently problematic for steps to be taken to address them.

Against the backdrop of key gaps in our overall knowledge and based on a review of the literature and discussions with scholars working in the field, the following provide at least partial answers to some key issues about aid, poverty and disability particularly applicable to the NGOs, which further research could confirm, refine or even refute.

There is a widely shared view among agencies that the aid available for their work on disability and poverty falls well short of the amount needed. This is in spite of the steady increase in income from private donations and legacies for the largest agencies in recent years, as well as income flows from official donor agencies.

The contribution that official aid makes to the aggregate income of NGOs and DPOs varies from country to country, though the overall figure is probably not more than 15 per cent of total income.[34] For the poorest countries, and consistent with the wider picture of NGO funding, aid comprises a major, and for most, still the most important source of income for nationally based NGOs and DPOs. Although a significant proportion of this income comes from northern NGOs, a share comes from official donor agencies. However, in recent years some of the larger NGOs have been able to source funds from poor country governments; for instance, in 2007 Sightsavers was able to obtain funds from the Nigerian government for more than half its projects (Sightsavers International, 2008).

To what extent do official donors influence the priorities of NGOs? The answer is almost certainly less than for NGOs in general, for two reasons: first because, excluding Scandinavian countries, the share of total income from official donors is less than it is for generalist NGOs[35] and, second, because a high proportion of the funds provided by official donors from Scandinavian countries is not earmarked. The dominant criticism is that insufficient official donor funds are allocated to NGOs to support disability and poverty initiatives. In 2007 a grant-making body, the Disability Rights Fund (n.d.), was established exclusively for the purpose of receiving and channelling funds from donors (official and private) to disability initiatives, including those in poor countries, based solely on work to promote the objectives of the CRPD. In December 2008, it received a grant of US$1.3 million from DFID.

As for the future, in the short term there is a concern that the financial crisis and the recession across donor countries will adversely affect funding from private donations and probably from private foundations as well, though a sharp fall in official levels of aid is not expected. However, as the numbers of poor people are expected to rise and poverty already disproportionately affects disabled people, the gap between the aid needed and that provided is likely to widen further.

As the total number of poor people with disabilities in poor countries still remains unknown, it is not possible to give an accurate assessment of the proportion of disabled people directly reached by NGO activities. However, it is widely assumed that the proportion is still small, and probably less than half of all poor people in low-income countries are estimated to be touched by NGOs.[36] But is this the right sort of question to ask? In one interpretation the question, though often asked, seems to imply a model of engagement that assumes that it is exclusively through NGOs – and the continuing expansion of their activities – that improvements will come. This seems to be an underlying theme of the informational material put out by many NGOs working in all fields of development. In contrast, one of the objectives of the mainstreaming approach is to move away from the view that it is the NGOs' projects that will provide the answer, and towards the view that the outcome of more inclusive recipient government policies will be to reduce progressively the need for NGOs to try to plug the gaps in coverage.

The impact of aid used by NGOs on poor people with disabilities

There is one further central question that we need to answer: what is the impact of the work of NGOs, including DPOs, that are financed by aid funds, especially its impact on the lives of poor people with disabilities in poor countries – one of the core objectives that most agencies working in the field are striving to achieve? It is to this issue that we now turn.

Against the backdrop of the earlier discussion of the impact of official aid interventions, it is not surprising to find that forming a judgement on the overall impact of NGOs' efforts to reduce the poverty and improve the lives of poor people with disabilities is exceedingly difficult, because of the paucity of reliable and systematic data and information and in-depth evaluation studies.

Even if they are exclusively focused on disability and poverty issues, NGOs working on these issues are part of the wider world of NGOs engaged in development and poverty issues and share with them many attributes, especially when it comes to the monitoring and evaluation of their work. Although the field still remains under-researched, the following paragraphs provide a brief summary of what we know from studies, surveys and reviews of impact assessment among development NGOs.[37]

The evidence in the wider literature

In general, it was some years after official aid agencies began to undertake evaluations of their aid that NGOs first began to consider assessing the impact of their development work. From the 1990s the larger NGOs in particular started to think about and develop methods of assessing the impact of their work. However, to this day, few undertake systematic assessments of their work and most agencies, especially the smaller ones, still undertake little to no rigorous assessments of impact.

Another problem concerns accessing information about project performance. With very few exceptions, such as CARE, Oxfam and the Bangladesh Rural Advancement Committee (BRAC, the large Bangladesh NGO), most NGOs remain reluctant to share information on project failures and almost none regularly place in the public domain, or on easily accessible websites, systematic information on the impact of the full range of all their different activities – their discrete projects for poor people and poor communities, or their advocacy, lobbying and campaigning activities.

The assessments that have been made are dominated by assessments of discrete projects, where the methods used range from the crude to the more sophisticated. It remains a challenge to assess the impact of most NGO development interventions beyond simply recording aid inputs and immediate outputs because of the absence of reliable baseline data and incomplete monitoring of projects, notwithstanding the far greater rigour in approach of the larger NGOs. However, though they remain comparatively small in relation to the tens of thousands of discrete NGO projects implemented each year, there are some examples of in-depth assessments of NGO projects using both robust methods. Indeed, NGOs have probably made use of a far more extensive and richer array of approaches, notably participatory methods, to try to understand and assess impact.

What does the evidence we have – partial and patchy though it is – tell us about this impact? It suggests that most discrete projects for poor communities run by NGOs successfully achieve their immediate objectives, though a high proportion are not financially sustainable without continuing external help. However, exceptionally few discrete wealth-creating or service delivery projects on their own provide sufficient benefits to enable poor people to escape permanently from poverty, though very few NGOs would claim that this is their core purpose. What outsiders view as marginal changes could be of major importance, not least in building the participants' confidence to do more.

Does NGO campaigning, lobbying and advocacy work? This is an issue that most NGOs and CSOs have only recently begun to try to answer in any systematic way, though assessments of such activities have been undertaken for some considerable time.[38] The evidence is probably slightly more robust than might be thought, and the results are mixed. There appear to be far more claims of success than there is firm evidence for attributing such success solely to NGO activities. There have been successes, such as the debt campaign in which NGOs and CSOs were centrally involved; however, many successes constitute what outsiders might judge to be small gains at the local grassroots level, though these can often be crucial to poor communities. Most go unnoticed and unreported not only by the international media, but also often by the national media.

What effect and impact have aid funds used for capacity building and strengthening NGOs and CSOs had? This is an issue that few NGOs have begun to examine and the answers from the studies that have been undertaken are mixed. One of the difficulties in trying to answer this composite question is that there is no single, simple or agreed method of building NGO capacities. Indeed, one of the characteristics and strengths of NGO approaches to capacity development has been the development of customised, endogenous and specific approaches rather than using blunt, one-size-fits-all approaches, more common with official aid initiatives (see Bebbington and Mitlin, 1996).

There have been both successes and failures. If the more extensive but still relatively small assessments of evidence from official aid efforts in this area are a guide, it is likely that sustainable successes are not common. Yet, as with the case of official aid, this does not mean that capacity-building efforts should be abandoned. Most studies suggest that they ought often to be intensified (see World Bank, 2005). A common problem identified has been the failure of NGO capacity-development projects to specify precisely what they are aiming to achieve. For many, however, the more fundamental question that needs to be answered is not so much whether the large and growing amounts of aid used for capacity development achieve their immediate short-term objectives, but the extent to which these different initiatives ultimately contribute to improving the lives of the beneficiaries. Most

NGOs have not yet focused on this question, though the experience of NGOs like Pact, that have worked on this issue for some years, indicates that when the goals are carefully selected and constructed, the lives of poor people can not only be improved, but can be shown to have been enhanced.[39]

What is the overall impact of NGO development activities in a particular country? Here we find one of the sharpest differences from official aid agencies, as few, if any, attempts have been made even to try to assess the wider effects of NGO development interventions on development outcomes. Most studies that purport to assess impact at the country level turn out to be predominantly descriptive overviews of the number, type and range of NGO activities, provided as backdrop to a discussion of impact at the project levels. The way they might go about trying to assess the overall contribution of NGO development activities to broader development outcomes is, however, likely to be more demanding than assessing the overall contribution of official aid because of the centrality that many NGOs give to empowerment issues, the impact of which is not at all easy to assess.

Evidence from the literature from DPOs and NGOs working
on disability issues

Against this backdrop it is not surprising to find that, historically, the assessment of impact has not been a major priority for DPOs and NGOs working on disability and poverty issues. A trawl of the websites of the larger agencies failed to find a single instance where an agency provided access to independent evaluations of their work. In common with other NGOs, the information on impact that is provided tends overwhelmingly to comprise summary accounts of particular interventions, most commonly reporting the successes achieved and focusing, in particular, on the numbers of people reached, the inputs delivered and the immediate outputs achieved from the aid funds used. It is extremely difficult to find any discussion or evidence presented of the impact and effects of the aid provided on the lives and poverty status of those assisted. Data on projects or programmes that have not been so successful, or even where the results are uncertain, is usually neither volunteered by agencies nor accessible on their websites.

Another feature of the information provided by many of the websites of NGOs working in the disability and disability/poverty fields is the growing prominence given to advocacy, campaigning and lobbying, capacity-building and research activities. Mention is often made here of achievements – some both impressive and significant, such as changes in the law to remove discriminatory legislation or to promulgate new laws consistent with different UN conventions or covenants, improvements in access for those with physical impairments, or the implementation of more inclusive policies – for instance, for educating children with disabilities. Some research studies have had a profound effect on current practices, challenging conventional wisdom and contributing to new ways of approaching issues that take note of disability issues. One example of this is the World Vision-initiated study on education and disability that influenced prevailing practices at the World Bank (Bines, 2007). Yet such reports of success invariably fail to identify the specific contribution that the activities of the particular NGO or DPO had on the final outcome and none have been found that assess the effects of these achievements on the lives of poor disabled people.

It would be easy to conclude from a review of the information put out by the agencies that this is all that can be said of the impact of the work of these agencies. Yet this would be inaccurate, as there is some far more robust evidence of impact. Though still small in number, a range of evaluations have been conducted and are being undertaken that directly or indirectly have focused on impact, including some (though still too few) studies that have applied quite rigorous methods and that have assessed the impact of discrete interventions on the lives of the beneficiaries. One example of an in-depth study is a three-year study undertaken by the International Centre for Eye Health in London in Kenya, Bangladesh and the Philippines, which assessed the impact of cataract surgery on the lives and living standards of those who went through the surgical procedures.[40]

It is among these studies that assessments of interventions can be found that highlight the weaknesses and failures of projects and programmes, as well the evidence of their successes. Given the small number of such rigorous assessment studies it is simply not possible to know whether the studies that have been undertaken comprise a representative sample. What is more, one needs to be extremely cautious about drawing conclusions about the merits of undertaking projects for poor people with disabilities, even if (and we have no robust evidence to suggest this is the case) this is done on the basis of evidence of some project failures. Indeed, because people with disabilities tend to face more constraints to achieving sustainable paths out of poverty than do the general population, then, a priori, one would expect projects for poor disabled people to be far more challenging both to construct and to succeed. Boxes 2.5 and 2.6 provide extracts from a selection of evaluations of the impact of disability projects and programmes undertaken by NGOs and DPOs. Those in Box 2.5 focus on discrete projects for particular groups of disabled people; those in Box 2.6 focus on aid-funded interventions that have had an impact beyond particular groups of disabled people, in some instances contributing to the objective of mainstreaming the issue of disability.

Box 2.5 Examples of the impact of NGOs' projects for disabled people from impact studies

An evaluation of the Community Based Rehabilitation programme (CBRP) in the Occupied Palestinian Territories investigated the impact of the programme from the perspective of disabled people and their families. Its main purpose was to ascertain to what extent the CBRP has contributed to improving their quality of life and to suggest ways in which the programme can more effectively meet their needs.

Despite the unfavourable political conditions the CBRP has recorded significant achievements. The evaluation found that it has

---

empowered individuals and parents, improved basic daily living skills and coping mechanisms, reduced stigma and isolation and increased social inclusion. People with disabilities are more respected in their families and have become more visible and more vocal. Many have also been able to access education and rehabilitation services.

In regard to the programme's impact on the different aspects of quality of life, it has had an exceptional impact on their emotional well-being and self-esteem. It has also had a substantial but uneven impact on their interpersonal relations, social inclusion and personal development. It has had some impact on their physical well-being (access to medical treatment, rehabilitation services and assistive devices), especially in Gaza and Central Region. However, the CBRP has had a limited impact on their self-determination and influence, material well-being and rights. The least impact has been found on the quality of life of persons with hearing impairments and severe intellectual disabilities.

The strategies that were most successful in achieving positive changes were moral support in getting the family to understand and deal with the disability, breaking isolation and helping to change the attitudes in schools and communities.

The local rehabilitation workshop (LOREWO project) was initiated in 1999 as a pilot aid project, providing assistive devices, predominately wheelchairs, to meet the requirements of the local population with disabilities and to aid people with disabilities economically by employing them in Namibia and Zimbabwe.

The immediate objectives of the project were to: create employment for people with disabilities, establish a local rehabilitation workshop infrastructure, facilitate local manufacturing and the availability of assistive devices (technical aids) and conduct capacity building and training of local personnel.

The evaluation concludes that thus far the LOREWO project has made an invaluable contribution to the raising of self-esteem, levels of skills and active participation of a total of 17 people with disabilities in a project they collectively own and manage. LOREWO has been able to achieve its immediate objectives, which were to employ and empower disabled people. It has helped disabled people by creating jobs for them as well as facilitating the local availability of assistive devices. However, for the future, LOREWO's sustainability is under threat because of a lack of self-generating finance, although there have been positive indicators of where this might lie, such as in the development of the local three-wheeler wheelchair. For now, LOREWO still needs funding in order to continue operating.

An external evaluation of the Uganda National Association of the Blind (UNAB) was carried out in 2007. The UNAB was established in 1970 as one of the first DPOs in Uganda and has been a recipient of large amounts of aid from both official donors and NGOs. It remains in good standing with both donors, the African Union of the Blind, the World Blind Union and other DPOs in Uganda.

Key government ministries also speak highly of it both as a partner and as a watchdog advocating the rights of disabled persons. The evaluation concluded that the UNAB is a sustainable organisation both institutionally and financially, although it still does not have nationwide coverage. The rehabilitation services that UNAB offers its members have the greatest impact on the lives of individual blind or partially sighted persons. It is able to advocate with competence the rights of the visually impaired in Uganda, currently with its strongest focus on education. However it has been least successful in running income-generating projects.

Overall, UNAB was assessed as being a well-functioning member organisation, although improved planning and reporting skills linked more closely to its own aims and objectives than to the requirements of donors would improve its results.

In Mozambique the International Disability Equality Agency was contracted by an organisation called Power to deliver empowerment training for disabled people. Power found that the delivery of training by disabled consultants, including a woman using a wheelchair, brought radical and far-reaching results and led to kick-starting a movement for women with disabilities in Mozambique that is now growing and working to promote access to education for disabled children.

In Mali, WaterAid collaborated with Sightsavers International to adapt village wells for people with disabilities. In consultation with blind users, simple adaptations made the wells easier and safer to use – the opening of each well was narrowed to reduce the danger of falling into it, a metallic plate was installed above the pulley wheel, alerting the user to the position of the water container, and a trench was dug for disabled users to draw water easily to their gardens.

The Zambian National Library and Cultural Centre for the Blind has been funded (largely by Finnish NGOs) for over 10 years. Though the library was established, remained open and provided service to disabled people, it had to close because of the high running costs and because the expected takeover of the running of the Centre by the government did not take place. The outreach plans for the Centre never materialised.

Source: DFID (2007); Kittelson and Okungu (2007); Nilsson and Qutteina (2005); Ruotsi *et al.* (2001); Samaita Associates (2007).

**Box 2.6 Examples of the wider impact of NGOs'
aid programmes on disability**

The Young India Project (YIP) in partnership with ADD, India, has included people with disabilities in all its work, the aim being to facilitate the access of people with disabilities to the services, equipment and opportunities they need to improve their own lives. Opportunities are created for people with disabilities through union membership to form supportive and campaigning self-help groups and awareness-building groups. By early 1998 YIP had unions in 209 *mandals* (group of 30–50 villages) with a total membership of more than 355,235. Work with people with disabilities makes up 25 per cent of YIP's activities. Well over 600 self-help groups of people with disabilities have been formed, with a combined membership in 1998 of more than 11,000. YIP has proved to be successful in linking disability issues to mainstream debates. People with disabilities are forming their own groups as well as participating in the general ones. They are increasingly aware of their rights and are able to claim and advocate their entitlements.

Leonard Cheshire Disability established a five-year inclusive education project in Oriang in western Kenya government schools. Initially, five schools had 2,700 pupils, although before the project started only 45 of the students had disabilities. Over time, enrolments expanded to 10,000, including over 600 children with disabilities and, indirectly, approximately 10,000 other children, parents and community members with disabilities. A total of 45 teachers were also trained in special needs education, through Kenya's teacher training institutions, which facilitated a change in their teaching style to learner-centred approaches. Additionally, work with the community extended beyond education to include home-based activities through which trained community health workers formed a link between schools and families. In 2007 an enlarged five-year programme was launched in response to overwhelming demand after the success of the pilot project. International replication plans are already under way.

In Bangladesh ADD worked with local research organisation Unnayan Shamannay to conduct research with disabled people in 23 districts. Research findings were discussed at a round table meeting opened by the minister of finance, and led to the inclusion of key commitments in the PRSP: to improve disabled people's access to health, education and transport services, to collect better data on the numbers of disabled people in Bangladesh and to develop a national disability action plan.

In Zambia aid funds were used to facilitate consultation between DPOs and the government on the 5th National Development Plan to which DFID funding is aligned. This consultation resulted in a chapter on disability and the disability movement is now involved in the inter-departmental meetings that take place to discuss plans and set budgets.

Source: DFID (2000, 2007); Leonard Cheshire Disability (2007).

Mention also needs to be made of the undoubted successes that have been achieved increasingly over the past 10 to 15 years in raising awareness of disability issues in both rich and poor countries, including awareness within and across aid agencies, symbolised most vividly in the achievement of creating and promulgating the UN Convention. While the list of what still needs to be done remains long and there are still substantial gaps between policies agreed and current practice, it needs to be acknowledged that significant progress has been made. Much of this would not have happened without the insights, research, determination and actions of individuals, groups and networks of people with disabilities.

Though questions can legitimately be raised about the methods used and hence the quality of some of the evaluations that have been carried out, even the small number of evaluations that we do have, especially when placed alongside the undoubted successes surrounding the signing of the UN Convention, helps build a picture which suggests that NGOs have had a significant impact on disability issues in poor countries, in large part because of the work of people with disabilities themselves. There have undoubtedly been failures, and very many more poor people need to be assisted. But the evidence we have suggests that agencies should have confidence to undertake and commission more independent studies to assess the impact of their work, not least because, although these are likely to highlight weaknesses and gaps in current approaches, if lessons are learned from them then such studies can contribute to a far greater and more extensive impact in this area in the future.

Conclusions and some recommendations for the future

The discussion of aid, poverty and disability needs to be placed in the wider context of the more general problems of aid and poverty summarised above. There are a number of similarities and weaknesses common to both general aid and aid and disability. For instance, official donors are not providing sufficient aid to the world's poorest countries and they are not providing enough to tackle effectively the problems of poor people with disabilities. Likewise, the gaps in information and the paucity of data upon which to draw firm conclusions on the impact of aid on poor people with disabilities are mirrored in the general literature on aid impact. Yet we know that the impact of aid is adversely – and seriously – affected by the failure of donors to work more closely together and the still large gap between their stated intentions to work towards greater harmony and alignment of their activities and the reality on the ground. These weaknesses also adversely affect the potential impact for aid initiatives focused on poor people with disabilities.

Yet the discussion has also thrown up some sharp differences between the general literature on aid and the role and use of aid in addressing the particular problems of poor people with disabilities. The most fundamental problem is that, notwithstanding the rhetoric of donors, disability and the plight of poor disabled people remains, in practice, a marginal issue for almost all donors. Disabled people are largely excluded from the rhythm of aid decisions and from the consciousness of key decision makers in aid agencies: they are still largely ignored. Fundamental shifts have certainly occurred in the rhetoric of donors and in the policies that an increasing number have articulated – highlighting the importance of disability issues and signalling a shift from the medical/individual impairment model to the social/inclusive and rights-based one. However the twin-track approach that many donors have adopted has not resulted in sufficient aid funds for projects and programmes designed explicitly for people with disabilities who would benefit from them, the inclusion of significant numbers of poor disabled people in mainstream activities or institutions in poor countries, or the effective mainstreaming disability into the day-to-day activities and decision-making processes across agencies. There are some signs, for instance in Australia, that changes are occurring to narrow the gap between rhetoric and reality, but earlier periods provided waves of optimism of effective change that did not materialise, so there are grounds for caution.[41] What is more, effective change is not likely to occur unless there is joint action in the donor community, which is unlikely unless the OECD/DAC takes a more proactive role.

However – and this is a further lesson to be drawn from the wider debates about aid and poverty – it is important that the discourse about aid, poverty and disability does not fall into the trap of seeing aid as the solution to the problems faced by poor people with disabilities in poor countries. Faced, as they are, with insufficient resources to meet their basic needs and secure the fulfilment of their basic rights as citizens without external assistance, aid certainly has a role to play in addressing resource gaps and funding shortfalls to provide access to more services to more poor people, including those with disabilities. But simply providing more and more aid remains insufficient. Poor countries need to implement policies to increase wealth and set them on a self-sustaining path of growth, providing gainful employment and distribution mechanisms that enable all citizens to live above the basic poverty line. While aid can help to achieve this long-term objective it needs to be provided alongside and in a manner supportive of the achievement of such policy goals.

Yet, as industrialised country experience confirms, such policies on their own will not automatically lead to gains for people with disabilities. Also needed in poor countries are far-reaching changes to the processes, institutions, structures and systems, including the legal system, within which people with disabilities, and especially those living in poverty, experience life as second-class citizens; lives that are characterised by prejudice, ignorance, discrimination and exclusion.

It is in this wider context that we end this chapter with a number of explicit recommendations for how aid might contribute more to improving the lives of poor people with disabilities in poor countries. Some focus on doing more directly for more poor people with disabilities, some on narrowing the gap between the rhetoric and reality of mainstreaming, and some focus on doing things differently by focusing on systemic issues and processes that lie outside and beyond the narrower world of aid, poverty and disability.

Providing more aid for poverty and disability

Donors are not providing enough aid to help meet the needs of the poorest countries. But in addition, the amounts of aid being channelled to disability projects and programmes are disproportionately far lower than the crudely estimated share of poor people living in poverty in poor countries. As long as agencies continue to provide aid in the form of discrete projects, on both equity grounds and because of the additional constraints that poor people with disabilities face, both official donors and generalist NGOs need substantially to increase the amounts of aid they channel to projects and programmes aimed at enhancing the lives and well-being of poor people with disabilities and expanding the capacities and capabilities.

**Making aid more effective by taking further measures
to mainstream disability in donor agencies**

Most official and many large NGO aid agencies now accept that the issue of disability needs to be mainstreamed in their work. However, the gap between the rhetoric and what happens in practice needs to be narrowed substantially, if not bridged entirely. Aid agencies that have not yet adopted an approach to disability in conformity with the UN Declaration need to be persuaded (or shamed) into doing so. The question is precisely how this goal can be achieved. There is no space to discuss this here in any detail, and it is an issue around which there is a growing and evolving literature.[42] Chapter 3 in this book is devoted explicitly to this issue. However, the following factors merit consideration.

Two linked and root causes of the failure of aid agencies to mainstream disability issues are an insufficient understanding and awareness of the nature and extent of the marginalisation of people with disabilities in society. While this issue can be adequately addressed only by raising general awareness and increasing understanding in and across donor countries, rolling out and institutionalising disability awareness training in aid agencies can also help, as can institutional assessments of disability, especially when these are undertaken regularly and systematically, and include researchers with disabilities.

Mainstreaming disability requires all key senior managers and those responsible for decisions about how aid funds are allocated to ensure that all decisions, including project appraisals, monitoring and evaluations, country and regional strategies, address the issue of disability. At the least, they should assess the direct and systemic effect such decisions are likely to have on the agency's disability objectives. Doing so ought to form part of regular staff appraisal systems, and how it happens should be addressed by senior management as regularly as other mainstreaming issues are discussed.

Mainstreaming will be enhanced if there is a budget for mainstreaming, if more senior managers include people with disabilities and if all departments are trained to understand that disability issues are a constituent part of their activities, and not something merely to be channelled to the disability advisor.

Mainstreaming will also be enhanced if agencies undertake and commission research that analyses the extent to which disability has been mainstreamed in major regular programmes, and where it has not.

History confirms that using researchers with disabilities adds both additional depth and different insights to such analyses.

Mainstreaming will be further enhanced if initiatives are taken by and agreed among groups of agencies, and against which ongoing practice needs to be regularly assessed. For official donors it is recommended that the OECD/DAC prioritises the issue of disability. In practice it could do this in two ways: first, by creating an explicit work stream on disability issues that develops guidelines and codes of good practice for donor agencies; and second, by adding disability to the key issues used in the assessment of donors under the regular peer review process.

Providing aid funds to increase awareness of disability issues within aid-recipient countries

Mainstreaming disability in aid agencies is not an end in itself. One of its key objectives is for disability to be mainstreamed in aid-recipient countries, the aim being to change attitudes, policies, processes, structures and systems so that all persons with disabilities, and especially those living in poverty, are included. For this to happen, wider society needs to pay far more attention to persons with disabilities, to the marginal status they occupy, the discrimination they face and the lack of access they have to mainstream facilities; and persons with disabilities, DPOs and people and organisations who support such goals need to increase their political power and influence. Aid agencies can assist in the achievement of these objectives in three different though linked ways, noted below.

1. Aid agencies can deploy more aid funds to strengthen the capacity of organisations and agencies championing disability issues and these goals, increasing both their voice and their competence to undertake advocacy, lobbying and campaigning activities more effectively to accelerate the movement towards a more inclusive society. Enhanced capacity development should also be geared towards expanding agencies' ability to monitor more systematically how the government and other agencies extend the services and access to services to disabled people in compliance with the law and associated regulations. The

aid provided for such activities needs to include long-term institutional support to DPOs and to those undertaking research to identify gaps in current legislation and practice.

2. Aid agencies ought to focus more upon aid funds and expand them to help enhance and build the capacity of parliament and its different committees so as to accelerate a movement to a more inclusive society. This could, for example, include support for the analysis of current legislation to ensure its compliance with the UN Declaration and linked human rights covenants and conventions, support for research and analysis to identify key gaps in domestic legislation and ensuring that the effective monitoring of current statutes, regulations and standards takes place, calling government and its institutions to account where necessary.

3. Official donors need to use the power they undoubtedly have, especially when united, to protect DPOs, those championing their rights and those working for change, especially change that challenges the interests of powerful political groups, or is perceived by such groups as a threat to their interests. This can happen only if donors move markedly away from focusing their efforts and attention on their own aid projects and programmes and work towards developing holistic approaches and strategies more consistent with the move to greater harmony and alignment, to which they have formally agreed in the Paris Declaration.

Addressing missed opportunities: taking greater advantage of the new aid modalities to promote and champion disability issues and to encourage aid-recipient governments to champion and mainstream disability issues

Mention has already been made of the failure of donors to champion disability sufficiently and to address the linked issues of disability and poverty in some of the new ways of giving aid. Much has been made in the literature of two specific weaknesses. The first is the omission of any reference to disability in the MDGs. The second has been the almost complete absence, especially in the earliest PRSPs, of any reference to the issue of disability and the failure of donors and aid-recipient governments to engage with DPOs in the consultation processes that did take place with CSOs. It is within the power of the donor community to address both these weaknesses and gaps and, although DPOs are now consulted more today than they were five to seven years ago, there is still far more that donors can and are able to do, especially in relation to the new aid modalities.

A common criticism made of donors who have begun to reduce the share of aid they provide in project form and increase the share to different sectors and, more centrally, as general budget support, is that they have been exceptionally slow in aligning their aid to home-grown development and poverty-reducing policies and strategies and in encouraging recipient governments to take an increasingly dominant role in coordinating donor aid and activity, as agreed in the Paris Declaration (see Wood et al., 2008). Indeed, it has been argued not merely that donors have continued to impose conditions on recipients but that conditionality has been more all-embracing, as it applies to the overall setting in which the decision to provide programme aid is placed. This enables donors to engage with – in other words, lean on – recipient governments on matters that include macroeconomic policies, governance and human rights issues (see, for example, Fraser and Whitfield, 2009).

While the objective supported by many scholars and commentators on aid issues is for genuine recipient ownership to increase and for donor conditionality to decline,[43] this is unlikely to occur in the short term. Until it does, donors will continue to exert pressure on recipient-governments and try to influence their policies well beyond the aid relationship. What donors have singularly failed to do, but can, especially if they act together, is to use their combined power and influence to lean on recipient governments to take practical steps (that will differ from country to country) to make their overall development policies more alive to the issues of disability and poverty, and to make the economy and the wider society more inclusive. The success that the donor community has frequently had in helping to change perceptions and policies towards people with HIV/AIDS provides a precedent that these sorts of actions are an appropriate focus of donor, and especially joint-donor, actions and evidence that they can have notable tangible effects. Donors have the power to complement and assist the core objectives that underlie much of the aid they provide to civil society organisations, namely to champion and accelerate the mainstreaming of disability.

The recommendation here is simply that they should start doing so. An additional reason is that it is wholly consistent with Article 4 of the UN Convention that official donor countries have signed and a growing number are now in the process of ratifying:

[W]ith regard to economic, social and cultural rights, each State Party undertakes to take measures to the maximum of its available resources and, where needed, within the framework of international cooperation, with a view to achieving progressively the full realisation of these rights (UN, 2006).

Notes

1. The definition of ODA was agreed in 1969 and refined in 1972. See Führer (1994, p. 25).

2. The full details of the MDGs and the commitments of the international community to help achieve these can be found in the 2001 Report of the United Nations Secretary General to the UN General Assembly, *Road Map Towards the Implementation of the United Nations Millennium Declaration*, available online at http://www.un.org/documents/ga/docs/56/a56326.pdf [Accessed 15 March 2010].

3. See OECD *Donors' Mixed Aid Performance for 2010 Sparks Concern*, available online at http://www.oecd.org/document/20/0,3 343,en_2649_34447_44617556_1_1_1_37413,00.html [Accessed 19 March 2010].

4. Trends in development and humanitarian aid from study by Development Initiatives (2005). In recent years a growing share of aid used by NGOs has been provided by official aid donors (donor governments), probably accounting for upwards of 40 per cent of their total income (and more in some countries such as Norway and Sweden), and the rest coming from private donations. For further discussion on these issues see Riddell (2008, pp. 259, 317–8, 418).

5. For a recent overview and discussion of the quality of the information available on the impact of aid and the methodological challenges involved in assessing aid, see Riddell *et al.* (2008).

6. Statistics on the rise in the number of donors and donor proliferation at the country levels are summarised in International Development Association (2007) and Frot and Santiso (2010).

7. See Organisation for Economic Cooperation and Development/ Development Assistance Committee (OECD/DAC, 2005a) and http:// www.oecd.org/dataoecd/57/60/36080258.pdf [Accessed 16 March 2010].

8. See Wood *et al.* (2008) and the Accra Agenda for Action (AAA) agreed at the 3rd High Level Meeting on Aid Effectiveness, Accra, Ghana, September 2008, available online at http:// siteresources.worldbank.org/ACCRAEXT/Resources/4700790- 1217425866038/AAA-4-SEPTEMBER-FINAL-16h00.pdf (Accessed 15 March 2010]..

9. See, for instance, Devarajan *et al.* (2002), Anderson and Waddington (2006) and the UN Millennium Project (2005, pp. 193–210).

10. The financial crisis and the slowdown in growth in both the industrialised world and in poor countries are likely to widen even further the gap between aid needs and the amounts of aid provided. For an analysis of these problems undertaken in late 2008 see World Bank (2008), Dang, Knack and Rogers (2009) and Addison, Arndt and Tarp (2010).

11. In 1965 the average income per inhabitant in the main donor countries was 22 times greater than in the poorest countries: by 2005 it was 65 times greater (see Riddell, 2008, pp. 126–7).

12. Space does not permit a discussion of those extremely poor disabled people who have been affected by disasters and emergencies, and the extent to which such people have and have not been reached by aid agencies and their emergency aid programmes. Some of the issues are discussed in Chapter 10 in this volume. See also the chapter 'Disability and disasters: towards an inclusive approach' in *World Disasters Report 2007* in International Federation of Red Cross and Red Crescent Societies (2007, pp. 87–111).

13. The World Bank study by Elwan (1999) is widely quoted as an authoritative source on poverty and disability statistics, as are the World Health Organization (WHO, n.d.) figures on the numbers of people with disabilities.

14. The Convention does not provide a clear-cut definition of disability, noting that disability is an evolving concept. However, according to the Convention, 'Discrimination on the basis of disability' means 'any distinction, exclusion or restriction on the basis of disability which has the purpose or effect of impairing or nullifying the recognition, enjoyment or exercise, on an equal basis with others, of all human rights and fundamental freedoms in the political, economic, social, cultural, civil or any other field. It includes all forms of discrimination, including denial of reasonable accommodation' (Article 2). For the full text of the Convention see UN Enable (2006).

15. For an accessible discussion on the rights-based approach to poverty and development see Picod (2004) and Uvin (2004).

16. These initiatives would include work by the UN Statistical Division to develop the Disability Statistics Database, work by the WHO on the International Classification of Impairments, Disabilities and Handicaps (ICIDH), the work of the International Labour Organization (ILO, 2007) on employment statistics of those with disabilities and the work of the Washington City Group to develop standard

questions on disability for census and population surveys. For further information on these see, for example, Metts (2004), Eide and Loeb (2005), ILO (2007) Mont (2007), Braithwaite and Mont (2008) and the Washington Group homepage (n.d.).

17. As Harris-White (2003, p.3) points out, disability is a relative term because different cultures define differently their norms of being and doing.

18. In Zambia the response to the 1990 Census question whether someone was blind, deaf, dumb and so forth, showed the prevalence was 0.9 per cent. The 2006 Living Conditions Survey asked people whether they had 'difficulties in seeing, hearing, walking, and remembering' and the resulting prevalence rate was 13.3 per cent (ILO, 2007, pp. 54–5).

19. This work was funded by the UK's Department for International Development (DFID, n.d.). For more information see http://www.disabilitykar.net/research/policy_co.html [Accessed 15 March 2010].

20. OECD/DAC (2007, pp. 10, 19, 39).

21. Under Code 15164, 'Women's equality organisations and institutions', official donors are asked to provide data and information exclusively on 'Support for institutions and organisations (governmental and non-governmental) working for gender equality and women's empowerment' (OECD/DAC, 2007, p. 8).

22. Budget support can be provided to different sectors – where it is called sector budget support – or to ministries of finance as 'general budget support'. For further discussion of SWAps see Riddell (2007, pp. 3–15) and for further discussion of the different types of budget support see Lister (2006, pp. 5–9).

23. See http://www.un.org/esa/socdev/enable/dissre00.htm [Accessed 16 March 2010].

24. The do no harm approach was initially influential in the world of emergency aid. See Anderson (1999).

25. Additionally, the 2002 Biwako Millennium Framework (BMF) for Action towards an inclusive barrier-free and rights-based society for persons with disabilities in Asia and the Pacific (2003–12) and the Biwako Plus Five have been adopted by the large donors and recipients in the region and also provide guidance for the action needed to create an inclusive society for people with disabilities in the Asia and Pacific region. See http://www.unescap.org/EPOC/documents/L2.1_PacificResolution.doc [Accessed 16 March 2010].

26. For up-to-date figures on which countries have signed and ratified the Convention see http://www.un.org/disabilities/countries.asp?id=16 [Accessed 16 March 2010].

27. The overall weaknesses in the quality, reach and coverage of aid impact studies are discussed further in Riddell (2008) and Riddell *et al.* (2008).

28. For a succinct summary of PRSPs and their link to donors see Fraser and Whitfield (2009, pp. 74–107).

29. This assessment is similar to earlier, more in-depth ones made, for example, by Albert (2004) and British Council of Disabled People (2005).

30. Further information on these research projects and their emerging outputs can be found on their respective websites: RECOUP http://recoup.educ.cam.ac.uk/research/disability.pdf and Consortium for Research on Educational Access, Transitions and Equity (CREATE) http://www.create-rpc.org/research/index.shtml [Accessed 15 March 2010].

31. This is a consistent and clear conclusion from the country case study work undertaken by Thomas in Rwanda, Cambodia and India (Thomas, 2005a, 2005b, 2005c).

32. The term 'voice' was coined by Hirschman (1970) in his influential book *Exit, Voice and Loyalty.*

33. The general issues are discussed in some detail in Riddell (2008), especially chapters 16 and 17.

34. In the UK the disability NGO that probably receives the highest share of its income from official donors is Action for Disability and Development. In 2007 36 per cent of its income came from official donors (DFID and the EU), see ADD (2007).

35. According to official statistics in 2006 British NGOs principally working on disability issues were able to access only £1.3 million in funds given to NGOs and CSOs out of a total provided for non-emergency purposes of over £180 million. See DFID (2008, Table 19, pp. 113–114).

36. See Riddell (2008, pp. 269ff) for the wider discussion of NGOs and their ability to reach poor people in poor countries.

37. The summary points are drawn from three studies and synthesis reports undertaken or led by the author. See Riddell *et al.* (1997, 2008) and Riddell (2008), especially chapters 10, 16 and 17.

38. See, for instance, Covey (1994) and Miller (1994) and, more recently, Hovland (2007) and Lofgren *et al.* (2008).

39. For examples of Pact's work and successes see Pact (n.d.) and Riddell (2008, p. 286).

40. See Sightsavers International (2008, p. 15). Available online at http://www.sightsavers.org/Who%20We%20Are/About%20Us/Annual%20Review/43443Sightsavers_lores.pdf [Accessed 16 March 2010].

41. See particularly AusAID's disability strategy document, which 'takes a targeted and sequenced approach, initially building a strong foundation and then scaling up over time as Australia's aid program's capacity and knowledge grows' (Commonwealth of Australia, 2008, p. 2).

42. See, for instance, the UN Economic and Social Council, Commission for Social Development (2007) and Miller and Albert (2005).

43. See de Renzio *et al.* (2008) for how this might be achieved.

References

ADD (Action on Disability and Development) 2007. *Annual Report and Financial Statements.* Frome, UK: ADD. Available online at http://www.add.org.uk/downloads/2007%20ADD.pdf [Accessed 12 March 2010].

Addison, T. Arndt, C. and Tarp, F. 2010. *The Triple Crisis and the Global Aid Architecture.* Working Paper No. 2010/01. Helsinki: United Nations University, World Institute for Development Economics Research (UNU-WIDER). Available online at http://www.wider.unu.edu/publications/working-papers/2010/en_GB/wp2010-01/_files/82784791381278751/default/2010-01.pdf [Accessed 19 March 2010].

Albert, B. 2004. *Is Disability Really on the Development Agenda? A review of official disability policies of the major governmental and international development agencies.* London: Disability Knowledge and Research Programme. Available online at http://disabilitykar.net/pdfs/disability_on_the_agenda.pdf [Accessed 12 March 2010].

Anderson, E. and Waddington, H. 2006. *Aid and the MDG Poverty Target: How Much is Required and How Should It Be Allocated? Working paper no. 275.* London: Overseas Development Institute. Available online at http://www.odi.org.uk/resources/odi-publications/working-papers/275-aid-mdg-poverty-target.pdf [Accessed 12 March 2010].

Anderson, M.B. 1999. *Do No Harm: How Aid Can Support Peace – Or War.* Boulder, CO: Lynne Rienner.

Barron, T. and Amerena, P. (eds.) 2007. *Disability and Inclusive Development*. London: Leonard Cheshire International.

Bebbington, A. and Mitlin, D. 1996. *NGO Capacity and Effectiveness: A Review of Themes in NGO-related Research Recently Funded by ESCOR*. London: International Institute for Environment and Development.

Bines, H. 2007. *Education's Missing Millions. Including disabled children in education through EFA FTI processes and national sector plans main report of study findings*. Milton Keynes, UK: World Vision UK. Available online at http://www.worldvision.org.uk/upload/pdf/Education's_Missing_Millions_-_Main_Report [Accessed 12 March 2010].

Braithwaite, J. and Mont, D. 2008. *Disability and Poverty: A Survey of World Bank Poverty Assessments and Implications. Social Protection and Labor Discussion Paper, no. 0805*. Washington, DC: World Bank. Available online at http://siteresources.worldbank.org/DISABILITY/Resources/280658-1172608138489/WBPovertyAssessments.pdf [Accessed 12 March 2010].

Braithwaite, J., Carroll, R., Mont, D. and Peffley, K. 2008. *Disability and Development in the World Bank: FY 2000–2007. Social Protection and Labor Discussion Paper, No. 0808*. Washington, DC: World Bank. Available online at http://siteresources.worldbank.org/SOCIALPROTECTION/Resources/SP-Discussion-papers/Disability-DP/0808.pdf [Accessed 12 March 2010].

British Council of Disabled People 2005. *Improving DFID's engagement with disability*. (Mimeo.) London: British Council of Disabled People. Available online at http://www.dfid.gov.uk/pubs/files/bcodp-dfid-disability.pdf [Accessed 12 March 2010].

Commonwealth of Australia 2008. *Development for All: Towards a Disability-inclusive Australian Aid Program 2009–2014*. Canberra: AusAID. Available online at http://www.ausaid.gov.au/keyaid/pdf/ FINAL%20AusAID_Disability%20for%20All.pdf [Accessed 12 March 2010].

Covey, J. 1994. *Accountability and Effectiveness of NGO Policy Alliances*. Report No. 11.8. Boston, MA: Institute for Development Research.

Dang, H.-A., Knack, S. and Rogers, S. 2009. *International Aid and Financial Crises in Donor Countries*. Policy Research Working Paper No. 5162. Washington, DC: World Bank. Available online at http:// www-wds.worldbank.org/external/default/WDSContentServer/IW3P/ IB/2009/12/29/000158349_20091229212514/Rendered/PDF/ WPS5162.pdf [Accessed 19 March 2010].

Danish International Development Agency (DANIDA) 2004. *Inclusion of Disability Aspects in Danish Development Co-operation, 2004. Status since the Nordic Ministers' meeting in Copenhagen*. Available online at http://www.danidadevforum.um.dk/NR/rdonlyres/ C91644CF-A5F2-441F-96FB-2C1637149494/0/DisabilityAspects.pdf [Accessed 12 March 2010].

de Renzio, P., Whitfield, L. and Bergamaschi, I. 2008. *Reforming Foreign Aid Practices: What Country Ownership is and What Donors Can Do to Support It*. Briefing paper (June). Oxford: Global Economic Governance Programme, Department of Politics and International Relations, University College. Available online at http://www. globaleconomicgovernance.org/wp-content/uploads/Reforming%20 Aid%20Practices,%20final.pdf [Accessed 12 March 2010].

Devarajan, S., Miller, M.J. and Swanson, E.V. 2002. *Goals for Development: History, Prospects and Costs. Policy research working paper 2819*. Washington, DC: World Bank. Available online at http://www-wds.worldbank.org/servlet/WDSContentServer/WDSP/ IB/2002/04/26/000094946_02041804272578/Rendered/PDF/ multi0page.pdf [Accessed 12 March 2010].

Development Initiatives 2005. *Global Humanitarian Assistance Update 2004–2005*. Evercreech, UK: Development Initiatives. Available online at http://www.globalhumanitarianassistance.org/ analyses-and-reports/gha-reports/gha-2005 [Accessed 12 March 2010].

DFID 2000. *Disability, Poverty and Development*. London: DFID. Available online at http://www.dfid.gov.uk/Documents/publications/ disabilitypovertydevelopment.pdf [Accessed 12 March 2010].

DFID 2005. *Reducing Poverty by Tackling Social Exclusion*. DFID policy paper. Available online at http://www.dfid.gov.uk/Documents/ publications/social-exclusion.pdf [Accessed 12 March 2010].

DFID 2007. *Working on Disability in Country Programmes. How To Note*. London: DFID. Available online at http://www.dfid.gov.uk/ Documents/publications/DisguideDFID.pdf [Accessed 12 March 2010].

DFID 2008. *Statistics on International Development 2003/4 – 2007/8*. London and East Kilbride: DFID. Available online at http:// www.dfid.gov.uk/pubs/files/sid2008/FINAL-printed-SID-2008.pdf [Accessed 12 March 2010].

DFID n.d. *Policy Project: In-country Research*. Available online at http://www.disabilitykar.net/research/policy_co.html [Accessed 12 March 2010].

Disability Rights Fund. Available online at http://www. disabilityrightsfund.org/index.html [Accessed 12 March 2010].

Eide, A.H. and Loeb, M.E. 2005. *Data and Statistics on Disability in Developing Countries*. London: Disability Knowledge and Research Programme. Available online at http://www.disabilitykar.net/docs/ thematic_stats.doc [Accessed 15 March 2010].

Eilor, J. 2004. *Education and the Sector-wide Approach in Uganda.* Paris: International Institute for Educational Planning. Available online at http://unesdoc.unesco.org/images/0013/001397/139756E.pdf [Accessed 15 March 2010].

Elwan, A. 1999. *Poverty and Disability: A Survey of the Literature. Social Protection Discussion Paper, no. 9932.* Washington, DC: World Bank, Social Protection Unit. Available online at http://www-wds.worldbank.org/external/default/WDSContentServer/WDSP/IB/2000/12/15/000094946_0011210532099/Rendered/PDF/multi_page.pdf [Accessed 15 March 2010].

EU 2005. *Guidance Note on Disability and Development for EU Delegations and Services.* Brussels: European Commission Information and Communications Unit. Available online at http://ec.europa.eu/development/body/publications/docs/Disability_en.pdf [Accessed 15 March 2010].

Federal Ministry for Economic Cooperation and Development 2006. *Disability and Development: A Contribution to Promoting the Interests of Persons with Disabilities in German Development Cooperation.* Policy paper. Bonn, Germany: Federal Ministry for Economic Cooperation and Development. Available online at http://digitalcommons.ilr.cornell.edu/cgi/viewcontent.cgi?article=1454&context=gladnetcollect and http://www2.gtz.de/dokumente/bib/06-0868.pdf [Accessed 15 March 2010].

Foster, M. and Mackintosh-Walker, S. 2001. *Sector Wide Programmes and Poverty Reduction. Working paper 157.* Centre for Aid and Public Expenditure. London: ODI. Available online at http://www.odi.org.uk/resources/odi-publications/working-papers/157-sector-wide-programmes-poverty-reduction.pdf [Accessed 15 March 2010].

Fraser, A. and Whitfield, L. 2009. Understanding contemporary aid relationships. In Whitfield, L., *The Politics of Aid: African Strategies for Dealing with Donors.* Oxford: Oxford University Press, pp. 74–107.

Freeman, T. and Faure, S. 2003. *Local Solutions to Global Challenges: Towards Effective Partnership in Basic Education.* Joint Evaluation of External Support to Basic Education in Developing Countries. The Hague: Ministry of Foreign Affairs. Available online at http://www.dfid.gov.uk/pubs/files/basic-education-final-report.pdf [Accessed 15 March 2010].

Frot, E. and Santiso, J. 2010. *Crushed Aid: Fragmentation in Sectoral Aid.* Working Paper No. 284. Paris: OECD Development Center. Available online at http://www.oecd.org/dataoecd/0/37/44341102.pdf [Accessed 19 March 2010].

Führer, H. 1994. *The Story of Development Assistance: A History of the Development Assistance Committee and the Development Co-operation Directorate in Dates and Figures.* Paris: OECD (mimeo).

Guernsey, K., Nicoli, M. and Ninio, A. 2007. *Convention on the Rights of Persons with Disabilities: Its Implementation and Relevance for the World Bank. Social Protection Discussion Paper, no. 0712.* Washington, DC: World Bank. Available online at http://siteresources.worldbank.org/SOCIALPROTECTION/Resources/SP-Discussion-papers/Disability-DP/0712.pdf [Accessed 15 March 2010].

Harriss-White, B. 2003. *Poverty and Disability with Special Reference to Rural South Asia.* Paper presented to the Chronic Poverty and Development Policy Conference, University of Manchester, April. Available online at http://www.chronicpoverty.org/uploads/publication_files/CP_2003_HarrissWhite.pdf [Accessed 15 March 2010].

Hirschman, A.O. 1970. *Exit, Voice and Loyalty: Responses to Decline in Firms, Organizations and States.* Cambridge, MA: Harvard University Press.

Hovland, I. 2007. *Making a difference: M and E of policy research. Working paper no. 281.* London: Overseas Development Institute. Available online at http://www.odi.org.uk/rapid/Publications/Documents/WP281.pdf [Accessed 15 March 2010].

International Development and Disability Consortium (IDDC). Available online at http://www.iddcconsortium.net [Accessed 15 March 2010].

International Development Association (IDA) 2007. *Aid Architecture: An Overview of the Main Trends in Official Development Assistance Flows.* Resource Mobilization, IDA. Washington, DC: World Bank Group. Available online at http://siteresources.worldbank.org/IDA/Resources/Seminar%20PDFs/73449-1172525976405/3492866-1172527584498/Aidarchitecture.pdf [Accessed 15 March 2010].

International Federation of Red Cross and Red Crescent Societies 2007. *World Disasters Report 200. Chapter 4 Disability and disasters: towards an inclusive approach.* Geneva: IFRC, pp. 86–111. Available online at http://www.ifrc.org/Docs/pubs/disasters/wdr2007/WDR2007-English-4.pdf [Accessed 15 March 2010].

ILO (International Labour Organization) 2002. *Disability and Poverty Reduction Strategies.* Discussion paper. Geneva: ILO. Available online at http://www.ilo.org/wcmsp5/groups/public/---ed_emp/---ifp_skills/documents/publication/wcms_107921.pdf [Accessed 19 March 2010].

ILO 2007. *The Employment Situation of People with Disabilities: Towards Improved Statistical Information.* Geneva: ILO. Available online at http://www.ilocarib.org.tt/portal/images/stories/contenido/pdf/Disability/statsguide.pdf [Accessed 19 March 2010].

Jeffreys, E. and Walford, V. 2003. *Mapping of Sector Wide Approaches in Health.* London: Institute for Health Sector Development. Available online at http://www.sti.ch/fileadmin/user_upload/Pdfs/swap/swap319.pdf [Accessed 15 March 2010].

Kittelsen, T.C. and Okungu, P.A. 2007. Evaluation of the Uganda National Association of the Blind. External evaluation commissioned by the Norwegian Association of the Blind and Partially Sighted (NABP). Oslo: NAPB (mimeo). Available online at http://www.atlas-alliansen.no/novus/upload/file/Ressursbanken/NBF%2046702%20 v1%201080%20external%20evaluation%20final%20report.doc [Accessed 15 March 2010].

Kokkala, H. 2006. Five years after Dakar. In Savolainen, H., Matero, M. and Kokkala, H., *When All Means All: Experiences in Three African Countries with EFA and Children with Disabilities*, pp. 1–18. Helsinki: Ministry for Foreign Affairs of Finland. Available online at http://formin.finland.fi/public/download. aspx?ID=12351&GUID={2035FE30-30CA-4390-A0F9-CA243B327AC1} [Accessed 15 March 2010].

Leonard Cheshire Disability 2007. *Inclusive Education in Kenya: Brian's Story*. Available online at http://www.lcint.org/?lid=3069 [Accessed 15 March 2010].

Lister, S. 2006. *Evaluation of General Budget Support: Synthesis Report*. Birmingham, UK: IDD, School of Public Policy, University of Birmingham. Available online at http://www.dfid.gov.uk/aboutdfid/ performance/files/general-budget-support/synthesis-report.pdf [Accessed 15 March 2010].

Loeb, M.E., Eide, A.H. and Mont, D. 2008. Approaching the measurement of disability prevalence: the case of Zambia. *Alter, Revue européenne de recherche sur le handicap*, 2(1), 32–43.

Lofgren, G., Lumley, T. and O'Boyle, A. 2008. *Critical Masses. Social Campaigning: A Guide for Donors and Funders*. London: New Philanthropy Capital.

Lwanga-Ntale, C. 2003. *Chronic Poverty and Disability in Uganda.* Paper presented to the international conference, 'Staying Poor: Chronic Poverty and Development Policy', held at the Chronic Poverty Research Centre, University of Manchester, UK. Available online at http://www.chronicpoverty.org/uploads/publication_files/CP_2003_lwangaNtale.pdf [Accessed 19 March 2010].

Metts, R. 2004. *Disability and Development.* Background paper prepared for the Disability and Development Research Agenda meeting, World Bank, November 2004. Washington, DC: World Bank. Available online at http://siteresources.worldbank.org/DISABILITY/Resources/280658-1172606907476/mettsBGpaper.pdf [Accessed 15 March 2010].

Miller, C. and Albert, B. 2005. *Mainstreaming Disability in Development: Lessons from Gender Mainstreaming.* London: Disability Knowledge and Research Programme. Available online at http://disabilitykar.net/docs/gender.doc [Accessed 15 March 2010].

Miller, U. and Ziegler, S. 2006. *Making PRSP Inclusive.* Munich: Handicap International and Christoffel-Blindenmission Deutschland. Available online at http://siteresources.worldbank.org/DISABILITY/Resources/280658-1172608138489/MakingPRSPInclusive.pdf [Accessed 15 March 2010].

Miller, V. 1994. NGO and Grassroots Policy Influence: What is Success? *IDR Reports*, 11(5). Boston, MA: IDR. Available online at http://www.justassociates.org/whatissuccess.pdf [Accessed 15 March 2010].

Ministry for Foreign Affairs of Finland 2007. *Government of Finland Development Policy Program 2007.* Towards a Sustainable and Just World Community: Government Decision-in-Principle 2007. Available online at http://formin.finland.fi/public/default.aspx?nodeid=15319&contentlan=2&culture=en-US [Accessed 15 March 2010].

Mont, D. 2007. Measuring health and disability. *The Lancet,* 369(9573), 1658–63.

Narayan, D. 2000. *Voices of the Poor: Can Anyone Hear Us?* New York: Oxford University Press.

Nilsson, A. and Qutteina, M. 2005. *Evaluation of the CBR Programme in Palestine – from the Perspective of Persons with Disabilities Themselves* (PAL-0028). Oslo: NORAD. Available online at http://www.norad.no/en/Tools+and+publications/Publications/ Publication+Page?key=117352 [Accessed 15 March 2010].

NORAD (Norwegian Agency for Development) 2002. *The Inclusion of Disability in Norwegian Development Co-operation: Planning and Monitoring for the Inclusion of Disability Issues in Mainstream Development Activities.* Oslo: NORAD.

NORAD) home page. Available online at http://www.norad.no/en [Accessed 15 March 2010].

O'Keefe, P. 2007. *People with Disabilities in India: From Commitments to Outcomes.* Washington, DC: World Bank. Available online at http://www-wds.worldbank.org/servlet/main?menuPK=64187510 &pagePK=64193027&piPK=64187937&theSitePK=523679&entityl D=000310607_20071121124147 [Accessed 15 March 2010].

OECD/DAC 2005a. *Paris Declaration on Aid Effectiveness.* Paris: OECD, March. Available online at http://www.oecd.org/ dataoecd/11/41/34428351.pdf [Accessed 15 March 2010].

OECD/DAC 2005b. *The OECD DAC Handbook on Security System Reform.* Paris: OECD.

OECD/DAC 2007. *Reporting on the Purpose of Aid: Classification by Sector of Destination.* Paris: OECD, Development Assistance Commitee, pp. 10, 19. Available online at http://www.oecd.org/ dataoecd/40/23/34384375.doc [Accessed 15 March 2010].

Pact. Available online at http://www.pactworld.org/ [Accessed 15 March 2010].

Picod, A. 2004. *Approaches to Poverty: A Note from the Human Rights Perspective.* Researchers' meeting, Geneva, 24–25 November 2004. Geneva: International Council on Human Rights Policy. Available online at http://www.ichrp.org/files/papers/145/121_ Picod.pdf#search='poverty' [Accessed 15 March 2010].

RECOUP n.d. *Social and Human Development Outcomes of Education for Poor People with Disabilities in Ghana, India, Kenya and Pakistan.* Available online at http://recoup.educ.cam.ac.uk/ research/disability.pdf [Accessed 15 March 2010].

Riddell, A.R. 2007. *Education Sector-wide Approaches (SWAps): Background, Guide and Lessons. Education Policies and Strategies 12.* Paris: UNESCO. Available online at http://unesdoc.unesco.org/ images/0015/001509/150965e.pdf [Accessed 15 March 2010].

Riddell, R.C. 2008. *Does Foreign Aid Really Work?* Oxford: Oxford University Press.

Riddell, R.C., Kotoglou, K., Basu Ray, D. and Bategeka, L. 2008. *Measuring Impact: The Global and Irish Aid Programme.* Dublin: Advisory Board for Irish Aid. Available online at http://www.opml. co.uk/policy_areas/aid_policy/measuring_impact.html [Accessed 19 March 2010]

Riddell, R.C., Kruse, S.-E., Kyllönen, T., Ojanperä, S. and Vielajus, J.-L. 1997. *Searching for Impact and Methods: NGO Evaluation Synthesis Study* (Main report and Volume II). Paris and Helsinki: OECD DAC and Department for International Development Cooperation, Ministry for Foreign Affairs of Finland.

Ruotsi, J., Lindberg, P., Segerström, O., Mbozi, D. and Laxén, J. 2001. *Evaluation of the Development Cooperation between Finland and Zambia. Evaluation report 2001: 9.* Helsinki: Ministry for Foreign Affairs of Finland.

Samaita Associates 2007. *Evaluation Report for the Capacity Building in the Area of Rehabilitation Services and Provision of Assistive Devices in Namibia and Zimbabwe.* East London, South Africa: Samaita Associates. Available online at http://www.atlas-alliansen.no/novus/upload/file/Ressursbanken/LOREWO%20 EVALUATION%20REPORT%20for%20NAMIBIA%20and%20 ZIMBABWE-FINAL%20REPORT%207%20OCT%2007.pdf [Accessed 15 March 2010].

Savolainen, H., Matero, M. and Kokkala, H. 2006. *When All Means All: Experiences in Three African countries with EFA and Children with Disabilities.* Helsinki: Ministry for Foreign Affairs of Finland, Development Policy Information Unit. Available online at http://formin.finland.fi/public/download. aspx?ID=12351&GUID={2035FE30-30CA-4390-A0F9-CA243B327AC1} [Accessed 15 March 2010].

Sen, A. 2009. *The Idea of Justice.* London: Allen Lane.

Shepherd, A. *et al.* 2008. The Chronic Poverty Report 2008–9: Escaping Poverty Traps. Manchester, UK: University of Manchester, Chronic Poverty Research Centre. Available online at http://www. chronicpoverty.org/uploads/publication_files/CPR2_ReportFull.pdf [Accessed 19 March 2010].

Sightsavers International 2008. *Annual Report and Financial Statements 2007.* Hayward's Heath, UK: Sightsavers International. Available online at http://www.sightsavers.org/learn_more/ publications/9664_SSI_Accounts_web2007.pdf [Accessed 15 March 2010].

SDD (Social Development Direct) and OPM (Oxford Policy Management) 2008. *Making Aid More Effective through Gender, Rights and Inclusion: Evidence from Implementing the Paris Declaration.* Oxford: OPM. Available online at http://www.oecd.org/ dataoecd/47/20/41047104.pdf [Accessed 19 March 2010]

STAKES (The National Research and Development Centre for Welfare and Health in Finland) 2003. *Label Us Able: a pro-active evaluation of Finnish development co-operation from the disability perspective. Evaluation Report No. 3.* Helsinki: Ministry for Foreign Affairs of Finland, Department for Development Policy. http://formin.finland.fi/Public/download.aspx?ID=13528&GUID={C2043295-F121-4ED1-984D-B394F821C13D} [Accessed 15 March 2010].

Swedish International Development Cooperation Agency (SIDA) 2005. *Children and Adults with Disabilities. Position paper 23244.* Stockholm: SIDA. Available online at http://www.make-development-inclusive.org/docsen/SWChildrenandadultswithdisabilities.pdf [Accessed 19 March 2010].

Third High Level Forum 2008. *Indicators of Progress to be Measured Nationally and Monitored Internationally.* Available online at http://siteresources.worldbank.org/ACCRAEXT/Resources/4700790-1217425866038/AAA-4-SEPTEMBER-FINAL-16h00.pdf [Accessed 15 March 2010].

Thomas, P. 2005a. *Mainstreaming Disability in Development: India Country Report.* London: Disability Knowledge and Research Programme. Available online at http://www.disabilitykar.net/docs/india.doc [Accessed 15 March 2010].

Thomas, P. 2005b. *Poverty Reduction and Disability in Cambodia: Enabling Disabled People to Play a Role.* London: Disability Knowledge and Research Programme. Available online at http://www.disabilitykar.net/docs/cambodia%20.doc [Accessed 15 March 2010].

Thomas, P. 2005c. *Mainstreaming Disability in Development: Country-level Research. Rwanda Country Report.* London: Disability Knowledge and Research Programme. Available online at http://www.disabilitykar.net/docs/rwanda.doc [Accessed 15 March 2010].

UN 2001. *End Poverty by 2015.* Available online in the *Road Map Towards the Implementation of the United Nations Millennium Declaration,* at http://www.un.org/documents/ga/docs/56/a56326.pdf [Accessed 15 March 2010].

UN 2006. *Convention on the Rights of Persons with Disabilities and Optional Protocol.* Available online at http://www.un.org/disabilities/documents/convention/convoptprot-e.pdf [Accessed 15 March 2010].

UN Economic and Social Council, Commission for Social Development 2007. *Mainstreaming Disability in the Development Agenda.* New York: Economic and Social Council (E/CN.5/2008/6). Available online at http://www.un.org/disabilities/documents/reports/e-cn5-2008-6.doc [Accessed 12 March 2010].

UN Enable 2006. Available online at http://www.un.org/disabilities/default.asp?id=259 [Accessed 15 March 2010].

UN ESCAP 2006. *Selected Resolutions and Other Decisions Adopted by the Commission.* Excerpt from the 2006 Annual Report of the Economic and Social Commission for Asia and the Pacific (E/2006/39 and E/ESCAP/1390) and 2004 Annual Report of the Economic and Social Commission for Asia and the Pacific (E/2004/39 and E/ESCAP/1330). Available online at http://www.unescap.org/EPOC/documents/L2.1_PacificResolution.doc [Accessed 12 March 2010].

UN General Assembly 1993. *The Standard Rules on the Equalization of Opportunities for Persons with Disabilities* (A/RES/48/96). New York: UN. Available online at http://www.un.org/documents/ga/res/48/a48r096.htm [Accessed 12 March 2010].

UN Millennium Project 2005. *Investing in Development: A Practical Plan to Achieve the Millennium Development Goals.* London and Sterling, VA: Earthscan. Available online at http://www.unmillenniumproject.org/documents/MainReportComplete-lowres.pdf [Accessed 15 March 2010].

UN Statistical Division. Available online at http://unstats.un.org/unsd/demographic/sconcerns/disability/ [Accessed 15 March 2010].

UNDP 2005. *Human Development Report 2005: International Development at a Crossroads.* New York: Oxford University Press.

UNDP 2007. *Human Development Report 2007/2008: Fighting Climate Change: Human Solidarity in a Changing World.* New York: Palgrave Macmillan.

USAID (US Agency for International Development) 1997. *USAID Disability Policy Paper.* Available online at http://pdf.usaid.gov/pdf_docs/Pdabq631.pdf [Accessed 15 March 2010].

USAID 2003. *Third Report on the Implementation of the USAID Disability Policy.* Washington, DC: USAID. Available online at http://pdf.usaid.gov/pdf_docs/PDACA180.pdf [Accessed 15 March 2010].

USAID 2005. *Fourth Report on the Implementation of the USAID Disability Policy.* Washington, DC: USAID. Available online at http://pdf.dec.org/pdf_docs/PDACF599.pdf [Accessed 15 March 2010].

USAID 2008. *Fifth Report on the Implementation of the USAID Disability Policy.* Washington, DC: USAID. Available online at http://www.usaid.gov/about_usaid/disability/modules/disreport08.pdf [Accessed 19 March 2010].

Uvin, P. 2004. *Human Rights and Development.* Bloomfield, CT: Kumarian Press.

Walford, V. 2007. *A Review of Health Sector-wide Approaches in Africa. Technical paper.* London: HLSP Institute. Available online at http://www.hlsp.org/LinkClick.aspx?fileticket=6G8sLo59BYl%3d&tabid=1796&mid=3485 [Accessed 14 July 2010].

Washington Group National Center for Health Statistics. Available online at http://www.cdc.gov/nchs/citygroup.htm [Accessed 15 March 2010].

West, R. 2003. *Education and Sector-wide Approaches (SWAp) in Namibia.* Paris: International Institute for Educational Planning. Available online at http://unesdoc.unesco.org/ images/0013/001376/137670e.pdf [Accessed 15 March 2010].

WHO. Available online at http://www.who.int/classifications/icf/en [Accessed 15 March 2010].

Wood, B., Kabell, D., Sagasti, F. and Muwanga, N. 2008. *Evaluation of the Implementation of the Paris Declaration. Phase One: Synthesis Report.* Copenhagen: Ministry of Foreign Affairs of Denmark. Available online at http://siteresources.worldbank.org/ACCRAEXT/ Resources/Evaluation-of-the-PD-English.pdf [Accessed 15 March 2010].

World Bank, Disability and Development Team 2004. *Poverty Reduction Strategies: Their Importance for Disability.* Washington, DC: World Bank. Available online at http://handicap-international. fr/bibliographie-handicap/4PolitiqueHandicap/hand_pauvrete/prsp/ Bonnel_PRSPddteam.pdf [Accessed 15 July 2010].

World Bank, Operations Evaluation Department 2005. *Capacity Building in Africa: An OED Evaluation of World Bank Support.* Washington, DC: World Bank. Available online at http://lnweb90. worldbank.org/oed/oeddoclib.nsf/24cc3bb1f94ae11c852568080 06a0046/5676a297fe57caf685256fdd00692e32/$FILE/africa_ capacity_building.pdf [Accessed 15 March 2010].

World Bank 2007. *Social Analysis and Disability: A Guidance Note.* Washington, DC: World Bank. Available online at http:// siteresources.worldbank.org/DISABILITY/Resources/280658- 1172606907476/SAnalysisDis.doc [Accessed 15 March 2010].

World Bank 2008. *The Implications of Global Crises on Developing Countries, The Millennium Development Goals, and Monterrey Consensus.* Washington, DC: World Bank. Available online at http://web.worldbank.org/WBSITE/EXTERNAL/NEWS/0,,contentMDK:21996735~pagePK:64257043~piPK:437376~theSitePK:4607,00.html [Accessed 15 March 2010].

Yeo R. and Moore, K. 2003. Including disabled people in poverty reduction work: 'nothing about us, without us'. *World Development*, 31(3), 571–90.

Governments must promote rights, not just ban discrimination
Photo: Joyce Browne

Chapter 3

Mainstreaming and Inclusive Development

Charlotte McClain-Nhlapo

Summary

Simply prohibiting disability discrimination through legal redress is not sufficient to achieve equality in practice, as has been acknowledged by many development workers, governments and policy makers. Furthermore, implementing and enforcing policy that seeks to mainstream people with disabilities is not enough to tackle the multifaceted and deep-rooted patterns of inequality they experience. Policies that mainstream disability into generic publically funded development initiatives need to complement the rights of people with disabilities, as contained in the United Nations Convention on the Rights of Persons with Disabilities (CRPD), with wider measures designed to promote and advance equality. This chapter explores some of the ways in which this mainstreaming can be advanced and explores approaches that should be considered in addressing the needs of people with disabilities.[1]

Introduction

Governments, donor agencies and development practitioners are increasingly recognising disability as a key issue, inexorably linked to poverty, the extension of human rights and citizenship (Heinicke-Motsch and Sygall, 2004). In 2002, James Wolfensohn, former President of the World Bank, stated that unless disability issues were addressed, the UN Millennium Development Goal targets (MDGs) would not be met.

Notwithstanding the high profile given to disability and development issues, there remains scant consensus on the most appropriate, sustainable strategies and operational modalities that should be employed for effective interventions within the disability sector. In 2000, the Department for International Development (DFID) published its issues paper on disability and development, advocating a 'twin-track approach' whereby DIFD would fund projects specifically targeted at disabled people, as well as encouraging mainstream development projects to incorporate a disability component (DFID, 2000). Since its publication, more emphasis has been placed on mainstreaming, in the belief that including disabled people in generic development activities will ultimately result in building more inclusive, sustainable societies. Nevertheless, development agencies are struggling to develop effective, sustainable operational modalities for mainstreaming disability issues into generic development programmes. This can be partially explained by the contention that surrounds precisely what is meant by 'mainstreaming' (Albert, Dube and Riis-Hansen, 2006).

There is currently no officially accepted definition of mainstreaming disability. However, the experience with defining gender mainstreaming may provide an insight about how to proceed to define disability mainstreaming. The concept of gender mainstreaming was defined in July 1997 by the Economic and Social Council in the agreed conclusions on mainstreaming a gender perspective into all policies and programmes of the United Nations system. The definition says that mainstreaming a gender perspective is the process of assessing the implications for women and men of any planned action, including legislation, policies or programmes, in any area and at all levels. It is a strategy for making the concerns and experiences of women as well as of men an integral part of the design, implementation, monitoring and evaluation of policies and programmes in all political, economic and societal spheres, so that women and men benefit equally, and inequality is not perpetuated. The ultimate goal of mainstreaming gender is to achieve gender equality. The process of mainstreaming disability in the development agenda may be viewed in a similar manner (Commission for Social Development, 2008).

Mainstreaming disability within social and economic policies is both an objective and a tool to promote equality for people with disabilities and for society as a whole. Approximately 10–12 per cent of the world's population has a disability, and as much as a quarter of all households have a member with a disability. The majority of people with disabilities live in developing countries and are disproportionately represented among the poor. Any initiative to alleviate poverty on a global scale therefore should include the needs of people with disabilities in its overarching objective.

> Mainstreaming disability means addressing inequalities between disabled and non-disabled people in all strategic areas of our work to promote disability equality. (DfID, 2007)

People with disabilities in all societies are systematically disadvantaged because they are discriminated against. Discrimination occurs everywhere at an institutional level; for example, within the legal, health and education systems, as well as in people's immediate communities and even sometimes in their homes. This systemic discrimination of people with disabilities has brought not only social exclusion from society, but has also raised barriers that significantly impede their economic and political participation. As a result, people with disabilities are more likely to be poor and denied access to income, assets and services. This in turn invariably leads to more entrenched levels of social exclusion and a violation of their inherent human rights.

The mainstreaming of disability in development cooperation at the programme and project levels is relatively new to most development partners and remains an ongoing process. Many development agencies have taken significant steps to mainstream disability at the policy level as part of an integrated approach to development cooperation, advocating the promotion of disability-inclusive development. The regional initiatives for mainstreaming disability in development cooperation, often in the context of a regional decade on disability – such as the African Decade of

Persons with Disabilities, the Arab Decade of Persons with Disabilities, the Asian and Pacific Decades of Persons with Disabilities – have been crucial for raising awareness and establishing support networks for mainstreaming (Commission for Social Development, 2008).

An important approach that can assist in reaching people with disabilities is 'inclusive development'. Inclusive development promotes the mainstreaming of disability. Mainstreaming disability describes a process in which projects and generic development policy and programmes, designed to benefit everyone in a specific geographical area, explicitly include people with disabilities in their design, taking into account their specific needs at all levels. The conceptual philosophy underpinning mainstreaming disability is that the same rights and opportunities accorded to others should be available to people with disabilities with the necessary accommodations. Such a philosophy explicitly endorses a 'rights-based' approach to the design and implementation of public policy. This approach contributes to the empowerment and participation of individuals with disabilities as agents and beneficiaries of development rather than as 'vulnerable' subjects requiring special care, protection or services. Consequently, rather than being perceived as passive recipients of charity, people with disabilities constitute a key stakeholder group within the development process. The adoption of the principles of an inclusive development approach prioritises the non-tokenistic participation of people with disabilities, as both contributors and beneficiaries. Furthermore, this approach enhances human rights through development and enhances development through human rights. Hence, the planning and implementation of policies and programmes in health or education, rural development or improved sanitation must anticipate the needs of people with disabilities, not as a distinct group, but as active and full members of any community.

The principle of inclusive development is a consistent and comprehensive approach; it acknowledges that reaching the most marginalised people in society is necessary for successful poverty reduction and more equitable development. It pulls together diverse aspects of social and economic development and provides a conceptual framework and practical guidance for development. It builds on stakeholder engagement, seeking to strengthen local institutions in practical ways. Engaging at the microlevel and addressing systemic changes is essential to its success. Inclusive development recognises that disability is a cross-cutting issue affecting all aspects of planning and implementation. It requires innovation, flexibility and evidence-based practices as well as a multisectoral approach. Inclusive development can be enhanced by tools such as Poverty Reduction Strategy Papers (PRSPs), MDGs and the CRPD.

As disability mainstreaming continues to gain acceptance in the field of international development, it must be applied using a long-term perspective to create new and more comprehensive programmes. This will mean ensuring above all that: a) people with disabilities are at the centre of the development; b) the development process respects all human rights; c) people with disabilities participate at various levels of the design (e.g., in implementing, monitoring and evaluating projects and programmes); and d) that the field of development seeks to protect and promote social justice and inclusion.

To mainstream disability we must analyse the current situation to establish the differential impact of policies (disaggregating statistics by disability and funding). People with disabilities must participate in the decision-making process. Success relies on the commitment of international, national, regional and local authorities to achieving these objectives and the acknowledgement that implementing a mainstreaming strategy is a complex and long-term process. It also relies on addressing stigma and the lack of awareness about disability among policy makers, who often see 'disability' as a profession. This is important because the conventional wisdom in mainstream development policy and practice is that people with disabilities are incapable of earning an independent living, are economically dependent and require care. Throughout the world, this simplistic view means that people with disabilities remain marginalised, stigmatised and denied opportunities that have benefited other poor people.

To date, in many cases governments have ignored this population, even where progressive disability legislation has been enacted. This further compounds the extent to which people with disabilities live in poverty, which further precludes them from benefiting from any expanding opportunities that economic development often brings. They are least likely to achieve empowerment even when other poor groups do and are most likely to remain vulnerable to economic shocks and other types of insecurity. A recent World Bank study in India found that disability is a stronger correlate of non-enrolment in school than either gender or class. It also found the employment rate of people with disabilities is 60 per cent lower than that of the general population (World Bank, 2007a). Similarly, in Uganda, people with disabilities are nearly 40 per cent more likely to be poor, and children living in households with disabled family members are less likely to attend school (Hoogeveen, 2005).

Consequently, people with disabilities are more likely to suffer from malnutrition and have limited access to health services, education, food and opportunities for employment. This multiplicity of deprivations translates into more extreme levels of poverty for people with disabilities. It is not

Disability in one member can affect whole families
Photo: Sudhindra CN/Leonard Cheshire Disability

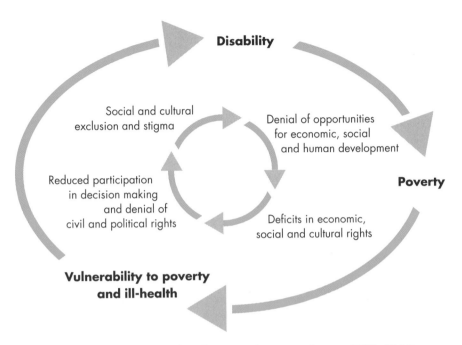

Figure 3.1: The vicious cycle of exclusion and poverty *Source*: DFID, 2000.

lack of income alone that causes high levels of poverty among people with disabilities but, more importantly, inaccessible and inadequate services, a lack of voice and profound stigmatisation in society. The social stigma attached to disability has served systemically to deprive people with disabilities from accessing public amenities and enjoying their rights. People with disabilities find themselves in a vicious cycle of exclusion and poverty from which it is difficult to escape without external help.

The chronic and vicious cycle of disability and poverty shown in Figure 3.1 is a barrier to the eradication of poverty and the enhancement of sustainable development, an international objective, in most of the world's poorest regions. According to World Bank estimates, people with disabilities constitute almost 20 per cent of the poorest of the poor in the world and make up one in five people living on less than one dollar a day (McClain-Nhlapo, 2006). Until this cycle is broken, people with disabilities will continue to be over-represented among the poorest of the poor.

The marginalisation of people with disabilities is increased if they do not know about their rights and how to access existing services. Even in countries where the disability movement is strong, such as Uganda, many people with disabilities are unaware of their rights, particularly those living in rural areas. People with disabilities are often found in communities that have weak institutions, that have low levels of social capital and relational bonds and where exclusionary social norms are commonplace. For example, in Croatia two thirds of people with disabilities live with their families and most view their financial situation as very unfavourable (UNDP, 2006). In Tanzania, survey data showed that households with a member who has a disability have a mean consumption of less than 60 per cent of the average and include 20 per cent more members than average (Elwan, 1999). In Poland, research shows that there is a strong negative correlation between average household income and disability. Disability may be likelier in lower-income households, and disability may also increase the likelihood of lower incomes (Hoopengardner, 2001). In Romania, nearly 30 per cent of wage earners who have disabilities are in the poorest quintile. In Honduras, 51 per cent of people with disabilities are illiterate, compared to 19 per cent among the general population.

Box 3.1 Social exclusion

Social exclusion is a process by which certain individuals are pushed to the edge of society and prevented from participating fully by virtue of their poverty, lack of basic competencies and lifelong learning opportunities, or as a result of discrimination. This distances them from work, income and education opportunities, as well as social and community networks and activities. They have little access to power and decision-making bodies and thus frequently feel powerless and unable to take control of the decisions that affect their day-to-day lives (UNDP, 2004).

Box 3.2 The cost of exclusion

The global annual loss of gross domestic product through the exclusion of people with disabilities from the labour market is between US$1.37 and $1.94 trillion (Zadek and Scott-Parker, 2001). In 1999, research highlighting the importance of taking disability into account in assessing poverty found that 23 per cent of UK households with disabled members earned less than 60 per cent of the median income, but when adjustments were made – such as workplace adaptations, work-related equipment and support to workers (including readers, communicators and personal assistants) – that rose to more than 47 per cent. This suggests that if people with disabilities had better access to services and opportunities, they could contribute more to growth and development.

A World Bank paper estimates that gross domestic product lost as the result of labour costs alone is in the range of five to seven per cent world-wide (Metts, 2000). This loss is the result of both inadequate access to the labour market and the lack of services for people with disabilities, which compels other household members to withdraw from the labour market, in order to compensate for potential foregone income.

Stigma and discrimination are at the core of the social exclusion of people with disabilities. Stigma and shame remain huge barriers to the mainstreaming of disability and contribute to the negative or paternal attitudes adopted towards people with disabilities, limiting their potential and creating a Catch-22 situation that keeps them marginalised. The new CRPD explicitly prohibits discrimination on the basis of disability and places the duty on governments to prevent it by taking certain actions.

The social and economic cost of segregating and excluding people with disabilities has substantial adverse effects upon other development processes. These include the negative effects of globalisation, which make significant changes in the daily life of individuals with shifts in social, cultural and political systems of support and participation (UNCTAD, 2007), as well as significant changes in information and communication technologies. It is anticipated that these changes will be further exacerbated by environmental degradation and climate change, which will have a disproportionate impact on the very poor, especially those persons who are both poor and with disabilities (United Nations General Assembly, 2008). However, the long-term impact of climate change upon the livelihoods of people with disabilities remains an under-researched area.

The economic costs of disability could be summed as 1) the direct costs of treatment, including travel and incidental expenses; 2) income foregone due to disability; and 3) indirect costs to others who provide care and support to the individual with a disability (Erb and Harriss-White, 2001), as well as the cost of stigma and discrimination, which is a lot more difficult to quantify.

Opportunities for mainstreaming in policy and planning

It is widely accepted that governments have the primary responsibility for ensuring development at national level, while their efforts and approach can be bolstered through appropriate international policies and cooperation. This section attempts to assess the extent to which existing international aid modalities have incorporated disability, and what strategies can be adopted to make this more effective. The effectiveness of mainstreaming disability, for example, can be improved by paying more systematic and widespread attention to disability issues in the context of various poverty reduction initiatives such as PRSPs, among others. The most successful interventions are either strategic, responsive to the circumstances of specific countries, or those in which international cooperation policies, processes and resources are aligned in support of such interventions. For example, ensuring that PRSPs mainstream disability throughout is strategic. Another important approach would be to ensure the empowerment of disabled people's organisations (DPOs) and to create enabling environments that are responsive to the needs of people with disabilities. Practical guidelines on how to make the PRSP process more inclusive by incorporating people with disabilities have been developed (CBM and Handicap International, 2008).

The links between poverty and disability are widely recognised among DPOs, non-governmental organisations (NGOs) and international NGOs, and limited policies are in place to include people with disabilities in development. This is perhaps best illustrated by the MDGs. As the biggest promise of humanitarian relief and development organisations ever made, the MDGs constitute a global agreement to reduce poverty and human deprivation at historically unprecedented rates through collaborative multilateral action (Hulme, 2008). However, they do not explicitly mention disability, despite the strong likelihood that many of the goals will not be achieved unless people with disabilities are explicitly included. This is best illustrated by the MDG on universal primary education. UNESCO estimates that 72 million children are currently out of school worldwide, and one third are children with disabilities (UNESCO, 2010). The MDG on universal primary education therefore cannot be met unless children with disabilities are included in national education plans and reforms. One can conclude that without the systematic inclusion of people with disabilities in development plans and programmes it will be impossible to attain the MDGs. Kate Gooding and Dianne Mulligan, in a think piece developed for the High Level Policy Forum held in Brussels in June 2009, have produced an insightful analysis of the impact and relevance of disability upon the MDGs (Gooding and Mulligan, 2009).

Box 3.3 Inclusive education for achieving universal primary education

Research from Uganda and Nicaragua shows that there are significantly higher rates of children out of school in households that contain a person with a disability.

> Inclusive education challenges the appropriateness of segregated education both on the grounds of effectiveness and from the perspective of respect for human rights (UNESCO, 2005, p. 9).
>
> As to effectiveness, current research suggests that states are increasingly realising that multiple systems of administration, organisational structures and services in education are inefficient and that special schools are financially unsustainable (Peters, 2004). Inclusive education can be both cost-efficient and cost-effective (Skrtic, 1991, quoted by Peters, 1991, pp. 148–206).

A PRSP is a key policy instrument for achieving sustainable development and poverty reduction. PRSPs are the operational framework for implementing MDGs.

National and international policy makers have a comparative advantage, in that they can raise the issue of disability with governments through sector-wide approaches such as developing PRSPs and similar overarching initiatives. More and more PRSPs mention disability, yet they are not always supported by disability-inclusive policies. Without the enabling policies these strategies are often not operationalised at national and international level and therefore are not entirely inclusive. Three key constraints hinder the participation of people with disabilities in the creation of PRSPs and other poverty alleviation activities: 1) they are economically excluded from pro-poor growth initiatives; 2) they are socially excluded and do not benefit from publically funded education and health programmes; and 3) they have a weak political voice. An examination of 29 African PRSPs showed that – apart from some notable exceptions – people with disabilities have again been either 'forgotten' or treated in a way that does not correspond to their aspirations to socio-economic integration (ILO, 2002). People with disabilities are of course included whenever PRSPs mention 'vulnerable groups', 'marginalised groups of society' or 'disadvantaged groups', but experience shows that whenever the specific exclusion mechanisms and specific needs of people with disabilities are not explicitly identified, the related strategies and programmes also miss their specific target. A category like 'vulnerable groups', while useful at certain levels of analysis, becomes an obstacle when it hides essential differences in poverty determinants of various vulnerable sub-groups, such as people with disabilities.

An analysis of PRSPs shows that when DPOs do participate in PRSP consultations, the social focus of the disability policy decreases and the economic focus increases. For example, the Honduras PRSP reports explicitly that consultations with civil society lead to the recognition of people with disabilities as a special target group for the PRSP, resulting in a chapter on people with disabilities in its poverty diagnosis. Further, this PRSP distinguishes itself by proposing the creation of a National Disability Council as well as a National Information System for Persons with Disabilities. It also calls upon the National Statistics Institute to include a range of disability-related issues such as geographic location, socio-economic and demographic characteristics when conducting surveys. This PRSP includes a comprehensive programme on prevention, care and integrated rehabilitation of persons with disabilities that includes key elements for their social and economic integration.

DPOs should be involved not only in preparing PRSPs but also in the policy discussions that follow their development to ensure they are implemented in appropriate ways.

Governments, development agencies and service providers either omit people with disabilities from their development programmes or create special disability projects that often ghettoise people with disabilities within mainstream society. In many cases, these programmes are often small in scale, fragmented and reach only urban people with disabilities. They typically depend heavily on donors for funding. This means not only that programmes are unlikely to be mainstreamed (given the project-based nature of funding), but also that they may be placed under the responsibility of under-staffed and under-resourced departments in selected ministries. This approach continues even though specialised disability services, where they exist, further segregate and hide people with disabilities rather than reducing inequality and promoting their empowerment. These institutional inequities undermine development and the inclusion of people with disabilities, thus reinforcing, rather than breaking, the cycle of poverty and disability.

The neglect of disability in development planning reflects a broader tendency to undervalue the capacity of people with disabilities and a failure to see them as full citizens with dignity, rights and abilities who can and should have the opportunity to contribute to their society. The discrimination and stigma faced by people with disabilities are well known. Only when the barriers facing people with disabilities are recognised and eliminated within programmes can there be substantive or sustainable change in the marginalisation and poverty they experience. It is therefore important to ensure that people with disabilities – who make up more than ten per cent of the world's population – are included in all dimensions of poverty reduction mechanisms and infrastructure.

The need to consider and include people with disabilities in general development projects led to the concept of inclusive development more than ten years ago. Today the inclusive development approach is increasingly recognised as an essential feature of successful and sustainable development. This is evidenced by a suite of policies mainstreaming disability in development cooperation. The first policy to appear came from the United States Agency for International Development (USAID) in 1996. Soon after, similar initiatives appeared from the UK DFID, the Nordic development agencies, the *Deutsche Gesellschaft für Technische Zusammenarbeit* and most recently AusAID. In addition to the policies developed, many donors have programmes, including DFID, New Zealand Aid, USAID, Japanese International Cooperation Agency (JICA), Canadian International Development Agency (CIDA) and those of EU countries. Many of these have specific disability funding windows, programmes and partnerships that form part of the global recognition that taking disability into account is fundamental to inclusive development and the overall effectiveness of aid. In Accra, Ghana, in 2008, ministers of developing and donor countries and heads of multilateral and bilateral development agencies endorsed the Accra Agenda for Action (AAA) on Aid Effectiveness and the acceleration of the implementation of the 2005 Paris Declaration on Aid Effectiveness.

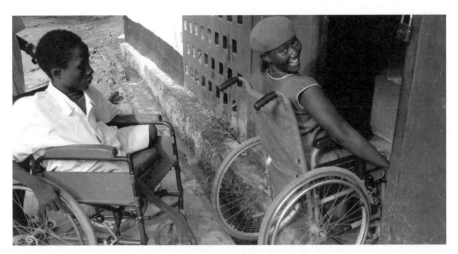

Inclusion is an essential feature of sustainable development
Photo: Jenny Matthews/Leonard Cheshire Disability

Over the years, knowledge and awareness of the mutual causality of poverty and disability has increased at the World Bank, which recognises that disability issues extend across many sectors of its work. In 2002 a disability and development team was established to support and coordinate the mainstreaming of disability into the World Bank's work. Located in the Social Protection and Labour unit of the Human Development Network, the team's mandate is to help ensure that disability issues are appropriately addressed in the World Bank's efforts to mainstream poverty alleviation. A key function of the team is to coordinate and seek synergies among the various areas and sectors of the World Bank. In addition to the disability and development team, regional coordinators are working on mainstreaming disability in all the World Bank regions (Africa, Latin America and the Caribbean, the Middle East and North Africa, East and Central Asia, East Asia and the Pacific and South Asia region). The World Bank has a three-pronged approach to mainstreaming inclusive development: 1) continuing its recent efforts to mainstream disability into existing programmes and research; 2) improving its evidence base through data collection and measurement and the analysis of programmes and policies; and 3) continuing its outreach and awareness raising of disability as a development issue that is crucial for achieving a sustainable reduction of poverty as well as reaching some key MDGs.

Making effective legislation

Although developments in policies and legislation can articulate the rights and entitlements of people with disabilities, experience shows that, without implementation and enforcement, policies and legislation are insufficient to make a real difference for most people with disabilities. Unimplemented policies and legislation may do more harm than good, as such documents breed complacency or cynicism, and potentially remain misunderstood. The absence of complaints and legal action by people with disabilities cannot be equated with the absence of discrimination and exclusion; rather, it should be seen as an indication of the lack of an enabling environment, relevant legislation, or people's awareness of their rights and the legal remedies available to them.

Legislation and policies need to contain provisions facilitating individual litigation in alignment with the principles of the Optional Protocol of the CRPD. They should protect complainants from victimisation or allow the burden of proof to be reduced when complainants produce the facts on which the claimed discrimination has occurred. With enforceable justice, trusted institutions and a legal system oriented towards the rights of people with disabilities, disabled people may be in a position to hold duty bearers accountable for guaranteeing their rights, as spelled out in the CRPD and national legislation. It is worth noting that many of the legislative and policy changes that have taken place, for example in Uganda and South Africa, are the result of the advocacy work of DPOs.

The CRPD and inclusive development

The CRPD constitutes a universal and comprehensive commitment to the rights of people with disabilities. It is consistent with current development thinking around reaching the poorest and most marginalised people. Governments that ratify the treaty are legally bound to treat people with disabilities not just as victims or a minority, but as subjects possessing all human rights, including civil and political rights as well as economic and social rights. As such, people with disabilities have the right to full participation in formulating and carrying out plans and policies affecting them, including policies related to poverty reduction.

The CRPD moves beyond the traditional concept of access to the physical environment to broader issues of equal access, social opportunities, health, education, employment, political, economic and social development and the elimination of legal and social barriers to equal participation.

In addition to being a human rights instrument, the CRPD has a social development perspective – a response to a clarion call from the majority of people with disabilities who live in developing countries, often in poverty. The CRPD is thus a constructive instrument for formulating inclusive development practices. It provides a minimum threshold criterion, or social floor, determines who is accountable, evokes the principle of non-discrimination and addresses the most vulnerable in society.

Further, it sets a benchmark for inclusive development to be supported and promoted by governments in partnership with relevant regional and international organisations. Supporting the notion that implementation of the CRPD requires not only appropriate national policies, but also suitable international cooperation such as Article 32 of the CRPD, recognises that implementation is a shared responsibility (McClain-Nhlapo, 2007).

In this regard the CRPD requires individual states and the international community to formulate appropriate development policies. The preamble recognises the importance of international cooperation for improving the conditions of people with disabilities in all countries, particularly developing countries, and highlights the fact that the majority of people with disabilities live in conditions of poverty. The CRPD thus recognises the critical need to address the negative impact of poverty on people with disabilities. As the individual is at the centre of development, the CRPD also considers the importance of the processes through which policies are developed and notes that they should be participatory. The rights of women and children with disabilities to participate, and the duty of individual states to ensure their participation, are also emphasised.

Legal empowerment, however, is not enough to eradicate the social exclusion and discrimination encountered by people with disabilities. The guiding principle of the roadmap, as set out in the Convention, is to move forward decisively to combat discrimination and all other forms of social exclusion. This framework compels us to look at inclusion and non-discrimination as both legal obligations and moral responsibilities. There is also a need to make economic arguments to support inclusive development – not as justifications per se, but as part of an overall strategy to raise awareness and strengthen implementation of the CRPD. Although there is a great deal of anecdotal evidence supporting the notion that disability is both a cause and a consequence of poverty, there are not yet enough statistical data to identify firm causal links. What is known is that people with disabilities find it extremely difficult to secure credit effectively from mainstream microfinance institutions (Marsland *et al.*, 2008) and that, in the vast majority of developing countries, with few notable exceptions, there are no social protection programmes for people with disabilities (Mitra, 2008). Furthermore, it must be noted that there are additional economic costs associated with having a disability. Harriss-White and Erb, in their social anthropological study of disability in Tamil Nadu, noted that there were additional direct costs for medical treatment and indirect costs regarding the provision of care, as well as the opportunity cost of income foregone, which is a direct result of having an impairment (Erb and Harriss-White, 2001).

Ensuring effective inclusive development

Box 3.4 An inclusive policy environment – South Africa

A policy environment that is conducive to inclusion was set up during the development of South Africa's Integrated National Disability Strategy. The policy development process was led by a team of people with disabilities in the Office of the Presidency, and the policy was finalised after robust consultation with people with disabilities throughout South Africa. It provides the country with a blueprint for mainstreaming disability in every aspect of governance. One notable feature of the policy is its articulation of a shift away from dealing with disability-related issues solely in the context of health and welfare towards a rights-based integrated approach. The process was supported financially by the Swedish International Development Authority.

Inclusive participation programmes

From the point of view of programme design, participation is needed to generate broader ownership of goals and to strengthen consensus on action. People with disabilities do not constitute one homogeneous group; they comprise many individuals with diverse backgrounds, interests and disabilities. The skills base in this community requires much improvement, mainly because people with disabilities have been systematically excluded from education and labour markets. Among disabled people, there are vast disparities in terms of basic human rights, resources, economic opportunities and political voice, despite recent gains. People need to be legally empowered so that they can claim their rights against national and international duty bearers. In many ways the CRPD addresses the issue of equality of voice and seeks to capture the ability to influence and contribute to the political discourse and the development process.

It is important to ensure that effective measures are in place for women with disabilities to play an active role in the development of inclusive participation programmes. Pilot projects to foster the participation of women with disabilities in such processes would be useful. Given the unique and often more complicated issues associated with poverty reduction for women with disabilities, research should be undertaken on the changes in gender roles as a result of disability, its implications for all members of the household and implications for poverty reduction.

Additional research needs to be undertaken on sexuality and reproductive health issues for women with disabilities in this region, especially in light of the overwhelming presence of HIV/AIDS.

Increasingly, the issue of women with disabilities is entering the mainstream development agenda. At the 2009 UN Commission on the Status of the Women, the United Nations Population Fund (UNFPA) referred to disability issues in several of its conclusions (UNFPA, 2008). UNFPA has also included women with disabilities in their *Strategy and Framework for Action to Addressing Gender-based Violence Strategic Plan (2008–11)*.

Forging partnerships

The potential and importance of collaborative work through partnerships is huge. Partnerships can create a valuable pool of resources from different organisations in the area of mainstreaming disability and these potential synergies need to be fostered and capitalised upon. Partnerships should be extended to governments, DPOs and donors, especially in the context of development projects or programmes, including formulating the PRSPs. Examples of partnerships include the Global Partnership on Disability and Development, the International Disability and Development Consortium and the International Disability Alliance Forum (IDA CRPD).

Developing operational tools and methodologies to mainstream disability

Examples of good practice from country experiences on how to mainstream disability must be compiled, such as policy development and PRSPs that have included people with disabilities. There are instructive examples of good practice from Tanzania, Cambodia and Vietnam and a useful handbook, *Making PRSP Inclusive* (Handicap International and the Christoffel-Blindenmission Deutschland, 2006), financed by the World Bank and the German Government.

Capacity building in implementing agencies

Methods for providing technical advice and training opportunities on mainstreaming disability into programme design and on monitoring its impact should be examined and made available to implementing agencies, such as governments, DPOs and donors.

Participatory budgeting to include people with disabilities

Participatory budgeting is an approach that brings local communities closer to the decision-making process of the public budget. This innovative financial practice has the potential to enhance the citizens' voice in budget decision making and to help government improve budget transparency, efficiency and accountability. There are no exact or precise participatory budgeting models. It is, rather, a mechanism that allows the citizens of a specific jurisdiction to participate in decisions on the allocation and management of all or part of the local government's available public financial resources. Participatory budgeting aims to increase transparency, accountability and social inclusion in local governance and is a tool with the potential to be useful in mainstreaming disability. Another tool that has been used to mainstream people with disabilities in the budgetary processes is the Gender Specific Budget in Uganda (Byanyima, 2004).

Monitoring and evaluating progress

An effective system of monitoring and evaluation, which includes assessing the results of existing programmes, is needed. Monitoring can help assess who has access to opportunities that allow people to exit the poverty trap, pursue their own lives and avoid extreme deprivation in outcomes. This can be monitored on an ongoing basis at all levels and by all relevant stakeholders. The CRPD could be used as a frame for developing disability-based indicators, targets and benchmarks for monitoring. The process should involve people with disabilities, improved targeting and building an appropriate enabling environment. There is specific reference to disability under the marginalisation section of the *Global Monitoring Report* (UNESCO, 2010, pp. 181–184).

Launching effective social safety-net programmes

Safety-net programmes, such as food and healthcare subsidies, cash transfers and unemployment assistance, are needed for people with disabilities who are unable to meet their own essential needs through exclusion and poverty. Such an approach would need to integrate micro and macro interventions and balance participatory processes with social protection mechanisms designed to include people with disabilities.

Mainstreaming and the twin-track approach to inclusive development

The philosophy of mainstreaming requires governments to view disability as a cross-cutting issue and to grasp that it goes beyond anti-discrimination legislation and needs to be supported by an enabling environment that includes policies, laws, regulations, administrative provisions and activities in the area of development.

While the term mainstreaming describes a broad-reaching goal, the actions required to achieve it consist of measurable concrete steps taken by individuals such as government ministers, department heads, directors of organisations and team leaders. Disability issues need to be incorporated into organisational policy and practice in the form of job descriptions, mission and vision statements and budget allocations (Commission for Social Development, 2008).

The twin-track approach combines specific targeting with mainstreaming approaches. Under this model, funding is provided for programmes that are specifically targeted at people with disabilities (for example, community-based rehabilitation programmes), as well as providing funding to ensure that people with disabilities are explicitly included in mainstream development initiatives (such as providing universal primary education in a designated geographical area). This strategy targets people with disabilities and integrates their voice and needs within the broader project cycle. This has the potential of creating a strong enabling environment, where disability concerns are mainstreamed into

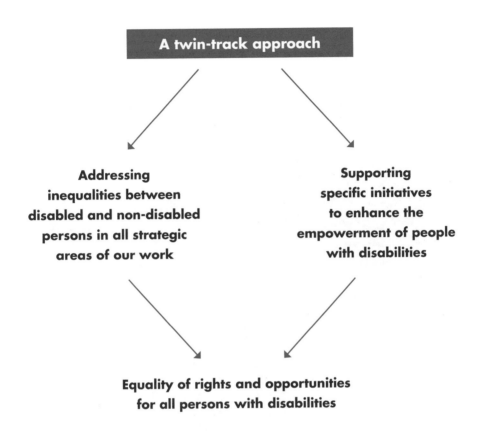

Figure 3.2 A twin-track approach Source: Handicap International, 2006: Twin-track approach to disability and development (adapted from DFID, 2003, p. 4)

institutional frameworks and supported by progressive legislation. To ensure sustainability, the involvement of multiple stakeholders such as local government, civil society organisations and the private sector, as well as DPOs, is also important. The twin-track approach is also useful in identifying and removing barriers that prevent people with disabilities from full participation and inclusion. It can be used to address institutional, environmental and attitudinal barriers in all sectors and at all levels of society. The two tracks are mutually reinforcing.

Mainstreaming disability is an issue of development effectiveness
Photo: Jenny Matthews/Leonard Cheshire Disability

A prerequisite for the successful application of the twin-track approach is creating an international and national policy environment that is conducive to inclusion. This is the responsibility of the national governments and civil society institutions of developing countries as well as the international community. At the international level, this implies the sustainability of measures to promote the inclusion of people with disabilities in policies and programmes and to provide the necessary training for agency and donor staff. Nationally, it implies that governments should adopt enabling policies as a basis for addressing discrimination and promoting equal opportunities for people with disabilities. This will require an increased focus on capacity building among people with disabilities to ensure their broad participation in policy decision making and the implementation of policies. It also requires strengthening the governance frameworks and institutions that increase the accountability of governments to this group and strengthening in turn the capacity of people with disabilities to place effective demands on service providers. There needs to be an emphasis on improved targeting and the building of supportive enabling environments. An enabling environment that includes the legal and regulatory framework, as well as organisational strengthening and institutional development of government, private and civil actors, plays a crucial role in promoting the inclusion of people with disabilities. For example, Yemen's strong network of NGOs and DPOs allowed the Yemen Social Fund for Development Project (YSFDP) to learn and gain momentum from their experiences. The project played a significant role in the promulgation of the disability law in 1999. In partnership with the Ministry of Education, NGOs and the National Union of Disabled, the project has been able to mainstream education for children with disabilities at the policy and practice level. In its next phase, the project will build the capacity for local governments to manage inclusive school systems and strengthen its efforts to meet the MDGs (World Bank, 2005).

Conclusions

Mainstreaming disability and promoting equality are issues of development effectiveness, not just a matter of political correctness or kindness to people with disabilities. When people with disabilities are treated equally (as is the case with other marginalised groups), economies tend not only to grow faster, but also to move quickly out of poverty, and the well-being of societies at large is enhanced. The basic principles described by the UN Division for the Advancement of Women of the Department of Economic and Social Affairs and adapted for disability are as follows.

1. Responsibility for implementing the mainstreaming strategy is system-wide, and rests at the highest levels within agencies.

2. Adequate accountability mechanisms for monitoring progress need to be established. Initial identification of issues and problems across all areas of activity should be such that differences and disparities between persons with and without disabilities can be diagnosed.

3. Clear political will and allocation of adequate resources for mainstreaming – including additional financial and human resources, if necessary – are important for translation of the concept into practice.

4. Disability mainstreaming requires that efforts be made to broaden the equitable participation of persons with disabilities at all levels of decision making.

5. Mainstreaming does not replace the need for targeted, disability-specific policies and programmes and positive legislation; nor does it do away with the need for disability units for focal points.

Inclusion is not only a goal in itself, but is also closely linked with and a means for the achievement of other key development goals set by the international community, such as those reflected in MDGs and PRSPs. It aims to generate benefits throughout society, including people with disabilities, who are often excluded and marginalised. This cannot be done by way of a trickle-down process – it needs to be complemented by targeted policies and practices.

There is a widely held perception that success in poverty reduction resulting from market-driven economic development automatically takes care of all vulnerable groups. This may account for the lack of action in specifically including people with disabilities in development. However, this ideological position fails to address three points. First, poverty reduction takes time. There are many contesting issues and people with disabilities often do not have the voice to articulate their needs. Second, contrary to the beliefs of many, the cost of inclusion, if factored in at the design stage of poverty reduction initiatives, does not have to be monumental. For example, using universal design requires additional costs of approximately one per cent if it is incorporated from the outset of a project. On the other hand, not incorporating universal design can incur significant human and opportunity costs due to inaccessibility (Snider and Takeda, 2008). Third, poverty is as much a cause as an effect of disability. Unless specific measures are taken to include people with disabilities, development will continue to exclude at least ten per cent of the world's population.

The concept of mainstreaming disability is not without its critics. Its novelty means that it is considered controversial in some quarters. A report from India reveals some confusion over the understanding of the terms 'mainstreaming' and 'inclusion'. It concludes that the confusion is largely semantic, resting on whether mainstreaming is the goal and inclusion the strategy, or vice versa. However, while the terminology may be contested, the meaning of the overall objective is clear: namely, the realisation of the rights of people with disabilities to full participation and equality of opportunity (Thomas, 2005).

Despite the frequently voiced concerns about mainstreaming people with disabilities in development, the literature offers very little systematic treatment of this issue. Notwithstanding, disability is moving up on the international agenda with a far greater visibility than before. However, disability issues should not be viewed merely as add-ons or luxuries to be provided once a certain level of economic development has taken place. Equitable development and poverty reduction will be achieved only if people with disabilities are included in economic development from the start.

Given the multitude of factors that have conspired and continue to conspire against integrating people with disabilities into society, stakeholders at all levels must collaborate in a comprehensive, multisectoral, participatory response. The CRPD offers a framework for such action. A twin-track approach is required for rapid success in promoting inclusion and mainstreaming disability into development. One track would create opportunities for people with disabilities to improve their livelihood by promoting development, particularly human development, through policy reform and investments in development. The other track would involve direct and immediate action to empower people with disabilities and enhance best practices, in turn increasing the productive potential of people with disabilities and allowing them to take advantage of the opportunities offered by development. Ultimately, society must stop seeing people with disabilities as objects of pity but rather as capable individuals with rights who can and do contribute immensely to its development.

Notes

1. The findings, interpretations, and conclusions expressed in this article are those of the author and do not necessarily reflect the views of the International Bank of Reconstruction and Development, the World Bank and its affiliated organisations, or those of the executive directors of the World Bank or the governments they represent.

References

Albert, B., Dube, A.K., and Riis-Hansen, C. 2006. Has disability been mainstreamed in development cooperation?, in Albert, B. (ed.), In and On the Mainstream? Lessons from Research and Development. Leeds, UK: The Disability Press.

Byanyima, W. 2004. *The Forum for Women in Democracy (FOWODE)'s Gender Budget Project.* Presentation to the World Bank.

CBM and Handicap International 2008. *Making PRSP Inclusive.* Washington, DC: World Bank.

Commission for Social Development 2008. *Mainstreaming Disability in the Development Agenda.* Economic and Social Council, 46th session, February 2008. New York: United Nations.

DFID 2000. *Disability, Poverty and Development.* London: DFID.

DFID 2007. *How to Note ... 2007.* London: DFID.

Elwan, A. 1999. *Poverty and Disability. A Survey of the Literature. Social Protection Discussion Paper Series, 9932.* Washington, DC: World Bank.

Erb, S. and Harriss-White, B. 2001. *Outcast from Social Welfare: Adult Disability and Incapacity in Rural South India.* Bangalore, India: Books for Change.

Gooding, K. and Mulligan, D. 2009. *What Has Been the Impact of Poverty on the MDG Paradigm?* Think piece prepared for the High Level Policy Forum – After 2015, Promoting Pro-Poor Policies after the MDGs. Available online at http://www.eadi.org/fileadmin/MDG_2015_Publications/Gooding_and_Mulligan_THINKPIECE.pdf [Accessed 25 February 2010].

Handicap International and the Christoffel-Blindenmission Deutschland 2006. *Making PRSP Inclusive Handbook.* Washington, DC: World Bank. Available online at http://www.making-prsp-inclusive.org [Accessed 25 February 2010].

Heinicke-Motsch, K. and Sygall, S. (eds.) 2004. *Building an Inclusive Development Community: A Manual for Including People with Disabilities in International Development Programs.* Eugene, OR: Mobility International USA.

Hoogeveen, J. 2005. Measuring welfare for small but vulnerable groups: poverty and disability in Uganda. *Journal of African Economies,* 14(4).

Hoopengardner, T. 2001. *Disability and Work in Poland. Social Protection Discussion Paper Series, 0101.* Washington, DC: World Bank.

Hulme, D. 2008. *The Making of the Millennium Development Goals: Human Development Meets Results-Based Management in an Imperfect World* (December 5, 2007). Brooks World Poverty Institute Working Paper No. 16. Manchester, UK: Brooks World Poverty Institute, University of Manchester. Available online at http://ssrn.com/abstract=1246696 [Accessed 25 February 2010].

ILO 2002. *Disability and Poverty Reduction Strategies: How to ensure that access of persons with disabilities to decent and productive work is part of the PRSP process.* Geneva: ILO.

Marsland, R. *et al.* 2008. *Access to Mainstream Micro-Finance Institutions: Lessons from Uganda.* Paper presented at the Joint UNECA/Leonard Cheshire Disability Conference 'UN Convention on the Rights of People with Disabilities: A Call for Action on Poverty, Lack of Access and Discrimination', Addis Ababa, May 2008.

McClain-Nhlapo, C. 2006. *Training on Inclusive Development.* PowerPoint presentation available online at http://siteresources.worldbank.org/DISABILITY/Resources/News---Events/463933-1147810251877/Charlotte.ppt [Accessed 25 February 2010].

McClain-Nhlapo, C. 2007. Towards inclusive development: the implementation challenge. *International Rehabilitation Review,* 56(1), 17–18.

Metts, R.L. 2000. *Disability Issues, Trends and Recommendations for the World Bank.* Washington, DC: World Bank.

Mitra, S. 2008. *Reaching Persons with Disabilities through Social Safety Nets in Developing Countries.* Paper presented at the Joint UNECA/Leonard Cheshire Disability Conference 'UN Convention on the Rights of People with Disabilities: A Call for Action on Poverty, Lack of Access and Discrimination', Addis Ababa, May 2008. Available online at http://www.lcint.org/?lid=4908 [Accessed 1 July 2010].

Peters, S.J. 2004. *Inclusive Education: An EFA Strategy for All Children.* Education Resources Center. Washington, DC: World Bank. Available online at http://eric.ed.gov/ERICWebPortal/custom/ portlets/recordDetails/detailmini.jsp?_nfpb=true&_&ERICExtSearch_S earchValue_0=ED485591&ERICExtSearch_SearchType_0= no&accno=ED485591 [Accessed 25 February 2010].

Peters, S.T.M. 1991. The special education paradox: equity as the way to excellence. *Harvard Educational Review,* 61(2), 148–206.

Snider, H. and Takeda, N. 2008. *Design for All: Implications for Bank Operations.* Washington, DC: World Bank. Available online at http://siteresources.worldbank.org/DISABILITY/Resources/Universal_ Design.pdf [Accessed 25 February 2010].

Thomas, P. 2005. *Mainstreaming Disability in Development: India Country Report.* London: DFID.

UNCTAD 2007. *Trade and Development Report, 2007 UNCTAD/ TDR/2007, Sales No. E.07.II.D.11, A/62/119 and A/62/266.* Geneva: UNCTAD.

UNDP 2004. *Joint Report on Social Inclusion.* Brussels: EU. Available online at http://ec.europa.eu/employment_social/soc-prot/soc-incl/ joint_rep_en.htm [Accessed 25 February 2010].

UNDP 2006. *Survey: Quality of Life and Risk of Social Exclusion in Croatia (Social Welfare Service Providers). The Right to Live in a Community: Social Inclusion and People with Disabilities.* Brussels: EU. Available online at http://ec.europa.eu/employment_social/ soc-prot/soc-incl/joint_rep_en.htm [Accessed 25 February 2010].

UNESCO 2010. *Reaching the Marginalized, EFA Global Monitoring Report 2010*. Paris and Oxford: UNESCO. Available online at http://www.unesco.org/en/efareport/reports/2010-marginalization/ and http://www.unesco.org/fileadmin/MULTIMEDIA/HQ/ED/GMR/pdf/gmr2010/gmr2010-highlights.pdf [Accessed 14 July 2010].

UNFPA 2008. UNFPA *Strategy and Framework for Action: Addressing Gender-based Violence 2008–11*. Gender, Human Rights and Culture Branch. Geneva: UNFPA Technical Division.

United Nations General Assembly 2008. *Overview of Progress Towards Sustainable Development: A Review of the Implementation of Agenda 21, the Programme for the Further Implementation of Agenda 21 and the Johannesburg Plan of Implementation – Report of the Secretary-General*. E/CN.17/2008/2. New York: United Nations.

World Bank 2005. *Community Driven Development Examining Inclusion: Disability and Community Driven Development. Social Development Notes 33013, 100*. Washington, DC: World Bank.

World Bank 2007a. *People with Disabilities in India: From Commitments to Outcomes*. Human Development Unit, South Asia Region. Washington, DC: World Bank.

World Bank 2007b. *Global Monitoring Report, 2007. Millennium Development Goals: Confronting the Challenges of Gender Equality and Fragile States*. Washington, DC: World Bank. Available online at http://siteresources.worldbank.org/INTGLOMONREP2007/Resources/3413191-1176390231604/1264-FINAL-LO-RES.pdf [Accessed 25 February 2010].

Zadek, S., and Scott-Parker, S. 2001. *Unlocking Potential: The New Disability Business Case*. Geneva and London: ILO and Employers Forum on Disability.

Further reading

Loaiza, C. and Cappa, E. 2005. *Measuring Children's Disability via Household Surveys: The MICS Experience.* Paper presented at the UNICEF 2005 Population Association of America (PAA) meeting, 30 March–2 April, 2005, Philadelphia, PA.

McClain-Nhlapo, C. 2007. *Including People with Disabilities in Actions to Reduce Poverty and Hunger. Focus Brief on the World's Poor and Hungry People.* Washington, DC: IFPRI. Available online at http://www.ifpri.org/publication/including-people-disabilities-actions-reduce-poverty-and-hunger [Accessed 25 February 2010].

Pradesh Tribes. Available online at http://www.aptribes.gov.in/html/tricor-ceo.htm [Accessed 25 February 2010].

O'Toole, B. and McConkey, R. 1995. *Innovations in Developing Countries for People with Disabilities.* Electronic book. Enabling Education Network. Manchester: University of Manchester. Available online at http://www.eenet.org.uk/resources/docs/inno_dev_coun. php [Accessed 25 February 2010].

Sen, A. 2001. *Development as Freedom.* Oxford, UK: Oxford University Press.

UN Enable 2006. *Convention on the Rights of Persons with Disabilities and Optional Protocol. Article 32.* New York: UN Enable. Available online at http://www.un.org/disabilities/default. asp?navid=12&pid=150 [Accessed 25 February 2010].

World Bank 2006. *World Development Report on Equity.* Washington, DC: World Bank.

Lifelong learning builds economic opportunity
Photo: Bob Ransom

Chapter 4

Lifelong Learning in Education, Training and Skills Development

Bob Ransom

Summary

This chapter outlines the components of lifelong learning that people with disabilities in developing countries can use to escape from poverty and dependence. These are competencies and qualifications. After discussing the various types of skills that people need to make a livelihood, the author shows that they can be acquired in non-formal ways at home and in the community, and in formal technical and vocational education and training institutions. The next section analyses the advantages and disadvantages of different institutions in training people with disabilities for a livelihood. The author then sketches a number of success stories: a skills transfer programme in Cambodia, a programme in Ethiopia that trains very poor women with disabilities in business skills, a community-based vocational rehabilitation programme in Nigeria and on-the-job training in a large company in Brazil. The last section focuses in detail on the National Centre for Persons with Disabilities in Trinidad and Tobago. The author concludes by emphasising that people with disabilities can learn skills in numerous ways to reach their full potential, earn a livelihood and contribute to their family and community. The key to this is to ensure equality of opportunity at every level while making adaptations according to needs.

Lifelong learning and skills development for people with disabilities

Basic education and skills development are paths by which people with disabilities and their families in developing countries can escape from poverty. They are also part of a new paradigm for education and training in the 21st century called 'Lifelong Learning'. Lifelong learning, according to the International Labour Organization (ILO), 'ensures that the individual's skills and competencies are maintained and improved as work, technology and skill requirements change; ensures the personal and career development of workers; results in increases in productivity and income; and improves social equity' (ILO, 2000, para. 5).

Lifelong learning encompasses all learning activities undertaken throughout life, including developing the competencies and qualifications for practising a livelihood and participating successfully in the world of work. 'Competencies' cover the knowledge, skills and know-how applied and mastered in a specific work context. 'Qualifications' are the formal acknowledgement of a worker's vocational or professional skill that are recognised at international, national or sectoral levels (ILO, 2005, para. 2).

A livelihood is the way in which an individual secures the necessities of life. It may involve working at home or in the community, working alone or in a group, for an organisation, a government or an enterprise. It may be paid in kind or with cash, by a daily wage or with a salary. But a livelihood is not just any kind of work – it means decent work that is freely chosen under conditions of equity, security and human dignity.

To be able to maintain a livelihood and earn a living, whether you have a disability or not, you need competencies. These have become increasingly important in obtaining work or engaging in a business activity. Competencies fall into three categories: technical or vocational skills and know-how; entrepreneurial and management skills; and core life and work skills and attitudes.

Types of skills

Technical or vocational skills and know-how are the individual work skills you need for producing goods or providing some kind of service. In developing countries these skills are needed in basic manual and craft occupations such as farming, woodworking, metalworking, leather-working, pottery-making, tailoring or dressmaking, weaving and fabric dying, as well as in construction, plumbing, electrical and electronic work. Service activities typically include repairing vehicles, bicycles, electrical goods and computers as well as retail sales, marketing, transport, telephone, secretarial, food and laundry services. Some skills, like repairing bicycles, are relatively easy to learn. Others, like repairing computers, are more complex and require advanced training. Advanced skills usually need more formal training, which often takes place in technical institutions and results in a formal certification of competencies.

Self-employed people working in a microbusiness or small business activity need entrepreneurial or business management skills to succeed. Basic management skills include managing finance and people as well as planning and organisational skills. They involve collecting, analysing and using supply, service and market information, planning and initiating business activities, applying knowledge and skills to new situations, making decisions and solving business problems. Management skills are crucial to any business. People who have these skills can organise their own development according to their situation and strengthen their survival and self-help capabilities. They can develop creative ways of earning a livelihood by making the best use of skills and resources available to them.

Although these two kinds of skills are important, equally important is the category of skills called core skills, key competencies, life skills or foundation skills. Core or life skills are part of general skills development. They complement technical skills, help people to develop their potential and enhance their ability to integrate into society and the world of work. Life skills consist of the attitudes, knowledge and skills needed to function in the world, to cope in changing circumstances and to translate practical skills into a livelihood.

Core life and work skills are often formed by family, friends and the community, and are reinforced in the framework of vocational training, career guidance and adult basic education, as well as in youth and community development programmes. They include various interrelated skills: learning how to learn; competence in reading, writing and computing; effective listening and communication skills; adaptability through creative thinking and problem-solving; self-confidence and self-esteem; personal management and discipline; interpersonal and social skills; the ability to work in teams or groups and having a work ethic; as well as basic awareness about how things work in a community. 'Life skills training adds value to technical skills training' (Lobner, 1997, p. 21).

Ways to acquire skills

People of all ages and abilities can learn and develop knowledge, skills and know-how in two general ways: through non-formal and formal technical and vocational skills training. Non-formal skills can be developed at home in the family, through community-based training, including formal or informal apprenticeships with individuals in the community, and by participating in small enterprise development programmes that include basic business skills training, business development services and mentoring. Formal skills can be learned in special or mainstream vocational training centres and through formal and on-the-job training in an organisation or enterprise. Choosing the most appropriate method of skills development depends upon the individual's interests, capabilities and resources, as well as the opportunities and support available in the community. In addition, an individual may benefit from both non-formal and formal skills development at various times during his or her lifetime.

Basic education and skills development

A basic education is the key to success in the world of work. It provides a foundation from which to develop or upgrade technical skills and to acquire core or life skills. Children, young people and adults with disabilities who have had a basic education have foundational literacy and numeracy as well as a basic knowledge about the world:

> The foundation of any skills [development] strategy is basic education, which lays the basis for all future learning, inculcates the values and skills needed for active participation in social and political life, and enhances generic capabilities such as language, communication and problem-solving skills. (Department of Labour, South Africa, 1996, p. 11)

Basic education is an

> essential prerequisite and foundation for access to education and further training as a basic right for unlocking other rights, such as the right to decent work, employment, cultural and political participation, economic wellbeing and security. (Singh, 2007, p. 30)

In order to extend access to quality and relevant training for people with disabilities, efforts need to start with extending access to quality basic education. As well as promoting equitable access to basic education for people of all ages with disabilities, vocational skills training needs to include elements of basic education, such as functional literacy, to facilitate the acquisition of skills by those who have not already acquired a basic education.

Access to mainstream education is essential. Ordinary secondary schools sometimes offer vocational education courses as well as vocational assessment and career guidance and counselling services. Students with disabilities should have the opportunity to enrol in such vocational courses and to benefit from career guidance services. They should also have an opportunity to benefit from mainstream programmes for youth to make the transition from school to work.

Non-formal skills development

Home-based skills development

In developing countries many people learn traditional vocational and life skills through home-based agricultural, manufacturing and other activities. Farm-related activities typically include cultivating cash crops (like cocoa, coffee, cotton and tea), growing vegetables and flowers, beekeeping, silkworm production, rearing livestock and poultry, and producing milk, butter, cheese and eggs. Examples of home-based productive activities include spinning and weaving, knitting, sewing, basketry, fishnet making and repair, as well as food preparation and preserving. Other home-based activities include drying fish, making candles, soap and pottery, taking in laundry and childcare. Home-based knowledge, skills and know-how are passed on from family members to children and young people in the home.

Often, however, children and young people with disabilities are excluded from this process of learning by doing. Parents often want to protect the child with a disability from harm and work. They may believe their child is unable to learn or contribute to the household; they may discourage, neglect or simply ignore them. As a result, family members with a disability do not learn useful skills and behaviour and are prevented from making a contribution to the household. This exclusion impacts negatively on their self-confidence and the self-esteem necessary for their further growth and active participation in the family and community.

Parents need to be helped to understand that family members with a disability have potential, and to be encouraged to teach them home-based skills so they can contribute productively to the household. Specific suggestions can be made to parents about the kinds of activities the family member with a disability might be taught and engage in, based

Gaining skills helps to contribute to family income
Photo: Bob Ransom

upon their capabilities. Children with intellectual disabilities can take care of animals, collect eggs and grow vegetables; visually impaired children can garden, weave, knit and sew; mobility-impaired children can help prepare food and other products and hearing impaired children can do just about anything. Home-based learning and doing is fundamental in preparing an individual for further skills acquisition in the world of work.

Non-formal skills development in the local community

One of the most effective ways that young people and adults with disabilities can develop the competencies necessary to engage in productive work is by taking advantage of the training opportunities available in the local community. Opportunities for formal, salaried employment are often very limited for any job-seeker in the rural areas, towns and cities of developing countries. As a result most people seeking work in developing countries, including people with disabilities, find it in the informal sector or economy.

Many men and women in search of work and income find that there are not enough jobs to go around and, eventually, create their own employment. That is, they start a micro-enterprise, usually in an urban area, in which they will work alone, or with one or two others, possibly apprentices. The multitude and diversity of unincorporated, household-based, small ventures, that are typically unregistered, and at least initially, overlooked by public authorities, such as statisticians and tax people, are hard to miss in the teeming cities of sub-Saharan Africa. Unsophisticated perhaps, they are the producers and traders providing essential goods and services to large numbers of customers, in markets, along major boulevards, and wherever their peers have their homes. They sell whatever sells. They dress the nation and they keep the cars on the road. They make pots and pans. They paint signs and they dye cloth. They run mobile restaurants, open-air barber shops, and, increasingly, cyber cafés. They produce and distribute medicine. And so on, and so forth. They are the working poor in what is widely known as the urban informal sector, or informal economy. (Fluitman, 1989, p. 24)

The economy of a local village, community or town offers many opportunities for people with disabilities to learn skills and become self-employed. Some examples of these activities include haircutting and hairdressing, cleaning and laundry, secretarial and bookkeeping or accounting, operating an Internet café or a telephone call centre, repairing electrical appliances, radios and televisions, sharpening scissors and knives, preparing and serving food in a canteen or restaurant, operating a small retail shop and producing and selling various items made from leather, wood, metal or pottery.

There are several ways to assist people with disabilities to find skills development and work opportunities in the community. One way is to arrange for the individual to participate in a traditional apprentice-ship under a master trainer engaged in a local production or service business. You can help individuals with disabilities anxious to learn a skill to identify:

- their interests, what they want to learn and do, what skills they already possess, and what family support is available

- training opportunities with someone in the community who is already engaged in that occupation or providing training, and encourage them to take on an apprentice who has a disability

- solutions to potential obstacles to becoming an apprentice, including the cost, access, mobility and support required (transport, sign language interpreter, special equipment).

The next step is to provide the financial or material support to the master trainer and the support the individual requires to becoming an apprentice. Finally a follow-up must be made with the master trainer and trainee to help overcome any problems and to ensure that learning and training are taking place. The challenge is to build upon the unique strengths, experience, capabilities and interests of individuals with disabilities and to find master trainers willing and able to impart their competencies to them.

Traditional apprenticeships offer both advantages and disadvantages. They can provide skills training at appropriate levels of technology, using equipment and techniques that are already in use in the community. The training often includes exposure to organisational, management and business skills, including costing, marketing, money management and consolidating supplier and customer relations. Apprentices have the opportunity to build the social and economic networks that are essential for successfully starting and running their own informal activities when their training is complete.

However, there are disadvantages. Training quality varies and there is no guarantee that a definite set of skills will be transferred. There is no certification process, so that apprenticeship graduates in the same trade may not have the same skills. Training is based on traditional technologies and techniques and does not readily permit the introduction of new technologies, methods and designs.

Finally, training is usually available for only a small number of trades and tends to benefit young men more than young women. Despite these drawbacks, informal, traditional apprenticeships often provide the first and sometimes the only available opportunity for many informal economy workers, including people with disabilities, to learn skills and to work their way out of poverty.

Box 4.1 Alleviating Poverty through Peer Training (APPT) project in Cambodia

Using a methodology called Success Case Replication (SCR), the APPT project in Cambodia is funded by the Finnish Embassy. People in Cambodia have traditionally transferred skills on an informal, personal basis. While the SCR methodology does not replace the system of formal, classroom-based vocational training, it does offer certain benefits, especially for the rural poor and for people with disabilities.

APPT project field workers first seek out successful microbusinesses, farmers and artisans and interview them. They include duck and pig farmers, barbers, wood carvers and producers of cement jars, rattan mats and joss sticks. The field workers analyse the businesses to determine their viability and profitability and then assess the local market to determine if it can sustain another similar business. The field workers then identify successful entrepreneurs who are willing to train others. Many entrepreneurs with disabilities are willing to train people with disabilities. Some entrepreneurs are willing to offer training at no cost, while others ask for a fee or charge for training materials. These fees tend to be higher for more profitable businesses. The trainers selected must agree to teach the business and technical aspects of the business and to share their trade secrets.

Village leaders, local government officials and non-governmental organisations (NGOs) help APPT project field workers to identify

---

people with disabilities who would like training. The field workers interview candidates and explore their interests, abilities and skills, and then match the candidates with trainers based on such factors as mutual interest and geographical proximity. Many trainees already know of successful entrepreneurs in their own or nearby communities with whom they want to train. When the trainer, trainee and the field worker agree to the length of training and costs, a simple agreement is signed between trainer and trainee.

APPT project field workers provide support to the trainer and trainee during the training period and intervene if problems or special needs arise; they also determine that the trainee is acquiring the necessary skills.

An evaluation of the APPT project revealed that over 750 people with disabilities or with a family member with a disability (52 per cent women) received peer training, and that 82 (37 per cent women) received other types of training. A total of 609 (60 per cent women) started their own microbusinesses. Another 126 (35 per cent women) enhanced their existing businesses through participation in the project. Some 70 per cent of participants had mobility impairments and 15 per cent had visual impairments.

The SCR methodology adopted by the APPT project is a simple concept that addresses the particular skills development needs of people with disabilities in rural communities. It uses the human resources found at the village level and overcomes the barriers of inaccessibility, negative attitudes and lack of services. Learning by doing is an approach that suits many people with disabilities and those with limited education. The project replicates the skills and practices of businesses known to be successful, although careful planning is required to ensure that markets are not flooded by too many new businesses offering similar products or services.

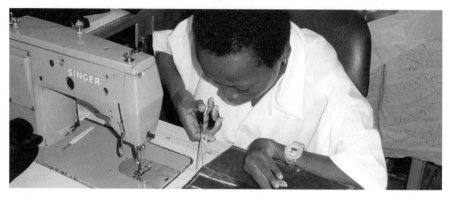

Skill building supports self-employment. Photo: Bob Ransom

Non-formal business skills training for self-employment

Micro and small enterprise development programmes are now found in most developing countries and are often linked to microfinance schemes. Self-employment through creating and operating a small business activity is often the most viable way of earning a livelihood for many people with disabilities. They can be helped to participate in existing mainstream programmes in the community. These need to be identified and encouraged to include entrepreneurs and potential entrepreneurs with disabilities. The programme personnel need to be sensitised to disability issues and helped to develop ways in which individuals with different types of disabilities can participate in the programme. Obstacles to their participation should be identified and overcome, and relevant support (such as transport, sign language interpreters and suitably adapted materials) is provided as required.

Box 4.2 Developing Entrepreneurship among Women with Disabilities (DEWD) programme in Ethiopia

The three-year International Labour Organization (ILO) DEWD programme in Ethiopia was funded by Irish Aid and implemented by two organisations of people with disabilities (DPOs) working under contract to the ILO: the Ethiopian Federation of Persons with

Disabilities (EFPD) and the Tigray Disabled Veterans Association (TDVA). In each DPO a project management committee composed of women with disabilities was formed. Women leaders in EFPD and TDVA and their member associations were trained in gathering information on the business aspirations of both women with disabilities and women having a dependent with a disability, as well as the business constraints facing them through situation analyses and case studies.

Over 450 women were then trained in basic business skills. They included women with disabilities, mothers of children with intellectual disabilities and wives of war veterans with disabilities. Some 20 women were trained to be basic business skills trainers. The business skills training, using a curriculum designed for illiterate women and delivered in the local language, was provided by experienced master trainers using ILO-designed training materials.

Market surveys were also conducted to identify new production and service opportunities that women entrepreneurs with disabilities could incorporate into their business plans. Twenty women entrepreneurs with disabilities were trained in product design and marketing in local trade fairs, and 55 women with disabilities were trained in vocational skills by local private training centres or through apprenticeships with local women already engaged in a business activity. Following this training over 200 of the women were given loans to implement their business plans through local microfinance institutions.

The DEWD programme demonstrated that women with disabilities in Ethiopia who are very poor can learn business skills, manage credit and start or develop small business activities. It also demonstrated that DPOs in Ethiopia can effectively coordinate the delivery of business skills training, access to credit and follow-up business advisory services to women entrepreneurs with disabilities.

Formal skills training: Mainstream technical and vocational education and training (TVET)

An integral part of the formal educational opportunities available in most countries is TVET, which includes

> the study of technologies and related sciences, and the acquisition of practical skills, attitudes, understanding and knowledge relating to occupations in various sectors of economic and social life. It is understood to be an integral part of general education, a means of preparing for occupational fields and for effective participation in the world of work, an aspect of lifelong learning and a preparation for responsible citizenship, an instrument for promoting environmentally sound sustainable development and a method of facilitating poverty alleviation. (UNESCO and ILO, 2002, p. 7)

An emerging training priority is giving young people and adults with disabilities access to mainstream TVET. Skills are usually acquired best by individuals with disabilities when they are trained together with their non-disabled peers. Formal TVET training centres are often located in towns and cities, and are geared to the skills needs of large urban enterprises. However, government, NGO and community-operated as well as private commercial vocational skills training centres in smaller towns and rural communities can also provide useful training in technical and life skills.

Barriers to trainees with disabilities in accessing TVET

Trainees with disabilities often face many obstacles in trying to access formal mainstream training in both formal TVET institutions and local skills training centres. Such barriers include high academic entry requirements, inaccessible buildings and classrooms, high tuition fees and training costs, a lack of adaptive aids and equipment, negative attitudes of centre staff and other trainees towards individuals with disabilities, lack of policies that support the training of people with disabilities and mainstream trainers' lack of confidence and experience in teaching trainees with disabilities.

Given such obstacles, special measures need to be taken to ensure access and the participation of trainees with disabilities in mainstream training. Access in its fullest sense refers to physical access, communication access and social access to facilities, services, training and work opportunities. Affirmative action is one way to overcome barriers to equal access through positive steps to eliminate or compensate for any inequalities faced by a disadvantaged group and to increase its opportunities to participate. Affirmative action is needed to encourage and facilitate mainstream formal training centres and courses to include trainees with disabilities.

Affirmative action in the institution

An enrolment policy can set a specific target each term for enrolling people with disabilities as trainees. The availability of these places could be publicised in local schools, DPOs, NGOs and organisations for women and youth. The awareness of parents and community groups of the importance of vocational skills training should be increased. Flexible entry requirements could be set and remedial basic education courses provided. Instructors should be given disability awareness training on the adjustment needs of trainees with different types of disabilities.

Affirmative action towards the trainees

Trainees with disabilities, especially women and girls, should be supported in applying for enrolment and for financial aid. They should be given guidance on various skills development opportunities, avoiding disability- and gender-based stereotypes. The accessibility and adaptation needs of individual trainees need to be assessed. Some trainees using wheelchairs may be integrated easily if the courses are on the ground floor and the toilet facilities are accessible. A separate class for deaf trainees who require sign language interpreters could be organised for trainees interested in the same course to minimise the expense of a sign language interpretation. Braille materials and information in electronic format or adaptive equipment should be provided to blind and visually impaired trainees as required. Finally, support during training from a local NGO or social service agency should be arranged to help trainees with disabilities succeed and to help instructors to resolve any difficulties that may arise.

Box 4.3 Community-Based Vocational Rehabilitation (CBVR) programme in Ibadan

The Ibadan CBVR programme, initiated by a joint ILO–UNDP technical cooperation project, encouraged representatives of various DPOs, relatives of people with disabilities, community elders, development NGOs, representatives of financial institutions and federal and state government officials to form a committee to design and implement a skills training programme for people with disabilities in the city. The CBVR programme committee chairperson was a non-salaried community elder and most of the volunteer committee members were representatives of DPOs and NGOs. The government provided office space and paid the salaries of the social workers attached to the programme, while the committee raised funds from the community for the training.

To initiate the programme community members and representatives of DPOs organised public sensitisation campaigns, including public marches, in target communities in the city to encourage people with disabilities to register to be trained for work. Upon registration the CBVR committee assessed their capabilities and vocational interests and the level of family support available to them. Selected participants were placed in local mainstream vocational skills training centres. While in training they received an allowance from the committee. The training period ranged from six months to a year, depending on the skills to be acquired, and the courses included carpentry, making and repairing shoes, keeping poultry, making tie-dyed textiles and catering.

The committee encouraged trainees to save a portion of their allowance by helping them to open bank savings accounts and arranging with the mobile unit of the People's Bank to visit the CBVR office on the days in which the allowances were paid. Upon graduation, most of the trainees used their savings to buy the items they needed to start work. The committee established a revolving loan scheme for their graduates. The bank disbursed its own funds to graduates, using ILO-UNDP project funds as collateral. During its first ten years of operation the CBVR programme trained over 200 people and at its tenth anniversary celebration it was found that a large number of former trainees had themselves become trainers in the programme. Both non-disabled workers and apprentices with disabilities were found to be working for them.

Enterprise-based training

Enterprise-based training (EBT) is widespread and is often the most common form of skills training in many developing countries, with in-firm, informal training predominating. EBT provides both firm-specific and general skills training. Local firms that have in-house skills training and upgrading programmes often offer useful ways for people with disabilities to be trained.

The local business community can provide valuable support by providing on the job training, hiring workers with disabilities, mentoring entrepreneurs with disabilities and providing advice on current and emerging skills requirements to vocational training centers. (ILO, UNESCO and WHO, 2004, p. 21)

Businesses in the community, as well as NGOs, can be approached to explore and initiate on-the-job training opportunities for individuals with disabilities. These could be in the form of a short-term attachment following the completion of school, or a long-term apprenticeship or internship. Employers might be willing to pay a training stipend to the trainee or a local sponsoring organisation might offer similar support. Experience in some countries shows that following successful on-the-job training the employer often hires the trainee, having seen at first hand what the trainee is capable of doing.

Box 4.4 On-the-job training by Serasa, a large private sector company in Brazil

Serasa is a leading Brazilian economic and financial analysis and information company. It has branches in 115 locations throughout Brazil and employs 2,400 people. The company has a strong commitment to social responsibility. As part of this, Serasa runs a six-month in-house traineeship on company premises for people with physical, hearing, visual and intellectual impairments. The programme provides industrial skills training and professional qualifications for people with disabilities in line with the needs of its industry. This leads to a recognised national qualification certificate. The programme is permanent and continuous with its own budget, which has increased by between 30 and 75 per cent every year since the programme started. Over 100 Serasa employees have disabilities, all of whom are graduates of the programme. Programme graduates who are not employed with Serasa enter the job market with a qualification and enhanced employability skills. The Serasa programme, and its emulation by other Brazilian businesses, has led to the establishment of the Forum of Employability, a group of representatives from several companies who meet four times a year to share their experience in developing employment programmes for people with disabilities.

Special training centres for people with disabilities

Some communities may have special training centres for people with disabilities, called vocational rehabilitation centres or vocational training centres. Such centres often offer a variety of services including vocational and life skills training. They are usually operated by governments, religious organisations, NGOs, parents' associations or DPOs. They may offer training to individuals with physical disabilities or to blind, deaf or intellectually disabled people; some may be for male trainees, some for female trainees, some for both.

The advantage of special training centres for individuals with disabilities is that their facilities are usually accessible and they have personnel, including instructors, who are experienced in training people with disabilities. However, such centres also often have drawbacks. They sometimes offer training in stereotypical and outdated skills such as broom-making and basket-weaving to blind trainees and woodworking to deaf trainees. They segregate people with disabilities from the rest of society, perpetuating societal lack of awareness of their needs and capabilities. They often fail to provide the necessary vocational skill certification that is required by some employers, and fail to help trainees with disabilities integrate into the world of work when their training is complete. Finally, the knowledge and skills development offered often do not correspond to local market needs and do not prepare the trainee for self-employment.

Despite these drawbacks, some specialised training centres for people with disabilities provide quality vocational assessment, skills training, work experience and job placement services among others. The programmes and activities of one such centre of excellence in the Caribbean region are described in detail to illustrate a complete and effective process of vocational rehabilitation, training and job placement.

National Centre for Persons with Disabilities (NCPD) Trinidad

The National Centre for Persons with Disabilities (NCPD) is an NGO in Trinidad and Tobago whose mission is to provide effective and efficient training and rehabilitation for people with disabilities to enhance their quality of life and promote their integration into the wider community. The NCPD mission is achieved through an extensive interview and assessment process, complemented by an individualised education and training plan that creates the foundation for successful training and job placement. Certified vocational training is used to access employment, remain in employment and advance in chosen careers. NCPD believes that people with disabilities have a right to decent work, not by virtue of their disability but by virtue of being qualified in their chosen field.

The NCPD was established in 1964 as a vocational rehabilitation centre primarily serving those affected by polio, and was registered in 1984 as a company limited by guarantee. It operates a multipurpose facility in the city of San Fernando in the southern part of the island of Trinidad. A major challenge for Trinidad and Tobago and other Caribbean countries is to develop their human resources and reduce their dependence on non-renewable natural resources, and to reduce poverty. In the long run, one of the most effective ways of breaking the cycle of poverty, disability and social exclusion is investing in all people, including people with disabilities.

The NCPD is governed by a nine-member voluntary board of directors composed of professionals with a range of experience in business, law, finance, special education, labour and project management. It has a good gender balance and includes people with disabilities. The board is involved in policy formulation and fundraising. The day-to-day administration of the NCPD is under the direction of a chief executive officer, supported by a team of 46 professional and administrative staff (30 female, 16 male), including persons with disabilities.

The NCPD annual operating budget comes from an annual subvention from the government. Its other major source of revenue is from its light manufacturing business. Other funds come from business and philanthropic organisations and from NCPD-organised fundraising events, such as an annual carnival fête and 'Tea by the Sea'.

NCPD programmes and services

The NCPD has four major areas of operation: vocational rehabilitation services, skills training, light manufacturing and community outreach. It has an annual client/trainee population of 170 individuals (60 women, 110 men) that includes people with various types of disabilities including hearing, visual, speech and language, and orthopaedic impairments. The centre also caters for people with intellectual disabilities and developmental disabilities, including Down's syndrome and autism, as well as serious emotional disturbance, traumatic brain injury, epilepsy, paraplegia, quadriplegia, cerebral palsy, muscular dystrophy, spina bifida, juvenile arthritis and multiple sclerosis. NCPD has a mixed gender population in which women outnumber men.

Vocational rehabilitation services

The vocational rehabilitation services include vocational assessment and guidance, situational assessment and counselling, leading to skills training and job placements. The NCPD uses a set of recruitment criteria to determine the programme or service to which someone seeking training should be directed. The criteria cover factors such as age (15–35), freedom from drug and alcohol abuse, ability to care for personal basic needs, willingness to follow medical treatment if prescribed, and ability to engage in and complete a two-year vocational skills training course for a maximum of eight hours a day, five days a week. Other factors, such as responsibility for their own transport to and from the centre, an assurance of continued support from parents, guardian, family members or referring agency and medical, social, economic and educational background information are also part of the basic criteria.

The NCPD believes that effective and efficient training can take place only against a background of solid vocational assessment. This includes a series of adapted standardised tests and work samples that give a comprehensive view of the client across a wide range of dimensions, including academic achievement, cognitive development, vocational interests, social behaviour, aptitude and attitudes, negative and positive learning behaviour and activities, life skills and physical capabilities. This information is used to prepare an assessment report, a client profile and an individualised education plan (IEP). The assessment report is a detailed confidential document that contains the client's personal data. The client profile, which is also confidential, gives concise information about the client and also provides a brief synopsis of the assessment. It helps the instructor to provide the best possible instruction to each trainee. The IEP is a tool that provides optimal management of the skills curriculum while setting realistic goals that allow trainees to perform to the best of their ability.

Once trainees are admitted to the centre, a one- to two-week situational assessment takes place. This monitors how well trainees adapt to their chosen skill area, through observations by the instructor of the instructor/trainee relationship, peer interaction, and their overall interest in the skill chosen. After this process is completed the trainee embarks on a two-year skills training programme. To foster holistic trainee development, each vocational skill training programme includes remedial education (basic numeric, reading and writing skills, social studies and science), information technology (computer literacy) and life skills. Trainees are also exposed to sports activities and extra-curricular activities such as dance and steel drumming. Training is offered in agriculture and horticulture, beauty culture, bookbinding, food preparation, garment construction, information technology, office administration, offset printing, upholstery, woodwork, welding and metal work.

The NCPD has referral relationships with the San Fernando Technical Institute and Trinzuela Secretarial and Technical Institute and places trainees at both institutions to pursue courses in repairing small appliances, technical drawing, electrical wiring and electronics. The NCPD offers accredited national and international certification for its skills training programmes. The centre is certified to offer the National Examination Council's (NEC) Craft Certificate, Trinidad and Tobago National Vocational Qualification Certification and the City and Guild

Training certificates increase the chance of getting a job
Photo: Bob Ransom

Pitman Typewriting Examination. The Caribbean Vocational Qualification system will ultimately provide certification that will be recognised in all Caribbean countries.

During a typical year the centre admits 85 new clients with different disabilities, offers training to over 300 trainees and presents over 50 trainees for the NEC Craft Certificate. Of the graduating trainees, some 50 obtain job placements. During a typical year over 600 people benefit from NCPD services, including counselling, assessment and work adjustment services.

As trainees proceed through their programme they are given regular, comprehensive progress reports. Evaluation and monitoring is ongoing and continuous throughout their training experience. Case conferences are held periodically by a multidisciplinary team (NCPD CEO, programme manager, vocational counsellor, relevant instructors and parents or guardians). The conference carefully considers the progress reports and the client's IEP. This allows the team to trace the trainee's progress and decide whether the trainee is ready to take the exams or needs to be relocated to another skill training area. It also allows the team to identify whatever changes may be necessary to redesign the IEP to ensure that the individual reaches his or her maximum potential.

As part of trainees' holistic development, the centre offers counselling services to the trainee and family members through its vocational counsellor. The counselling is designed to support and complement the training process. It offers a positive and sympathetic environment in which trainees can explore any issue at their own pace. It also helps to build the trainees' self-esteem, improve communication skills and foster individual empowerment by reinforcing socially appropriate behaviour. The content of all counselling sessions is confidential.

Apprenticeship programme

A trainee who successfully completes the training process and graduates is invited to participate for a year in the NCPD apprenticeship programme. This is an on-the-job training programme that allows trainees to experience a real work setting in which to master the skills acquired during training. This may take place at the NCPD, in government offices or in a collaborating business enterprise. Most placements are made in the private sector in companies in the oil and energy sector (as senior draughtsperson, receptionist, clerical officer and carpenter) the furniture manufacturing industry, including woodwork shops (as cabinet maker, joiner, sander, machine operator and furniture finisher). Placements also include the printing industry (as printing operator, binder, stitcher and desktop publisher), the garment industry (as stitcher) and the food and hospitality industry (as waiter or waitress, dishwasher, kitchen assistant, pastry cook and assistant cook). During their apprenticeship trainees learn how to cope with various challenges associated with employment on the open job market. They are guided to adopt positive work-related behaviour and job etiquette, and to understand labour laws. At the end of this programme each apprentice is taught how to prepare a résumé, complete job application forms, conduct a job search and handle job interviews.

Job placement

Job placement is seen as the final step in the skills training process. A multidisciplinary team (the CEO, vocational counsellor, programme manager and supervisor) evaluates the development of the apprentice based on progress reports from the supervisor. This evaluation is used to help the apprentice to secure a job. The job placement officer identifies job vacancies and conducts extensive discussions with prospective employers, establishing precise job descriptions, working hours, training process, dress code, work-related behaviour, safety measures, co-worker involvement and the social milieu. The prospective employer is made aware of the client's type of disability, their medication (if applicable), emergency phone contact and any accommodations that may be necessary. The job placement officer maintains contact with the employer and new employee for a period of six months. The vocational counsellor may also be actively involved in providing a follow-up service to help the former apprentice and the employer during this transition period.

Work adjustment programme

The NCPD offers a work adjustment service to individuals who have acquired a disability during their working life. It may entail intensive counselling with the individual and family members to help them adjust to their new circumstances. It may also lead to the acquisition of new skills that will enable a return to work and to regain a level of independence. The programme is personalised and as participants progress it is adjusted to suit their specific needs. This programme has no age restriction.

Independent living skills programme

The participants assigned to this programme are individuals who have reached their learning threshold vocationally, and who have been working for an extensive period of time but still need to acquire or reinforce independent living skills. It also includes people who have been identified during the interview as being unable to cope with skills training or open employment but who need independent living skills. It helps such people to acquire the basic skills (such as dressing themselves, making a bed, preparing a simple breakfast, housekeeping) they need to become assets at home and to live as independently as possible.

Light manufacturing business services

The NCPD light manufacturing section creates work opportunities for trained people with disabilities. It provides on-the-job training for apprentices and creates revenue for the institution. The centre offers a range of business services to individuals, government agencies and corporations. These services include:

- constructing and repairing wooden home and office furniture

- upholstering furniture for offices and homes, wheelchair seats and backs

- sewing industrial uniforms, curtains, bedspreads and conference bags

- printing offset (colour) brochures, letterheads, calling cards and forms

- bookbinding hard and soft covers, journal boxes and binders

- repairing wheelchairs

- manufacturing disability aids such as wheelchairs, wooden and metal crutches, walking sticks, metal walkers and orthopaedic shoes.

Community outreach

The NCPD has outreach activities at both the Caribbean regional level and at national level. It conducts training workshops and seminars for organisations of and for people with disabilities, employer and labour organisations and vocational training institutions in other Caribbean countries. It arranges study tours for interested people to observe the methodologies employed by NCPD in the areas of training and employment. It conducts research studies on training and employing people with disabilities, disseminates information about current trends on disability issues to both national and regional organisations, and promotes advocacy on equality issues and the rights of persons with disabilities. Finally, NCPD personnel and trainees participate in national radio programmes and career fairs.

Partnerships

The success enjoyed by the NCPD owes much to the partnerships it has forged in order to serve the community better. Current and ongoing partnerships include government, corporations, international agencies and organisations of and for people with disabilities as well as private citizens. These partnerships provide funding, technical expertise and job and business opportunities for the NCPD and its trainees. Other factors that have contributed to the success of the NCPD include an intensive trainee recruitment process, the tailored programmes designed for each trainee, a dedicated and effective management, keeping abreast with changing trends in the world of work and technology, certified and relevant vocational skills training and providing appropriate support to trainees.

Conclusions

There are a number of ways in which children, young people, and adult men and women with disabilities can learn and develop the vocational, entrepreneurial and core life skill competencies needed for a livelihood. They include learning traditional home-based skills such as agriculture and animal husbandry, vocational or technical skills to produce things such as chairs, tables, sweaters or food, or to provide services such as secretarial or hairdressing, repairing motor cars or TVs, as well as the entrepreneurial skills needed to buy and sell goods in the market or to run a business. They also include core or life skills, such as self-confidence, how to relate to people, how to network or work in a group or simply how to survive in a community.

The particular interests, talents and abilities of each individual help determine the skills development most suited to them. Everyone should be given an equal opportunity without being limited by traditional gender roles, and women and girls with disabilities may need special additional support. Maximum skills development options should be considered for each person, and these should not be based upon preconceived ideas of what the individual is capable of doing.

Skills development opportunities in the local community should be identified first. Existing mainstream training centres provide the most direct source of training and should be encouraged and assisted to take trainees with disabilities. Local people engaged in a production or service activity can also be used as master trainers. There are several ways to identify such trainers as well as the skills required in a community. They include market surveys and analysis of local demand for goods and services, studies of potential new products, services and markets currently unavailable or underserved, their related skill requirements, and actual or future local job opportunities. Training in technical or vocational skills for which there is no demand, or in skills for which the market may be saturated, is a frustrating waste of resources for all concerned. Equality of opportunity in training and work for people with disabilities should be a basic principle in local schools and training centres, and in local businesses and organisations working in close cooperation with the labour and social affairs government officials who are often responsible for programmes and services for people with disabilities.

References

Department of Labour, South Africa 1996. *Integrated Human Resources Development Strategy for South Africa.* Pretoria: Department of Labour and the National Training Board.

Fluitman, F. (ed.) 1989. *Training for Work in the Informal Sector.* Geneva: ILO.

ILO 2000. *Conclusions Concerning Human Resources Training and Development.* International Labour Conference, 88th Session. Geneva: ILO.

ILO 2005. *Recommendation Concerning Human Resources Development: Education, Training and Lifelong Learning (Recommendation 195).* Geneva: ILO.

ILO, UNESCO and WHO 2004. *CBR: A Strategy for Rehabilitation, Equalization of Opportunities, Poverty Reduction and Social Inclusion of People with Disabilities.* Joint position paper. Geneva: WHO.

Lobner, S. 1997. *Life Skills for the World of Work: Experiences in South Africa. ILO Action Programme on skills and entrepreneurship training in countries emerging from armed conflict.* Geneva: ILO.

Singh, M. 2007. *New Knowledge, Skills and Competence Requirements for the Informal Economy in the Context of Globalisation.* Paper presented at a conference on Approaching Inclusive Growth through Skills Development, 12–13 February. UNESCO, GTZ and Government of India.

UNESCO and ILO 2002. *Technical and Vocational Education and Training for the Twenty-first Century* (UNESCO and ILO recommendations), Paris: UNESCO and Geneva: ILO.

Further reading

Brewer, B. 2004. *Youth at Risk: The Role of Skills Development in Facilitating the Transition to Work.* ILO InFocus Programme on Skills, Knowledge and Employability. Working Paper No. 19. Geneva: ILO.

CINTERFOR 2001. *Training for decent work.* Montevideo: ILO.

Haan, H.C. 2002. *Training for Work in the Informal Sector: New Evidence from Kenya, Tanzania and Uganda,* ILO InFocus Programme on Skills, Knowledge and Employability Working Paper No. 11. Geneva: ILO.

ILO 1994. *We Can ... Given the Opportunity: Profiles on Eight Participants of the Community-based Vocational Rehabilitation Programme in Ibadan, Nigeria.* Lagos: ILO.

ILO 2003. *Doing Business in Addis Ababa: Case Studies of Women Entrepreneurs with Disabilities in Ethiopia.* Addis Ababa: ILO.

ILO 2004. *Lifelong Learning in Asia and the Pacific.* Report of the ILO Regional Tripartite Meeting, 8–10 December 2003, Bangkok and Geneva: ILO.

ILO 2007. *Strategies for Skills Acquisition and Work for People with Disabilities in Southern Africa – Malawi, South Africa, Zambia.* Geneva: ILO.

ILO 2008a. *Improving Skills and Productivity of Disadvantaged Youth Employment Sector.* Working Paper No. 7. Geneva: ILO.

ILO 2008b. *Recognising Ability: The Skills and Productivity of People with Disabilities. A Literature Review.* Employment Sector Working Paper No. 3. Geneva: ILO.

ILO 2008c. *Skills and Productivity in the Informal Economy.* Employment Sector Working Paper No. 5. Geneva: ILO.

ILO 2008d. *Skills Development through Community Based Rehabilitation (CBR): A good practice guide.* Geneva: ILO.

King, K. 2006. *Skills Development and Poverty Reduction: The State of the Art.* Post-basic Education and Training Working Paper No. 7. Edinburgh: Centre of African Studies.

King, K., and Palmer, R. 2006. Skills, capacities and knowledge in the least developed countries: new challenges for development cooperation. Background paper for the *2006 UNCTAD Least Developed Countries Report*. Edinburgh: Centre of African Studies.

Liimatainen, M. R. 2002. *Training and Skills Acquisition in the Informal Sector: A Literature Review*. In Focus Programme on Skills, Knowledge and Employability Working Paper No. 9. Geneva: ILO.

Middleton, J., Ziderman, A., and Van Adams, A. 1993. *Skills for Productivity: Vocational Education and Training in Developing Countries*. New York: Oxford University Press.

O'Reilly, A. 2007. *The Right to Decent Work of People with Disabilities*. Geneva: ILO.

Perry, D. (ed.) 2003. *Moving Forward: Toward Decent Work for People with Disabilities. Examples of good practices in vocational training and employment from Asia and the Pacific*. Bangkok: ILO.

Sim, F.G. 1999. *Integrating Women and Girls with Disabilities into Mainstream Vocational Training: A Practical Guide*. Geneva: ILO.

Werner, D. 1987. *Disabled Village Children: A Guide for Community Health Workers, Rehabilitation Workers, and Families*. Palo Alto, CA: The Hesperian Foundation.

World Bank 2004. *Skills Development in Sub-Saharan Africa*. Washington, DC: World Bank.

World Bank, Working Group for International Cooperation in Skills Development 2004. *Debates in Skills Development (Paper 7), World Bank Study on Vocational Skills Development in Sub-Saharan Africa: a Working Group Review*. Washington, DC: World Bank.

Zuniga, F.V. 2005. *Key Competencies and Lifelong Learning: Three Perspectives on These Subjects in Latin America and the Caribbean*. CINTERFOR. Montevideo: ILO.

Self-help groups can contribute to just societies
Photo: Sudhindra CN/Leonard Cheshire Disability

Chapter 5

Community Approaches to Livelihood Development: Self-help Groups in India

Peter Coleridge and Balakrishna Venkatesh

Summary

> Man can only liberate himself or develop himself. He cannot be liberated or developed by another.... The expansion of his own consciousness, and therefore of his power over himself, his environment, and his society, must therefore ultimately be what we mean by development (Julius Nyerere)
>
> To be human is to engage in relationships with others and with the world (Paulo Freire)

Poverty is not simply lack of income; it is a denial of the fundamental freedom and opportunity to develop as a human being. Discrimination on the grounds of race, religion, gender, class, caste and disability creates or exacerbates poverty for many millions of people around the world. The elimination of poverty lies, in large measure, in the creation of a just society in which all citizens have equal opportunity to develop their full potential.[1]

Global trends show both increasing support for and increasing obstacles to the creation of just societies. On the one hand international and national legislation outlaw discrimination and governments proclaim the values of equal opportunity, including equal opportunities for disabled people. On the other hand it is primarily economics, not human values, that drives much of global development and there is often little interest from those who have economic power in sharing it on an equitable basis. Poor people all over the world, from landless peasants in Brazil to *dalits*[2] and women in India, have learned that if equality is to become a reality it is they who must take the initiative through mobilising themselves for both political and economic power.

Disabled people are in the same position and have made the same discovery. It has become clear to them in many countries that it is they who must take the initiative to solve their own problems and create their own opportunities. In many parts of the world they have found that the most effective way to do this is through the formation of self-help groups (SHGs). SHGs open the doors of possibility to both individual and community development in the fullest sense. Through group membership and action disabled people gain increased confidence and self-esteem, create economic opportunities and make rights a reality.

This chapter takes the view that the development of livelihood goes well beyond the ability to earn an income. It involves creating opportunities to develop one's full potential as a social and political human being (political in the sense of having increasing control over the factors that shape one's life) and the ability to contribute to the development of one's community and society.

While SHGs have sprung up all over the world, the development of SHGs of disabled people is most advanced in India. For this reason this chapter uses India as a case study to examine the role of the SHG as a tool for both individual and collective empowerment. Each country has its own political, cultural and economic context and some contexts are more suited to this approach than others. It will be seen that the Indian context is especially conducive to it. The concluding section of the chapter points the way to a more universal application of the concept.

The history of SHGs in India

The term *sangha* or *sangham* has been used for centuries in India to describe a community or group with a shared vision and common purpose.[3] (While *sangha* is the word commonly used, *sangham* is used in some of the southern states of India, particularly Tamil Nadu.) Even before Independence in 1947 the word was used to describe a

A *sangha* can fight for full inclusion and participation. Photo: Peter Coleridge

group formed to address a particular issue or grievance shared by the group members, such as women mobilising against the practice of *sati* (widow immolation on their husband's pyre). In post-Independence India, self-help efforts by the people have augmented the state welfare system. Every community and village has its own systems for self-help in the economic, social, cultural and political aspects of day-to-day life. *Sanghas* have become the organisational identity of people, particularly those belonging to deprived or marginalised sections of society such as *dalits*, landless labourers, bonded labourers, women and now disabled people. A *sangha* is a class organisation formed to address the structural causes of oppression. For example, *sanghas* for women address gender discrimination and oppression manifested through bigamy, domestic and sexual violence, alcoholism and drug abuse, child marriage, dowry deaths and the pandemic of HIV/AIDS.

The use of groups to mobilise around social issues can be traced back to two main influences, Marxist and Gandhian. Even before Independence, Marxist principles of organising labour unions gained increasing accept- ance, and in the 1960s the Naxalite movement, influenced by Maoist ideology, gained momentum as an Indian expression and interpretation of Marxist ideology to change gross social inequalities. A spill-over effect of this was the emergence of various people's movements on issues of rights and justice. However, the Naxalites believed that radical change was not possible without violence and the movement has now been largely suppressed by the state.

Gandhi's ideas have had a more lasting and significant effect. His principles focused on self-help, local production and the use of non-violent disobedience (*satyagraha*) to bring pressure to bear to change an unjust social order. The best-known example was the Salt March in 1930, when Gandhi led a non-violent march protesting against the British salt tax. The salt tax made it illegal for Indians to sell or produce salt, allowing a complete British monopoly. Since salt is necessary in everyone's daily diet, everyone in India was affected. Gandhi and fellow believers in non-violence (*satyagrahis*) walked for 29 days to the sea, speaking in every village they passed through about what they were doing and gathering an ever-increasing crowd of followers. On reaching the sea Gandhi symbolically made salt, an act of non-violent civil disobedience. This and similar acts were part of the sustained process of making ordinary Indians aware of the power they had in their own hands to change the political order, a process that eventually led to Independence for India in 1947.

The ideas of Paulo Freire, a Brazilian educator who is one of the most significant influences on education and development thinking and practice in the 20th century, have also taken firm root in India since the 1960s. In Latin America, Marxist ideas of liberation from oppression through mass action by the oppressed were given contextual shape in a predominantly Christian subcontinent by liberation theology. Paulo Freire adopted and developed these concepts into a comprehensive and systematic approach. He underlined the importance of conscientisation, which means becoming aware of your own situation, analysing it and working to change it. Conscientisation enables oppressed people to use negative emotions creatively for social action. The analysis of an issue is not restricted to its cause and effect but includes how people feel about their situation, including their feelings of anger, fear, helplessness and anxiety. Combining the facts and emotions in the analysis generates positive energy for social action (Freire, 1970).

Freire also stressed the enormous importance of the collective rather than the individual:

In Freire's view of education, learning to take control and achieving power are not individual objectives, as in a 'boot strap' theory of empowerment. For poor and dispossessed people, strength is in numbers and social change is accomplished in unity. Power is shared, not the power of a few who improve themselves at the expense of others, but the power of the many who find strength and purpose in a common vision. Liberation achieved by individuals at the expense of others is an act of oppression. Personal freedom and the development of individuals can only occur in mutuality with others. In the experience of women's groups, civil rights workers, and many others committed to liberation from oppression, collective power protects the individual far more than authoritarian and hierarchical modes of organisation. (Heaney, 1995)

This philosophy has been used in particular in the development of SHGs of disabled people, and we return to Freire's ideas in more detail below. Freire's ideas were transmitted to India primarily through Jesuits in the 1960s. They recognised the similarity and power of both Gandhi's and Freire's ideas, and began to encourage the formation of community-based organisations like *sanghas* and trade unions. These were based on analysis, reflection and problem solving through struggle and mass action. This approach was especially adopted by the working class in the non-formal sectors of the economy, such as fishermen, domestic labourers and workers in the construction industry. The *sanghas* and trade unions formulated a charter of demands that they addressed to the state.

During the 1970s and 1980s the *sanghas* in India continued their focus on a struggle for rights. In addition, they began to include savings and credit as one of their objectives. This was especially the case among poor women, who sought more control over their meagre finances by collective savings in SHGs. SHGs are often described now as either issue-based or savings- and credit-based. While savings and credit has become the dominant reason for groups to form, many still retain a focus on issues, as we see below.

The profile of SHGs in India

We will first outline the characteristics of SHGs in India before coming to a more detailed look at SHGs for disabled people. An average SHG in India consists of 10–19 members. If the group has been formed for savings and credit, each member is required to pay into a common pot each week or each month the sum decided by the group. From this money loans are made to one or two members based on the consensus of the group. Members use the money for peak expenses such as school fees, as well as unforeseen expenses such as medical bills. The loans are repaid to the group in instalments, with interest as decided by the group, normally 24 per cent per annum or 2 per cent per month.

If this provision had not been available, members would be forced to borrow from local money lenders who charge interest as high as 120–150 per cent or more. This often results in borrowers being caught in a long-term debt trap, forcing them to mortgage vital assets. Since the borrower is invariably a woman it also exposes her to sexual exploitation. Savings through SHGs have therefore been an important mechanism for breaking the power of such money lenders and eliminating this reason for the perpetuation of poverty.

The popularity of such savings groups gathered pace as women realised that their collective savings gave them real bargaining power with banks to obtain loans. Now, under current state provisions SHGs can qualify for government subsidies once they reach a certain level of savings and have fulfilled other criteria.

In Bangladesh, Muhammed Yunus founded the Grameen Bank in the early 1980s to give loans to poor people whom the banks considered were not creditworthy. The Grameen system has now become the dominant mechanism for development in Bangladesh and other countries (Yunus, 1998, 2007). The Indian group savings system is different, however: Indian groups can access bank loans only once they have built up both group and individual savings. Initial loans are given equal to the amount of the savings, which the group then lends to its members. If there is no defaulting the size of loans may be progressively increased up to eight times the amount of savings (Tankha, 2002).

Critics of the Grameen system argue that as its emphasis is purely on loans, with no requirement for prior savings, very poor people may become trapped in a perpetual cycle of debt, needing a second loan to pay off the first and so on indefinitely. The Indian model of using savings as the primary method of raising loans is an inherently more sustainable and empowering approach since the group starts entirely with its own money and seeks loans only when it has enough savings to act as collateral. The risk of running into debt is thereby greatly reduced.

By 2003 over 700,000 groups in India had accessed over Rs20 billion (US$425 million) in top-up loans from banks, benefiting more than 10 million members across the country. Savings in these groups are estimated to be at least Rs8 billion (US$170 million) (Nair, 2005.) By present estimates (2008) there are more than 7 million SHGs in India, composed predominantly of women. These groups generally come together for economic development through savings and credit, but issues and rights in most cases continue to be a major part of their agenda.

With increasing economic power has come increasing political power. Evidence strongly suggests that women's SHGs in India have made it possible for their members to find their own voice. A study of the effectiveness of women's groups in 2003 found that in one quarter of the groups surveyed a woman ran for election at the *panchayat* level[4] and one fifth of the groups under review had a woman elected at this level (EDA, 2003).

One of the key characteristics of structural adjustment imposed by the International Monetary Fund (IMF) in the 1980s was a reduction in the welfare responsibility of the state. The privatisation of services began to substitute for state service sectors, especially in health and education. Self-help and micro-credit for entrepreneurship became the main strategies for development in the government as well as non-governmental sectors. The state changed its role from total responsibility for services, welfare and development to being just one of the players in development. Big players in development, such as the World Bank and the National Bank for Agriculture and Rural Development, began to fund large programmes based on micro-credit through SHGs. However, this has not always been in the best interests of the SHG movement and the original Marxist, Gandhian and Freirean principles have become diluted and eroded. The self-help initiatives of the individual, group and community have been subjected to an institutionalisation process through the formation of what have become universally known as SHGs. SHGs are now the symbol of community organisation but the main objective of those in the large programmes appears to focus on enabling their members to become consumers in the market economy through credit capacity building and increasing purchasing power.

Some recent studies on the impact of women's SHGs have revealed a gap between the claims for women's empowerment and poverty alleviation and the ground-level realities. For example, a study in 2007 by Nirantar, a centre for gender and education, found that although they may provide women with access to money, SHGs do not ensure their entitlement to the use of the resources or assets that the money provides. In other words, women still face problems in controlling family money and the assets that they have generated. Furthermore, the primary burden of repayment falls on women, adding to their already stressful lives. The study maintains that it is education, not finance, that empowers women, and a reliance on self-help savings groups as the main tool for women's empowerment does not deliver this. Instead this reliance relieves the government of its responsibility for providing proper education for girls and women (Agrawal, 2007).

These are serious criticisms, but we must not throw the baby out with the bathwater in a discussion of the SHG movement in India, and to dismiss the concept as flawed when the real problem is that it has been misunderstood and misused. By 2003 non-governmental organisation (NGO) programmes accounted for only a third of these groups in the country. Two thirds were initiated by the World Bank, government and other big players (EDA Rural Systems Pvt Ltd, 2003). The weaknesses reported almost certainly derive from a wholesale approach to group formation by the large agencies, which fails to understand the importance of the detailed work required by committed field workers to support group formation on a group-by-group and village-by-village basis. We explain what this detailed work entails below in relation to the formation of SHGs of disabled people.

The development of SHGs of disabled people in India

The criticisms of women's SHGs expressed above are comparatively recent. In the mid-1980s it was the successful example of the women's sanghas that inspired the use of the SHG approach in India for disabled people.[5] Three NGOs working in rural development in Andhra Pradesh and Tamil Nadu (the Young India Project, the Rural Development Trust and PREPARE) agreed to form and animate groups for disabled people in villages under the inspiration and training provided by Action on Disability and Development, India (ADD), led at that time by Balakrishna Venkatesh. At first the idea was neither understood nor accepted by disabled people themselves; they were accustomed to the charity and total dependency model that has been traditionally built into conditions of impairment, handicap and disability. The idea that they should take charge of their own development did not fit any of their previous experiences. But ADD India persisted in its efforts and the next 10 years witnessed a proliferation of SHGs for disabled people in South India. The SHG has now, in 2008, become the dominant strategy used by community-based rehabilitation (CBR[6]) programmes throughout India.

Initially these groups were issue-based and neither handled savings nor operated loans. Their primary concern was to obtain the benefits to which disabled people are entitled under the law from the state: medical certificates, bus passes, help with buying aids and appliances, income supplements (pensions) and scholarships for education. While these benefits are statutory entitlements, most of the disabled individuals and their families were not aware of them. The few who were aware and attempted to access them met with apathy, insensitivity and corruption in the government system. Meeting and negotiating with government officials needs courage and self-confidence, which an individual disabled person often did not have. SHGs provided both. The identity of an SHG as a community-based organisation provided the minimal degree of power that was imperative for meeting and negotiating with officials. While one individual with a disability was easily dismissed or ignored, a group could not be.

Experience has shown that these groups have revolutionised the way disabled people think about themselves, and also the way they are regarded in their communities. Forming a group makes them more visible in the community, showing that they are as capable as anybody else of managing their own affairs. They come together for the purpose of solving their common problems through mutual help and collective actions. Members can support one another by sharing information on the availability of services and resources. They reach a better understanding of disability, discrimination and human rights. They provide a means for disabled people to be part of the community decision-making process. Most of all, membership of a group gives a disabled person the experience of being a contributor rather than a passive receiver, which is the first essential step to personal empowerment.

Case Study 5.1, from a CBR project supported by Leonard Cheshire Disability in India, illustrates these points.

Case Study 5.1: SHG, Uppugundur Village, Prakasam, Andhra Pradesh, India

The group started in 2006 and has 14 members. It is composed of ten people with mobility impairments (almost all from polio), one with a visual impairment, one with mental illness, one with speech and hearing difficulties and one with an intellectual impairment (represented by her mother). They were given three days of training to start. This training covered how to develop an action plan, how to maintain records and how to keep the group animated.

There are 89 disabled people in the village (population 12,000, therefore 0.74 per cent), but this is the only SHG of disabled people. The members consider that 14 is the ideal number for a group: it is difficult to build a real consensus with a larger number and a smaller number is non-representative and precarious. So they are not planning to increase its size. Instead, they encourage disabled people who are not in a group to form another group.

The purpose of the group is to sort out their own problems by their own efforts. They say: 'We have demonstrated by our own experience that a group is stronger than an individual'.

They meet once a month. Besides the usual attention to medical certificates, bus passes and pensions, their activities also include identifying disabled people in the village, mainstreaming disabled children in schools, keeping group records, arranging opportunities for skills training, helping members with job applications, putting on film shows to inform and raise awareness about disability, sensitising other disabled people to form groups, arranging basic literacy training, forming links with the Association for Rural Poverty, organising training for writing requisitions to the local government and discussing the formation of a village organisation.

The members also participate in women's groups and arrange extra activities for disabled children. They have addressed not only the problems of disabled people but also general village problems, such as water supplies, electricity, housing, old age pensions, widows' pensions and road access. They each put in Rs30 per month to the group's savings account. They have not so far applied for any bank loans.

Since starting in December 2006, three of their members have obtained bus passes, three have obtained pensions, three were assessed for corrective surgery, one took a six-month computer training course, four disabled children were enrolled in mainstream schools and special educational material was provided to three disabled children. They have shown four films to raise awareness about disability issues and have also put on street theatre performances for the same purpose. In addition they have succeeded in getting more drinking water taps fitted in the village. They intend to put candidates up for election to the *panchayat.*

When asked what they valued most about being in the group the members mentioned personal gains such as pensions, bus passes, skills training, house improvement loans, how to save and how to manage their finances better. They also mentioned increased self-confidence, self-esteem and a significant change in the way they were regarded in the village. They showed a good level of knowledge about the legislation applicable to disabled people and were adamant that disability should be seen as a rights issue, not charity.

As a participant in a discussion about the Uppugundur Village programme put it:

Groups bring a change of concern about others. Self-help groups give their members the opportunity to learn, be aware and be exposed to wider realities of life and society. They discover that one person cannot raise his voice for everybody. Only a group can do this.

Over the two decades that SHGs of disabled people have been developing in India they have evolved in three significant ways. First, they have advanced from focusing on the personal needs of individuals to the collective needs of disabled people in the larger context of community and village. Second, they have moved into savings and credit, based on credit capacity building as a strategy for the economic self-reliance of the individual, family and group, replicating the successful model of women's groups. Finally, they have formed federations, which means that their voice is now raised above the village level to the district and sometimes the state level.

We discuss the last of these important developments, the formation of federations, in more detail below, but first we need to consider in more detail the process of group formation and, in particular, how the ideas of Paulo Freire have been applied in the context of forming SHGs of disabled people in India.

The application of Freire's ideas

Freire identified three levels of awareness that constitute barriers for poor people wishing to empower and liberate themselves. These are: magical, naive and fanatical thinking. In addition he identified a fourth level, that of critical awareness, which is the key to empowerment.

The magical level of awareness is characterised by fatalism, apathy, uncritical belief and a state of mind that cannot imagine an order of society different from what exists, which is ordained by God. When disabled people come together to form an SHG they are almost always apathetic. They may, for example, feel that it is quite legitimate for communities to call them by their disability and not by their name. The absence of a number of key factors in their upbringing and life experience can leave them psychologically stunted. These include, for example, a lack of stimulation in early childhood, companionship among peer groups, opportunities for play, education and childhood occupations such as looking after younger siblings. They may feel that they cannot do anything for themselves. They may believe that their disability is the consequence of 'sin' in either themselves or their parents. This is a form of deep conditioning resulting from their environment and the attitudes that surround them. It is often the case that family members of disabled people cannot imagine how disabled children can learn, move about, work and so on. This state of mind corresponds closely to what Freire calls the magical level of awareness.

The naive level of awareness is characterised by aping, copying structures or behaving without understanding their implications or consequences. For example, the oppressed person becomes the oppressor or an abused child becomes an abusive adult. A more common example is when individuals from a poor family go to the city for higher education, deny their roots in an attempt to climb up the social ladder and cut off contact with their home and family.

How does this apply to disabled people? As we have shown, disability SHGs are set up and operate like non-disabled groups, with an economic agenda including savings, loans and the pursuit of livelihoods. But if they leave it there, as many non-disabled groups do, they are still stuck in a naive level of awareness. While livelihood is very important in the context of poverty, equally important are the issues of discrimination, rehabilitation, education, early childhood stimulation, play and childhood activities. The double discrimination faced by women with disabilities and people affected by leprosy, against whom there is a particularly strong stigma, is often not on the agenda of disability groups at all. They need to see the full implications of stigma and discrimination in all their dimensions.

The third level is that of fanatical awareness. Here there is a sense of reverse exclusion; disabled people live in a world of their own, believing that only they can address their problems, and non-disabled people are seen as being outside their sphere of interest, perhaps even as the enemy. The attitude (evident at the extreme end of the disability movement) that non-disabled people have no right to involve themselves in disability issues will be familiar to many who work in this field. This kind of attitude is counter-productive because it misunderstands the purpose of the task or how empowerment can be achieved. Empowerment is not about exclusion and erecting barriers of any kind but about embracing differences. It is also about building alliances, in this case between disabled and non-disabled people.

If one form of exclusion (or oppression) is replaced with another, there is no empowerment, no fundamental transformation of society. In Freire's view an equal and just society is characterised by dialogue, debate, openness and accepting differences of opinion. An oppressive society is characterised by hierarchical, authoritarian, and alienating systems and organisations.

These three levels of awareness need to be recognised and dealt with on the road to the fourth level, which is critical awareness.

> This stage is characterised by depth in the interpretation of problems, by testing one's own findings, and being open to revision and reconstruction, by the attempt to avoid distortion when perceiving problems and to avoid preconceived notions when analysing them, by rejecting passivity, by the practice of dialogue rather than polemics, by receptivity to the new without rejecting the old, and by permeable, interrogative, restless, and dialogical forms of interaction (Heaney, 1995).

There is a tendency among both disabled and non-disabled people to remain stuck at the level of the impairment, to see disability in terms of different limitations imposed by different impairments and to think that the problem to be fixed is the impairment itself. A deeper level of awareness is to see being disabled as the target of another form of discrimination, in the same way that being a woman or an ethnic minority or a minority religious group are used as reasons for discrimination. But this level of awareness is not, in Freire's philosophy, attained by becoming bitter or angry but by 'permeable, interrogative, restless, and dialogical forms of interaction'. In other words, there is a powerful need for this kind of interaction between disabled people themselves and between disabled and non-disabled people.

We have emphasised the influence of Paulo Freire on the formation of disability groups and the training of disabled people because we believe that his ideas hold the key to healthy social and political development. The next section examines the political development of disabled people in India that has resulted from group formation. We see that Freire's concepts run right through this process.

Political empowerment through federations

The political voice of disabled people has been greatly strengthened by the formation of federations of SHGs. In the 1970s Father Cutinha, a Jesuit priest in charge of a school for blind children near Bangalore, joined others in trying to get legislation changed to allow grants in aid for special schools on the same level as mainstream schools. It meant adding just one sentence to the legislation but, despite intensive lobbying with legislators, they met with indifference. In 1992 Father Cutinha said:

> We went to every leader of every party and explained to them the position. We said, 'This is a common factor; disability has no party'. We worked for six months like this. We must have approached 200 politicians of different parties. It was just a matter of adding one sentence to the code. We waited with great apprehension for the crowning of our work. But when it came to the crucial moment, not a single person in the legislative assembly raised the matter. It was just not mentioned. No one, just no one mentioned it.
>
> I had a good friend among the Communist party members, a very progressive man. He called me and asked, 'You are disappointed?' I said, 'Of course, bitterly disappointed'. He said, 'Tell me: how many votes can you give me?' I replied, 'Well, four or five perhaps'. He said. 'You must learn this lesson: unless disability becomes a movement on its own, it will not survive as an issue. It must become part of the civil rights movement.' (Coleridge, 1993, p.158)

In 1992 disabled people had no real political voice in India. However, as SHGs of disabled people have proliferated across India, federations have been formed that combine a number of groups at and sometimes above the *mandal*[7] level. This has had a very powerful effect on their political profile. It has shown that they are organised, it has given them the courage and strength in numbers to challenge social and political issues in disability and beyond and, most significantly, politicians are increasingly taking disabled people into account because they realise that they constitute an organised constituency with the potential to deliver votes. In addition, the experience in forming federations has given disabled people the courage to stand for election to local government at the *panchayat* level and above.

Case Study 5.2 gives an example of these kinds of achievements through a federation that represents SHGs of disabled people in a CBR programme run by the NGO SACRED in Andhra Pradesh.

Case Study 5.2: Federation of Disability Groups, Anantapur District, Andhra Pradesh, India

The federation emerged from the periodic review meetings of disability SHGs of disabled people in a few *mandals* of the district. The reviews led to the finding that the problems related to disabled people are common in form and profile and hence the causes of and solutions to the problems are also logically common. The two major problems faced by the SHG members were the neglect and absence of home care for disabled children and adults and problems in access to education for disabled children.

This led to the SHGs forming a federation. The federation now has representatives from 20 SHGs and an executive body of 11 members. It meets once every three months. In 2007 they discussed in particular issues of education and mental health. Thirty children with hearing impairments have been integrated into mainstream schools as a result of their efforts. They petitioned successfully for the appointment of a psychiatrist and an ear, nose and throat specialist in the District Headquarters Hospital in Anantapur. These specialists are required to authorise the medical certification of disability, which is essential to access statutory entitlements.[8]

In 2007 the federation dealt with a legal case involving desertion of a disabled woman. The federation hired a lawyer to represent her in court. Justice was established when the court ordered her husband to pay maintenance for the children and awarded a share in the property owned by the man to the woman and her children.

A significant achievement of the federation relates to influencing a World Bank programme. As a result of pressure from the federation the World Bank has included disability as a statutory intervention

---

of the women's empowerment programme, implemented in the state of Andhra Pradesh. This project involves encouraging women to form SHGs around economic and livelihood issues. The criteria for entitlement for loans from this project is that the members save regularly, maintain records and lend money to members in need.

This project includes the empowerment of disabled people in selected *mandals* in Andhra Pradesh. Loans are given to SHGs of disabled people through the women's federation at the *mandal* level. Each village has a women's group called a village organisation (VO). The federation of women is made up of representatives from village SHGs of women. In order to get loans from the project, SHGs of disabled people need to become members of the VO. This strategy has meant that VOs and *mandal* women's federations involve themselves in supporting the activities of the SHGs and federation of disabled people. For example, they help SHGs of disabled people to increase their bookkeeping and facilitation skills, motivate individual households to continue with home-based rehabilitation interventions for disabled children and take up disabled women's issues, such as domestic violence.

The federation of disability groups also plays a relevant role in conflict resolution. This takes place both within a group and between one group and another, or even in situations involving a number of groups.

The risks of political empowerment

There is no doubt that the formation of disability SHGs and federations of groups has had a dramatic impact on the profile of disabled people in their communities, especially politically. However, their increasing political empowerment is double edged: it has real and present dangers as well as the considerable gains outlined above. Organised constituencies of any specific group are open to political manipulation. Because they now see disabled people as an organised constituency, politicians invent slogans and make promises without understanding the values that led to the formation of these groups in the first place. As we have seen, these values are based on self-help, self-advocacy, self-sufficiency and collective problem solving. However politicians are now making promises, such as a regular subsidy of Rs1000 a month for each registered SHG of disabled people. In the opinion of D.M. Naidu, director of the Bangalore-based NGO Basic Needs, India, 'Such subsidies will muddy the original purpose of setting up these groups and their ways and means of achieving their vision, mission and stated objectives' (Naidu, personal communication, Bangalore, 9 February 2008).

Size, rate of growth and resources are critical factors in determining the healthy existence of a group, and whether it survives beyond the programme that initiated it. Too much financial support too soon, and a lack of capacity to handle it, often mean that disability groups have a short lifespan. As we have seen, the institutionalised adoption of women's groups by the World Bank and other large players has had a mixed effect on their authenticity: they are in danger of becoming hostage to major sources of finance. It takes time for a group to mature and build capacity; if they are set up quickly with minimal follow-up they will also die quickly.

The concern of D.M. Naidu and others is that disability groups face a similar danger: they could become victims of their own success. Once substantial sums of money with political and other non-local agendas are involved, the group loses its independence and value base. How to keep a successful grass-root initiative authentic, alive, spontaneous and fresh in the face of such threats remains one of the great challenges of development everywhere. As Naidu says, 'The strength of a group is to say NO to a subsidy and other propositions, however tempting, if they are not in line with the ideology and values of the group'.

India, like many other developing countries, has adopted economic liberalisation. The resulting structural change is turning its people into consumers in a market economy by enhancing their motivation and power to buy. The wholesale approach to group formation with major funds attached is based on a materialist view of development. It does not understand or emphasise human processes, but aims at a product, a bottom line that can be measured in financial and numerical terms.

Development is a process of awakening in the individual and community. It is not a mechanical process of filling targets and ticking boxes. Global organisations like the World Bank set targets for the formation of thousands of groups at the level of a country and region. This may dilute or destroy the awakening process of the individual group. Authentic development is a balanced combination of material and human development. While money is necessary to meet the needs and wants of the individual and family, it is also necessary that the process of development should enable the individual to reach beyond the material level to enduring human values of cooperation and mutual support, and contribution to a caring, learning society. It is to this process of group formation and the nurturing of human values that we now turn.

The formation and development of SHGs

We need to emphasise that this chapter records and discusses the experience of SHGs of disabled people in India.[9] While many of the lessons learnt in India may be applicable elsewhere, each country has its own particular historical, political, cultural, social, economic and religious context that will influence the way SHGs form and operate there – and, indeed, whether they can operate at all. We are aware, for example, that the history, culture and politics of many countries in Africa make SHG formation very different from the Indian experience. We return to the point of how far lessons learnt in India can be applied elsewhere in the conclusions at the end of the chapter.

Self-help is as old as the idea of community itself. Through the centuries SHGs have come into being spontaneously, with no external instigation or facilitation. This continues to happen today in India (and elsewhere), despite the large number of NGOs that make group formation an important part of their programmes. Experience in India, however, shows that the formation of SHGs of disabled people is much enhanced by skilled and well-informed facilitation. But facilitating does not mean organising. The role of the facilitator is to enable the awakening process in the catalytic core of the group, which can spread to all the members and stakeholders who are to constitute the group. Facilitation requires patience, tact and a professional strategy in choosing the appropriate approach and methodology for the promotion of the group. Group situations differ from one to another. The composition of a group is organic and hence no two groups are similar; a group reflects the character of the individuals who constitute it. An effective facilitator is one who 'walks with the group with appropriate hand holding' (Venkatesh, see note 8). This is one of the reasons why wholesale, formulaic and top-down approaches do not work. They do not pay proper respect to the sense of identity, ownership and accountability that the group needs in order to grow organically. The basic qualification of facilitators is sensitivity to the group that they facilitate.

A professional and skilled facilitator begins with enabling the stakeholders of the group to internalise the purpose and scope of a group. This involves the members in developing, over a period of time, a vision for the group. The vision is the engine that drives any group or organisation. The process of developing a vision begins with informal interaction between the facilitator and members. The objective of these interactions is to make them feel comfortable. In the case of disabled people this may take more time and may need a planned strategy to achieve it. The idea of this informal interaction is to break the ice and enable members to develop a feeling of togetherness and trust in one other. At this stage the facilitator does not introduce any agenda other than getting every member in the group to feel comfortable and happy. Over a series of meetings they will begin to define their vision, purpose and goals.

This is followed by enabling the group to develop a mission for itself. A mission is what the group would like to achieve over a given horizon, such as a three-year period. The mission needs to be made concrete and achievable by the group setting objectives, which need to be specific, measurable, achievable, relevant and time-bound.

The facilitator next enables the group to develop a strategic plan to implement its objectives. A strategic plan details what the group wishes to achieve in a systematic way. The format for a strategic plan is to ask and answer the following eight questions: what, why, how, where, who, when, how much and how will we know we have achieved it?

SHGs of non-disabled people are often homogenous in the sense that the members come from similar backgrounds and have the same economic status. SHGs of disabled people, on the other hand, often come from diverse economic and disability backgrounds. For example, in almost every disability SHG in South India we find two or three people who come from households who are in trading, providing services or with small land holdings. These people, usually with mobility or visual impairments or non-disabled parents representing disabled children, have often been able to afford secondary education and therefore start with a major advantage in skills and leadership potential. This has both advantages and disadvantages. On the one hand, it means that such people inspire other members and become role models. They can be a useful resource to the group in providing not just leadership but also help with the enhancement of the literacy, motivation, unity and inclusion in the group. They may have particular skills, such as bookkeeping, which are very useful for the group. On the other hand it means there is a built-in inequality in the group from the start and this must be handled with sensitivity. In addition, members will have different types of impairment, which will affect how they interact with other members. For example, those with communication impairments will need particular understanding.

Three of the criteria for measuring the effectiveness of SHGs for disabled people in South India are: first, if disabled women are found in leadership positions; second, if people with severe disabilities have been effectively included; and third, if priority is given to the poorest of the poor in the group for appropriate assistance, financial or otherwise.

– It is likely that those who are brought together by the facilitator may not be used to the concept of working in a group. They may not be familiar with collective decision making and consensus and

Including disabled women in self-help groups is particularly important
Photo: Sunanda Mavillapalli/Leonard Cheshire Disability

they may feel uneasy listening to others. The few with a higher level of personal initiative will want what they say to be accepted by everybody; others may not have the confidence to speak at all. A lot of personal anxieties and agendas will be evident in the discussions. There may also be the issue of compatibility: among those present, some will support selected individuals and oppose others.

– The role of facilitators in the early stages is crucial. They should be able to exercise the right balance of control over the group and nurture the generative process by enabling members to express their opinions and mould them into a consensus. Differences in opinion should be acknowledged and the facilitator should be able to distinguish between divergence of opinions and a conflict. In the case of conflicts, the facilitator should be able to initiate conflict resolution as a group process. A well-facilitated conflict resolution in a group has high educational value.

- Professional facilitators divide their inputs to the group into hardware and software components. The hardware components include bookkeeping, maintenance of registers, data, documentation, concept formulation, policies and systems development. The software components include clarifying values, setting norms, developing a group culture and interpersonal relationships in the group.

A group that is facilitated successfully through the early stages grows in confidence and group solidarity, and it develops the strength to function without dependency on a facilitator. Ultimately, the group should be independent of the NGO that initiated it. As illustrated in Case Study 5.1, the ideal size of a group is 10–15 members. Groups larger than that require different and complex mechanisms for interaction, transaction of business, consensus and decision making. Groups with fewer than ten members may find it harder to establish a group identity. They lack the weight of numbers required to represent the members as a group, which is especially important with official bodies such as government departments, banks and the other institutions with which they wish to negotiate.

The facilitator should enable the group to take its own decisions. Decisions about the criteria for membership, schedules and agendas for meetings and the formulation of action plans should be taken by the group. As part of concept and policy, the group should be helped to decide its proportion of economic development (that is, savings and loan activities) versus issues. The facilitator should not rush the decisions of the group. It should have the necessary time and space to identify and analyse the different propositions and take decisions based on consensus.

In the early stages, action plans and their implementation will be on a trial and error basis. This is a healthy learning process and should be encouraged with appropriate guidance by the facilitator. It may be appropriate to start with straightforward cases of obtaining medical certificates, bus passes, pensions and the like. Success in obtaining such basic entitlements for individual members will give them the experience and courage to tackle other, bigger issues.

The needs of disabled people are various, but they fall within the broad spectrum of basic human needs – food, shelter, clothing, health, livelihood, education and relationships. The causes that hinder disabled people from accessing the existing opportunities in the family and community to meet these needs are rooted in attitudes, institutionalised concepts of charity, the environment or simply poverty. Skilful facilitation can often help members identify the common causes of their exclusion. When members share the problem that they are most afraid of or worried, angry or ashamed about, they begin to recognise that they have similar emotions. The sharing of individual experiences of exclusion and discrimination in this way is empowering because it takes the issue beyond the individual and makes it a group concern. Shared emotions give life to the group and become a source of motivation.

They will also have to consider the advantages and disadvantages of cross- and single-disability groups. There are arguments for both and they are not mutually exclusive. Blind people, for example, may belong to a blind union as well as their local disability SHG. Deaf people, in particular, may prefer to form their own groups but in a rural community their numbers may be too small or the distances between them too great to make this practical. Membership of different groups, both cross-disability and single-disability, is to be encouraged.[10]

What makes a group effective?

The over-riding principle for effectiveness is that the group has a strong sense of its own unity and identity and that its members truly own the decisions they make in the group. This includes setting its own standards and criteria for success. However, there are certain characteristics that can be considered essential if the group is to be regarded as effective. These include the following.

– *Setting clear goals* that are known, internalised and agreed by all members of the group. This can be achieved if all members genuinely play a part in formulating the goals and when the goal is realistic and based on the needs of the members.

- *Attaining consistent and stable membership* with regular attendance. This indicates unity and strength of purpose and a valuing of each individual member. The only reason for rejection should be the deliberate misuse of funds or some other major moral transgression detrimental to the values and principles of the group.

- *Addressing its own issues as a group.* As has been noted, individual needs will be seen to be common to the group, and the problems related to disability must be seen as part of a wider picture of poverty, but unless individual needs are met the group will not see itself as effective.

- *Communicating both ideas and feelings.* Members must feel able to express their feelings such as anger, frustration and anxiety, and not feel judged for doing so. This strengthens relationships and trust among the members of the group.

- *Achieving the active participation of all.* One of the most difficult things to achieve in any group, but especially in a group of disabled people (some of whom may have communication impairments), is to ensure that each member participates fully in discussions and decisions. The tendency of those with the best communication skills to dominate proceedings needs to be countered, but this requires patience and time to build up the confidence of the less confident. If people feel that they are listened to they will gain in confidence. The core value is that each member is important and has a contribution to make. Without this value the group will not develop a unity of spirit and purpose and it will be neither sustainable nor effective in the long run.

- *Distributing and sharing responsibilities.* The value of each member should be recognised by ensuring that clear roles and responsibilities are evenly distributed and rotated.

- *Managing conflicts constructively.* Conflicts will arise, and how they are dealt with will have a major impact on the effectiveness of the group. Conflicts need to be addressed through conflict resolution mechanisms involving the whole group.

– *Agreeing procedures and keeping to them.* It is important to have proper procedures without becoming hidebound or bureaucratic. Accurate records of meetings will help the decision-making process, regular elections are essential for keeping everybody involved, transparent bookkeeping is vital to keep the group's trust over finance. Transparency and financial accountability are vital for the credibility of the group, both to its members and to outside bodies.

– *Leadership.* In the absence of visible potential in members, quite often a few disabled people hold leadership positions for many years and sometimes for life. Progressive groups are aware of this and have deliberate practices of changing leaders periodically, for example once a year. This may mean that the group has ineffective leaders for a period, but groups can learn from such experiences and will be the stronger for it.

Connecting disability with wider development issues

It is important for SHGs of disabled people to see disability in the wider context of poverty, as one of the manifestations of poverty and deprivation. Addressing disability therefore involves addressing issues related to poverty and development. Interventions in the field of disability should join forces with other interventions on poverty and deprivation.

Disability groups need to become knowledgeable about all the issues they wish to address, starting with entitlements under the law and disability legislation and moving on to poverty alleviation programmes and statutory provisions for the poor, environmental issues and the issues that affect other deprived groups.

The group needs to focus on the analysis of situations they intend to change. The primary purpose is to help the group understand the cause and effect of a situation and how it is interlinked with other factors. For example, disabled children do not go to school because their parents cannot afford to pay for their uniforms or books. They cannot pay because they earn barely enough to survive. Wage opportunities are very limited because they do not have adequate skills. Thus the cycle of poverty is perpetuated. SHGs have a role in breaking this cycle by appropriate interventions, for example, by enabling access to primary education as a strategy and finding ways to increase the income of parents so that they can afford to send their children to school.

Practically this means that disability groups need to establish an effective system of public relations with government departments, duty bearers in local areas, service institutions such as banks, resource centres, media and other institutions in their operational areas. If discussions on poverty-related issues are already under way in the community they need to engage actively in these discussions. If they are not already under way, disabled groups need to initiate them.

It is likewise important for disability groups to develop alliances with people's movements in their area by joining in with campaigns and advocacy. For example, one significant linkage that disabled groups and their federations in India have built is with the Campaign Against Child Labour and the Campaign Against Violence on Women and Children.

Can and should disabled people be integrated into other SHGs?

An argument often put forward by non-disabled people working in development is that if we are aiming at integration, why form separate groups of disabled people? Why not integrate disabled people in so-called mainstream groups? This question does not have a simple answer and we need to consider different aspects of it.

As we have seen, women's empowerment has made huge strides in India through the formation of women's SHGs. Women argue that this would not have happened if these groups had been mixed, because men would have dominated them. Women need their own space in order to find their own voice. The same argument applies to disabled people.

We have already stressed the importance of linking disability with wider development issues and integration of disabled people in mainstream groups is to be encouraged. Some NGOs make this a programme aim. For example, Chetanalaya, an NGO working in the informal housing areas of Delhi on the economic and social empowerment of women, makes it a rule that six per cent of the members of the women's savings and credit groups formed in the programme should be people with disablities. However, there are a number of factors that need to be considered in this discussion.

First, it is important to distinguish between issue-based groups and savings and credit groups. Disability groups started in the 1980s as issue-based groups and it is still disability issues that propel them into being. Although they need to link to wider development issues they need to address their own issues first. These are unlikely to be addressed in a mainstream group where disabled people constitute a small minority.

Second, for a mainstream programme to say that its groups are open to disabled people does not mean that disabled people will join them. Group membership cannot be controlled by the NGO (despite the example of Chetanalaya above), and it is up to the members whom they accept. Generally speaking, programmes that say they are open to disabled people have great difficulty demonstrating that disabled people are actually included. The Grameen Bank in Bangladesh, for example, says disabled people are welcome in its programmes but it makes no special provision for them. It is also unable to say how many disabled people actually benefit from its programmes. Anecdotal evidence suggests that disabled people are generally excluded from Grameen groups.

Third, most savings and credit groups in India and often elsewhere are composed of women, which poses a real problem if disabled men wish to join. Finally, disabled people, especially those with communication impairments, may be reluctant to join mainstream groups if they have already had experiences of rejection. However, there is no reason why disabled people should not be members of several groups, including a disability group and mainstream groups. This is often the case, especially with women.

Some words of caution

This chapter has made strong claims for SHGs of disabled people in India. There are, however, a number of caveats that must be expressed about SHGs as the dominant strategy for CBR programmes; caveats that are generally acknowledged by NGOs in India themselves.

First, there is the question of who owns the groups. Is it the NGO or are they independent? This is of particular importance when it comes to collective economic enterprises. Some NGOs admit that although their intention is to foster groups that will be independent of the parent NGO, in reality this is difficult to achieve. There is the added problem that NGOs normally have to report numbers to donors, and they therefore count the groups they have set up as their groups. Genuinely independent groups are rare.

Second, as we have seen, SHGs are open to manipulation, either by external political forces, by members themselves or by the NGO through the facilitator. Awareness of the possibility of manipulation is the first step towards preventing it.

Third, using SHGs as a CBR strategy to lobby for the provision of rights under the law works only if rehabilitation services, in particular, are actually available. In practice, especially in remote areas, they may not be available, or there may be impossible travel costs and logistical problems for access. (This is even more likely in countries that do not provide benefits to disabled people, which includes most countries in Africa.)

Fourth, there may be a tendency for people with communication difficulties to be excluded from SHGs of disabled people. This especially applies to people with learning difficulties or such impairments as cerebral palsy. Related to this is the fact that SHGs tend to concentrate on adult membership and so the needs of children may be neglected. Finally, some professional therapists in India consider that the social model of CBR in the country has gone too far and has neglected the medical aspects of rehabilitation. In this view, making SHGs the main medium for CBR means that knowledge about the technicalities of rehabilitation is poor, with the result that important preventive work, early detection and, especially, attention to complex impairments like cerebral palsy are missing or inadequate.

Conclusions

CBR is sometimes criticised for being a western response to the problem of how to work with disabled people in developing countries. Mike Miles, for example, points out that many European and North American development workers do not know much about the cultures of the countries in which they are working, and try to impose methods and strategies that are inappropriate in those cultures, especially in approaches to disabled people. In particular, he criticises the global application of rights-based development on the grounds that rights is a western concept with limited applicability in poor countries that do not have the resources to provide for the rights of disabled people. He refers to CBR as a kind of cargo cult designed in the west and imported as a package to developing countries, whether it is suitable or not (Miles, 2003).

An important reason for choosing India as a case study for examining community approaches to livelihood development is to counter this kind of argument. While Miles undoubtedly has a point in some situations, especially Africa, the example of India illustrates a genuinely home-grown development movement. Despite the negative example of the World Bank given above, which through its massive programmes has tended to distort and dilute the essential values of human-scale development, India has, on the whole, been more successful than other low-income countries in fending off western approaches to development and has formed its own particular style of addressing social development issues. The hallmark of this approach is self-help and self-advocacy. The historical, cultural, political, economic and social circumstances of India make it very fertile ground for the development of SHGs. There are two factors in particular that have favoured the blossoming of such a vigorous grass-roots movement.

First, India is a democracy: not only does it have elections that are generally rated as free and fair, but it allows people from all sections of society to mobilise, to express their views and to work to address their grievances with a real prospect of making a difference. India is riven with social inequalities through its caste system and in other ways, but deprived groups have the freedom to express their grievances without fear of further oppression for the simple act of speaking out. Such freedom does not exist in many developing countries, especially in the Middle East and Africa.

Second, the main inspirations for the present SHG movement were Gandhi and Paulo Freire, from India and Brazil respectively. Gandhi demonstrated the power of ordinary people to change the social and political order. The influence of Paulo Freire is an illustration of how important cross-fertilisation is between countries with similar problems and levels of poverty. Indian development workers picked up on Freire's ideas because of their obvious applicability in the Indian context (there is a similar success story to be told about the mobilisation of peasant farmers and other workers in Brazil).

In the case of disabled people, two further factors in India have combined to encourage the growth of the disability movement through SHGs.

The first is that there are a range of benefits under the law, such as bus passes, assistance with aids and appliances and scholarships, which means that forming groups to lobby for and obtain these benefits gives visible, concrete and immediate results. The groups feel that they can achieve something tangible for their members and this is very motivational. In countries where these benefits do not exist group formation faces different challenges.

The second is that the profile of disability in India is itself helpful: these *sanghas* are dominated by people with mobility impairments, mainly as a result of polio, who have the ability to communicate well. In countries where polio has long been eliminated (such as Malaysia or Jordan), the profile of disability is very different: people with communication impairments (learning difficulties and communication problems, including cerebral palsy) tend to be in the majority. Forming SHGs in such countries will pose different challenges to those in India.

We seriously question the globalisation of development, the unquestioning standardisation of approaches to all countries and cultures, the uncritical assumptions behind the universal quest for a magic pill to eliminate poverty and the top-down, wholesale approaches espoused by large agencies such as the World Bank, which do not understand the detailed and patient work needed for authentic human development. If there is one thing that India teaches us it is the power that is unleashed when a country develops its own approach and grows its own methods, deeply rooted in its own history and culture.

However, having said all this, the Indian experience demonstrates principles that are applicable everywhere. This conclusion summarises some of these principles, divided into those relating to the formation of SHGs, and those relating to the general philosophy of SHGs.

In the formation of SHGs it is essential for an external facilitator to have a clear and deep understanding of the entire context in which the group is being formed. Besides the historical, political, social and cultural factors, this will include an understanding of the organisational structure behind the facilitation – who the facilitator reports to, whether the structure is donor driven, driven by political ideology or driven purely by the needs of people and their aspiration for social change.

It is seldom possible to achieve complete consensus in an SHG. Holding the tension arising out of differences among group members is crucial for its development; it gives room for reflection and analysis. Agreeing to disagree and to continue to work together in this framework is also a form of consensus – a sign of the level of maturity of any SHG. Respect for difference in the group mirrors the need for respect for difference in society at large, where disabled people are accepted for what they are and not rejected for what they are not. Groups need to demonstrate this value within the group itself.

The philosophy of self-help through group formation underlines more than anything else that livelihood is not simply a matter of earning an income; it is the way we live our lives in relation to our context, which includes how we sustain ourselves and how we contribute to our communities and society. If we restrict livelihood simply to individual income generation we miss out the larger and more important matter of how we foster the creation of cohesive communities, the values of mutual cooperation and, ultimately, a just society.

In *Creating a World without Poverty* the founder of the Grameen Bank and Nobel Prize winner Muhammed Yunus states:

> Capitalism takes a narrow view of human nature, assuming that people are one-dimensional beings concerned only with the pursuit of maximum profit. The concept of the free market, as generally understood, is based on this one-dimensional human being .... But mainstream free-market theory suffers from a 'conceptualisation failure', a failure to capture the essence of what it is to be human. [This view], to quote Oscar Wilde, knows the price of everything and the value of nothing. (Yunus, 2007)

The development of SHGs in India illustrates this idea perfectly. Poverty is far more than material deprivation and the route out of poverty is far more than the ability to earn an income. SHGs of disabled people, joining the growing groundswell of popular mobilisation in India, have demonstrated that it is possible to break out of the limitations imposed by society on disabled people through discrimination, neglect and overprotection.

The creation of just societies requires people at all levels who have progressed through Freire's levels of consciousness, from a fatalistic attitude that we cannot change anything to an awareness that by patient dialogue, openness to new ideas and respect of differences, we can progress to communities and societies that are truly human. Critical awareness 'proclaims the future as ours to determine and seeks the liberation of the human will to do so through learning and social action' (Freire, 1970, quoted in Heaney, 1995). Disabled people's groups provide an excellent laboratory for testing and developing such an approach.

Notes

1. In a recent study the World Health Organization (WHO) calculated the social determinants of health and revealed that social factors, especially poverty – rather than genetics – are to blame for huge variations in ill health and life expectancy around the world (WHO, 2008).

2. *Dalit* is the word now used for those at the bottom of the caste structure in India. The word refers to those who are outside and below the other castes, who in the past were called untouchables. The official terminology, somewhat illogically, is scheduled castes.

3. We are indebted to Ms V.A. Mary Vattamattam and Mr C.K. Ganguli of the Timbuktu Collective, Andra Pradesh, for a general outline of this history.

4. The full range of administrative areas in India in descending order of size is as follows: state, division, district, block or *taluk, mandal, panchayat,* village, hamlet.

5. For a fuller treatment of how disability *sanghas* were started and developed in India see chapter 10 of *Disability, Liberation and Development* (1993) by Peter Coleridge.

6. For a full discussion of the remit of CBR, please see the WHO website http://www.who.int/disabilities/cbr/en/ [Accessed 8 July 2010].

7. A *mandal* is the administrative area above a *panchayat* and on par with a block in India.

8. Mental illness is increasingly seen as a form of disability in India as a result of the work by Basic Needs, India, an NGO which promotes a CBR approach to people with long-term mental illness.

9. The ideas contained in this section come largely from the experience of Balakrishna Venkatesh, who initiated disability SHGs in the 1980s and still trains them. Another important resource has been G. Venkatesa Reddy, Senior Officer at the CBR Forum, Bangalore.

10. This still leaves open the question of whether to include people with mental illness. The decision belongs to the group.

References

Agrawal, R. 2007. Micro-finance is just band aid. *Civil Society*, May. Available online at http://www.civilsocietyonline.com/May07/may076.asp [Accessed 5 March 2010].

Coleridge, P. 1993. *Disability, Liberation and Development*. Oxford: Oxfam.

EDA Rural Systems Pvt Ltd 2003. *Self-help Groups in India. A study of lights and shades*. Research paper written by EDA Rural Systems for CRS, USAID, CARE and GTZ. Gurgaon: EDA.

Freire, P. 1970. *Pedagogy of the Oppressed*. London: Continuum.

Heaney, T. 1995. *Issues in Freirean Pedagogy*. Chicago, IL: Thresholds in Education. Available online at http://www.debtireland.org/resources/economic-literacy/Frieire-background-reading1.htm [Accessed 5 March 2010].

Miles, M., 2003. International strategies for disability-related work in developing countries: historical and critical reflection. *Zeitschrift Behinderung und Dritte Welt*. Ausgabe 3/2003, pp. 96–106.

Nair, A., 2005. *Sustainability of Microfinance Self-help Groups in India: Would Federating Help?* World Bank Policy Research Working Paper No. 3516. Washington, DC: World Bank.

Tankha, A., 2002. *Self-help Groups as Financial Intermediaries in India: Cost of Promotion, Sustainability and Impact*. A study prepared for ICCO and Cordaid, The Netherlands, August. Available online at http://www.sa-dhan.net/Adls/Microfinance/PerspectiveMicrofinance/Self-helpGroupsasFinancial.pdf [Accessed 5 March 2010].

WHO 2008. *Closing the Gap in a Generation: Health Equity Through Action on the Social Determinants of Health.* Geneva: WHO.

Yunus, M., 1998. *Banker to the Poor.* London: Aurum Press.

Yunus, M., 2007. *Creating a World Without Poverty. Social business and the future of capitalism.* New York: Public Affairs.

Further Reading

Barron, T., and Amerena, P. (eds.) 2007. *Disability and Inclusive Development.* London: Leonard Cheshire International.

With support, disabled people can participate in microfinance
Photo: Sudhindra CN/Leonard Cheshire Disability

Chapter 6

Microfinance for People with Disabilities

Enzo Martinelli and Roy Mersland

Summary

Microfinance is considered an important tool in reaching the United Nations' Millennium Development Goals (Littlefield *et al.*, 2003). Nevertheless, few people with disabilities have access to microfinance. This is in contrast to the United Nations' assertion that people with disabilities have the right to equal opportunities (UN, 1993, 2008). Anthony Mukungu in Lugazi, Uganda is an example of how people with disabilities are excluded from accessing microfinance. He packages and distributes flavoured drinking water. Mr Mukungu has a physical disability and moves in a wheelchair. He reports that the market is growing steadily and he now needs access to additional capital to boost his business. He has therefore approached several microfinance institutions '(MFIs) to apply for credit, but so far he has not succeeded. The reason he gives is that MFIs think we [persons with disabilities] are not creditworthy' (Mersland *et al.*, 2009, p. 3)

The aim of this chapter is, first, to provide the reader with basic knowledge about microfinance and how this is relevant for people with disabilities. Second, the chapter outlines the main mechanisms leading to exclusion from services and identifies strategies to improve the current situation. The overall objective is to give the readers a background to understand better how microfinance can be used as a tool to reduce poverty for one of the most marginalised social groups and to provide important knowledge useful in advocacy and project efforts.

Disabled People's Organisations (DPOs) in developing countries have long tried to advocate better access to microfinance for their members. However, if any answer is given at all, the message from the MFIs is normally that people with disabilities are a group too risky for lending and that their savings capacity is limited. Owing to the general misunderstanding within society that people with disabilities are 'destitute' and without the knowledge, skills and opportunities to operate businesses successfully, the MFIs generally shy away from clients with disabilities. However, in doing so they miss an important business opportunity, and fail to reach out to the poorest and the most marginalised – hence failing to implement the double bottom-line policy of reaching both financial and social objectives, with which nearly all MFIs claim to be acting in accordance (UN, 2006; Helms, 2006).

Adding to the challenge of persuading MFIs to target people with disabilities is the fact that DPOs, in their advocacy efforts, often demonstrate limited knowledge about microfinance. After all, microfinance is about the provision of working capital and financial services for sustainable businesses and individuals with lending and/or savings capacities. Advocacy to improve access to microfinance that fails to keep in mind the MFIs' business models (and the rationales behind them) risks being counterproductive. This leads to lost opportunities for both the MFIs and people with disabilities – the former miss out on an important market segment while the latter continue to be left out of the benefits of microfinance. A situation of asymmetric information is currently prevailing in the microfinance disability market. We therefore want to make the case for information dissemination and awareness creation among the microfinance providers as well as among DPOs and disabled people in general. In order to assure improved access to microfinance opportunities in the future, it is important to understand better what microfinance is and the reasons why people with disabilities tend to be excluded from it.

In developing countries most livelihood opportunities are generated in the informal sector, and people with disabilities have to compete within these constraints. Statistics show that 80–90 per cent of people with disabilities in these economies do not have a formal job, and as a consequence must turn to self-employment (UN, 2008). A main obstacle facing the self-employed is the lack of access to capital, either in the form of loans or accumulated savings. Without access to microfinance the economic activities of most people with disabilities tend to remain marginal and difficult to sustain (Handicap International, 2006; Mersland, 2005).

The idea of providing better access to microfinance services for persons with disabilities is not new. Several projects have been initiated to provide people with disabilities with a combination of training and subsidised credit from non-financially specialised organisations like community-based organisations (CBOs) or DPOs (Handicap International, 2006). The results from these efforts have been mixed. In some cases the results for the beneficiaries have been positive, but very few initiatives have been sustainable and able to reach out to more than a few people. Thus, when donor support ends, the provision of services is normally discontinued (Handicap International, 2006; Lewis, 2004).

Aside from Thomas (2000), Lewis (2004), Mersland et al. (2009) and Cramm and Finkenflugel (2008), the academic literature on microfinance and disability published in peer-reviewed journals is virtually non-existent. Thankfully, some reports like Handicap International (2006), MIUSA (1998), Dyer (2003) and Mersland (2005) do provide guidelines, conceptual frameworks, basic knowledge and, when available, some statistics. Most of the literature concerns the need to include people with disabilities in microfinance efforts but few studies provide evidence-based insights. Only Handicap International (2006) and Mersland et al. (2009) provide data to support their analysis.

All the studies, including those published in peer-reviewed journals, can be classified as 'expert opinion' and generally lack the theoretical rigour necessary in order to be classified as academic studies (Cramm and Finkenflugel, 2008). In particular, there is a considerable gap in the literature when it comes to empirical evidence of the market size, market served, exclusion mechanisms, and the effect of different inter-vention efforts.

The rest of this chapter proceeds as follows: in the next section we define microfinance and follow this with a brief history of microfinance. Later sections explain the reasons why poor people demand microfinance services and outlines the basics of savings, credit, insurance and money transfer services. The potential impact from accessing services is then explained and then the different providers of microfinance and their potentials are discussed. The barriers hindering disabled people's access to microfinance are presented and ideas are given on how the outreach to disabled people can be increased. The chapter concludes with a list of questions to stimulate debate and further research.

Defining microfinance

As will be outlined later in this chapter, the scope in terms of services, market segments and participating organisations involved in microfinance is increasing rapidly. Microfinance has therefore become a difficult term to define. Anything from member-owned savings and credit groups, where the members struggle to save ten US cents weekly, up to multi-million-dollar investments in huge banks, often serving medium-sized enterprises, are all referred to as microfinance. Nevertheless, it is important to start out by defining the term in order to structure the content of the chapter. Thus, in order to define microfinance we make use of the following short definition:

> Microfinance is the supply of financial services to micro-enterprises and poor families.

This definition is roughly the same as that used by recognised books such as those by Robinson (2001) and Ledgerwood (1999). It is a narrow definition, but it serves its purpose when understanding the core of microfinance. This is important since many socially oriented organisations, like DPOs interested in microfinance, often tend to neglect the technicalities, and keep their main focus on the proposed positive outcome of microfinance. Three areas in the definition stand out:

1. financial services (what kind of financial services are supplied?),

2. supply (who supplies the services?),

3. micro-enterprises and poor families (which market segments are being served?)

The best known microfinance service is microcredit, which is limited to the provision of capital. However, savings, micro-insurance and money-transfer systems can be equally important services, as will be outlined later in this chapter.

Suppliers of microfinance are a broad group of organisations and schemes, ranging from small informal self-organised groups to multi-billion international commercial banks.

Regarding the market, in principle all poor people, whether they are disabled or non-disabled, micro-entrepreneurs or not, are a potential market segment for microfinance services. The long-term overall micro-finance objective is to reach penetration rates for access to financial services similar to the ones experienced in several European countries. Here up to 99 per cent of the population have access to and make use of financial services, like savings accounts, money-transfer systems or housing credit.

The long-term objective is thus *access for all* (Helms, 2006) regardless of where people live, their poverty level or their physical or intellectual limitations. International development and financial service stakeholders know that to reach such an ambitious objective there is still a long way to go. However, several initiatives have demonstrated that it is possible to reach poor people with microfinance services, and also that people with disabilities can successfully benefit from microfinance. The noble objective of reaching all is therefore not an unreachable objective – and by sharing knowledge and lessons learned, the aim of this chapter is to provide the reader with information useful for increasing the outreach of microfinance to people with disabilities.

The history of microfinance

To understand microfinance one needs to know its history. First of all, microfinance is not a recent invention. For hundreds of years people of modest means have come together to organise savings clubs and small credit schemes (Bouman, 1995). In Europe the upper classes and authorities have been concerned with bringing financial services to the poor since at least the 16th century. As today, the objective then was also developmental.

Some of the historical pro-poor banking systems developed hundreds of years ago continue to be important banking organisations throughout the world. The savings banks, initiated more than 200 years ago, and the savings and credit cooperatives initiated 150 years ago were organised by people who had a real concern to help poor people escape poverty (Teck, 1968; Horne, 1947; Mersland, forthcoming). Similar to microfinance today, savings and credit were introduced as a self-help means to avoid poverty and to improve poor people's living conditions (Tucker, 1991; Rønning, 1972; Horne, 1947).

Modern microfinance as we know it today was born as a response to the frustrated development resulting from subsidised rural credit in the 1950s and 1960s (Adams and Fitchett, 1992). Over several years international donors and national governments invested billions of dollars in cheap credit to farmers. The results were disappointing. Corruption flourished, repayment of the loans was low and the overall development effect was negligible.

It was in this context that several pioneers started experimenting with new methods of issuing loans to poor people (mobilising savings or promoting other types of microfinance services were often not their initial concern). The Nobel Peace Price winner Mohammad Yunus, who started issuing small loans to poor women from his own pocket in 1976, is (together with his Grameen Bank in Bangladesh) the most well known of the pioneers (Yunus, 2003). Others, however, had preceded Mr Yunus, including a student organisation in Recife, Brazil, which later became Accion International (www.accion.org), and David Bussau and

Financial inclusion is vital for full participation in the economy
Photo: Jenny Matthews/Leonard Cheshire Disability

Al Whittaker, who in 1971 started issuing small loans to generate jobs. Their initiative later became Opportunity International, one of today's biggest international microfinance networks (www.opportunity.org).

Until the early 1990s, most microfinance initiatives were driven by donor-funded NGOs concentrating upon providing credit to entrepreneurial poor people, often women. Since then microfinance has gained a much broader scope, including all types of financial services, not only credit, and several kinds of actors, not only NGOs, are participating in it. Today the importance of microsavings is considered by many to be more important than microcredit, and, increasingly, services like micro-insurance and systems for money transfer are becoming available for the poor throughout the world. Moreover, most international banks are now becoming involved in microfinance and more than 100 international funds are investing in MFIs (www.mixmarket.org). Today more than 500 million poor people, including children, have a savings account (Christen *et al.*, 2004) and more than 100 million poor families have received loans (www.microcreditsummit.org).

Why do people demand microfinance services?

So, why do people demand microfinance services, and why is it also important that people with disabilities get access to microfinance? To answer these questions we refer to Rutherford (2000), who provides an excellent, down-to-earth introduction to understanding poor people and their money. His main answer is that people need access to microfinance because they frequently need access to lump sums of money. Such lump sums of money are larger amounts that cannot be drawn easily from the daily income and require sacrifice and planning. According to Rutherford, lump sums of money are needed for:

- life-cycle events: dowries, funerals, religious feasts, rites, marriage, etc.

- emergencies: healthcare, loss of work, climatic incidents, livestock diseases, loss of home (e.g. bulldozing in slum areas), etc.

- opportunities (either business or other types of opportunities):
  to buy a piece of land or a TV, to take advantage of
  fluctuations in food prices (e.g. grains), livestock, machinery,
  as incentives to get hold of opportunities, start a business,
  increase a business, etc.

As indicated in this list, business opportunities are only one of several reasons why people need access to microfinance. A first lesson from Rutherford is therefore to understand that microfinance is not only about supporting businesses. Other events or emergencies may equally trigger a need for a lump sum of money.

There are two traditional ways of getting access to lump sums of money; either through savings or via borrowing. A second essential lesson from Rutherford (2000) is to understand that accessing lump sums of money through savings or credit is basically the same. Either you save beforehand (Rutherford call this 'savings up') or you save (repay the loan) afterwards (what Rutherford calls 'savings down'). In any case, it is the user who is ultimately responsible for paying the lump sum of money. This is illustrated in Figures 6.1 and 6.2.

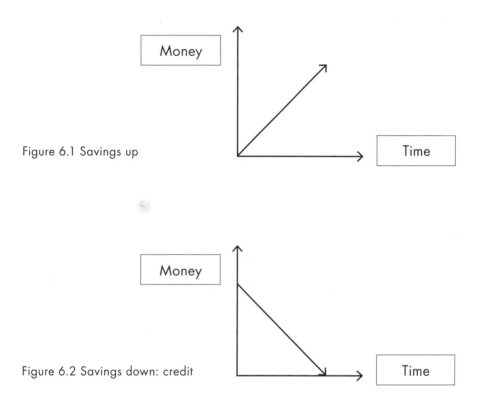

Figure 6.1 Savings up

Figure 6.2 Savings down: credit

As illustrated in Figures 6.1 and 6.2, the major difference between savings and credit is the time when a person gets access to the lump sum of money. By accessing credit a person immediately gets the money. For this advantage there is an associated cost referred to as 'interest'. In addition to the price involved with lending, another important 'disadvantage' of credit is the considerable risk associated with being indebted. If challenges arise when repaying a loan the borrower can easily become worse off than before. For economically marginalised people, including most people with disabilities, it can therefore be important to generate a good understanding of the concept of management of savings and credit before they actually access microfinance services.

The microfinance services

Nowadays, in addition to savings and credit, insurance and money transfers are also important microfinance services. In the following section we introduce important basic knowledge about each of these four services.

The basics of savings

Financially speaking, savings serve two main purposes. They enable future investments and they can smooth out consumption. For people who are poor, both of these are essential. The first gives access to lump sums of money that can be used for life-cycle events, emergencies or investment opportunities, while the second makes it possible to cover everyday basic consumption needs even when no daily income is available. The latter in particular is of utmost importance, because income for poor people tends to fluctuate considerably through the year. Particularly for farmers, the evening out of income between harvests is vital; during harvest, income and consumption can be abundant, while during the growing season, winter or drought many farmers depend totally on their savings, whether these are in cash, livestock or in grains.

Becoming disabled or discovering your child is disabled is normally associated with both a personal crisis as well as financial distress. Few people ever consider that one day they may become disabled. Often people do not even make financial plans for their old age. Probably the best preventive measure to avoid financial distress in case of disability is to learn to save.

Generally speaking, poor people want to save and in most cases they can save at least during some parts of the year. The claim that a person is too poor to save can in most cases be disproved (Rutherford, 2000). However, poor people don't necessarily save in cash. Saving in kind – like animals, grains and building materials – can be more common than saving in cash. Unfortunately saving in kind can be risky (e.g. animals can die) and, from an economic point of view, it is inefficient. If people save cash, in a system where the cash becomes available for others during the time when the saver does not need the money, the overall economy will grow. This, however, requires the intermediation of money.

Such intermediation can take place in a bank, a savings and credit cooperative, an MFI or through a Rotating Savings and Credit Association (ROSCA) or other self-managed financial schemes. In any of these systems the money being borrowed is provided by the savers. People will, however, only use such financial systems if they can trust them. Due to the inefficiency and insecurity associated with many financial systems, poor people may be perfectly rational in not using available financial systems but instead continuing to save in animals or building materials. Furthermore, inflation may deflate the value of the savings and, especially in rural areas, often there is no financial intermediation system available.

In livelihood projects the aim is often to start up new business ventures. Experience shows that practically all new successful business activities involve some kind of personal savings. However, this knowledge is often not incorporated when planning livelihood projects. What many seem to forget is that starting a new venture that is only financed with credit is extremely risky. Rarely do more than 50 per cent of new business ventures succeed. However, regardless of success a credit must be paid back. Increased misery instead of economic progress is too often the result of loans to finance the start-up of new businesses. Poor people, and particularly vulnerable persons with disabilities, should therefore not be enticed into contracting credit to initiate a new business, without sufficient safety nets in place. Savings, help from families and friends and sometimes grants are needed when a new business is to be initiated.

When persons with disabilities initiate business ventures they follow the same financial pattern as others without disabilities. This was recently revealed in a study from Uganda among 841 disabled persons involved in business (NUDIPU, 2009).[1]

Source of initial business investment	%
Personal savings	51
Support from families and friends	25
Sold a personal asset	17
Loan	7
Total	**100**

Source: NUDIPU, 2009

The numbers in the table above illustrate the personal sacrifice needed to get involved in business. Ninety-three per cent of the respondents depended on their own personal efforts or their own personal networks (families and friends) to enable their initial investment.

One important lesson from this study is the importance of promoting and cultivating a saving culture among prospective users of microfinance schemes. Furthermore, when a business is nurtured by the fruits of a person's own sacrifice the owner has strong incentives to protect and care for that business. The likelihood for success thereby increases.

The claim that disabled persons are too poor to save needs contesting. In the survey from Uganda already mentioned, 74 per cent of the respondents indicated that they saved regularly and, on average, they had one month's worth of income in cash deposits (NUDIPU, 2009). Generally, because of the risks and the costs associated with borrowing, most poor people prefer savings over credit (Hirschland, 2005; Rutherford, 2000). One therefore wonders why most donor efforts are for the outreach of credit and not for the promotion of savings. Strategies that promote savings before facilitating credit, especially for economically marginalised people, should be much more at the forefront of livelihood interventions. Poor people, including people with disabilities, *can* save and should be encouraged to save *more* in order to sustain their livelihoods.

Poor people demand the facility for both voluntary and compulsory savings. Most economic rationales indicate that consumers prefer flexibility, meaning voluntary savings that can be deposited and withdrawn whenever needed. However, many poor people are perfectly rational when they often indicate that they prefer compulsory savings that can only be withdrawn after some time. One of the reasons for this is that women who save often want outside pressure to protect their savings against the many daily claims for cash – for example, claims for food, healthcare or from their husbands, who often demand the money for immediate consumption (Anderson and Baland, 2002; Rutherford, 2000). When savings are compulsory, a person (often a woman) has the necessary argument to postpone immediate consumption in order to honour the compulsory savings contract.

Often poor people prefer participating in a group where they can save together with their peers (Eggen and Mersland, 2007). Gugerty (2007) and Ambec and Treich (2007) argue that the reasons why poor people save in groups is in order to cope with self-control problems. They argue that individuals simply cannot save alone since there are just too many claims on cash. Thus, poor people appreciate peer pressure. As many ROSCA participants put it 'you cannot save alone' (Gugerty, 2007) .

Group participation can promote saving
Photo: Sudhindra CN/Leonard Cheshire Disability

The extent to which people value the importance of having a place where they can save is illustrated in the following quote:

> If you live in an urban slum or in straw hut in a village, finding a safe place to store savings is not easy. Bank notes tucked into rafters, buried in the earth, rolled inside hollowed-out bamboo, or thrust into clay piggy banks, can be lost or stolen or blown away or may just rot. Certainly their value will decline, because of inflation. But the physical risks are the least of the problem. Much tougher is keeping the cash safe from the many claims on it – claims by relatives who have fallen on hard times, by important neighbours, by hungry or sick children or alcoholic husbands, and by landlords, creditors and beggars. Finally, even when you do a have a little cash left over at the day's end, if you don't have somewhere safe to put it you'll most probably spend it in some trivial way or other. I have lost count of the number of women who have told me how hard it is to save at home, and how much they would value a safe, simple way to save. (Rutherford, 2000, p. 2)

For most people saving is a habit that has to be learned. Regularly setting aside resources, even the smallest amount, that can be drawn upon when needed is essential, but difficult. However, there is very seldom a quick way out of poverty – sacrifices are needed. It is important to keep in mind that even if only a small amount can be saved every day or every week, over time it accumulates into important amounts. We all need to remember that 10 cents a day makes nearly 40 dollars in a year.

Furthermore, when poor people save together in groups their limited individual resources become important amounts when pooled together. For example, 20 persons each saving a dollar per week makes $1,000 a year. Development experts and the donor community have repeatedly been impressed when they learn about the resources being mobilised by the poor themselves. Persons with disabilities are no exception. The above-mentioned study in Uganda revealed that 50 per cent had a savings account in a formal financial institution like a bank, an MFI or a

SACCO (savings and credit cooperative), and as many as 71 per cent indicated that they participated in a ROSCA or other type of informal financial group. Their responses when asked about the value of their savings are shown in the table below (NUDIPU, 2009).

Current balance in savings account	%
Less than 46 dollars	55
Between 46 and 184 dollars	29
Between 185 and 322 dollars	8
Between 323 and 460 dollars	3
More than 460 dollars	5
Total	**100**

Source: NUDIPU, 2009

The survey from Uganda reveals that it is time to rethink the entrepreneurial potential of people with disabilities and their savings habits. Even though it does not represent all disabled people (only those involved in some kind of business, including the tiniest vegetable garden or the smallest tomato vendor at the market), the survey reveals that disabled people understand the importance of savings, and that they do save. Even if the amounts of money involved may seem small to some, the effort behind this is undeniably admirable. It is that type of effort that in the long run helps people to escape poverty.

The basics of credit

Credit is still the best-known microfinance service. Microcredit is normally a short-term, high-priced (high interest rate) loan for working capital to the self-employed poor. The main reason for the high interest rate is because of the high cost of handling many small loans. The average global interest rate in MFIs is close to 40 per cent p.a. (Mersland and Strøm, 2009). Figure 6.3 illustrates the virtuous potential of microcredit.

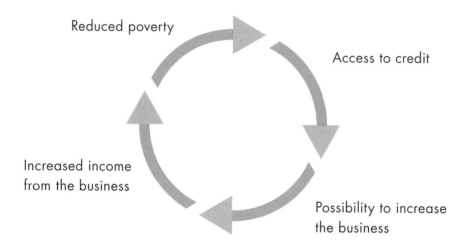

Figure 6.3: The virtuous circle of microcredit

First of all, Figure 6.3 indicates that a loan is something that should be used to *increase* a business (or expand into a new business line). Most poor people are farmers or are involved in other types of business activities. It can be a tiny garden where part of the harvest is sold at the market, a home brewery or selling charcoal in the street. A loan can fertilise such a business, or the existing income from the business can serve as a guarantee when a person wants to expand into a parallel business line (for example, to initiate some non-farm business alongside farming). As illustrated in Figure 6.3, access to credit can enable an increase in the total business size, which, in turn, makes possible an increased income from the business(es). Increased income reduces poverty, and people who are less poor get easier access to credit, thereby enabling them to have the continued possibility of increasing their outcome from business ventures. Access to credit can therefore be an important tool in reducing poverty.

However, a loan needs to be repaid. Thus, for those without repayment capacity, contracting credit can be a very risky strategy. 'Credit is also debt, and constitutes a risky strategy for the poorest and most vulnerable to economic stress' (Montgomery, 1996, p. 292). Most poor people know of peers who ended up in trouble because they could not repay their loans. Imagine disabled people who are already struggling in their daily life; if they were to fall into repayment problems on a loan they could end up in total misery.

Another downside of microcredit is the high interest rates. The benefit of receiving a loan can easily be lost in the face of the costs of the loan. Too often, when calculating the real return on a business loan, it is revealed that the associated increase in income is less than the real interest paid on the loan. Access to credit is not, therefore, an easy prescription for escaping from poverty and, in fact, Hulme (2000) suggests that microcredit should be renamed 'microdebt'. Nevertheless, as illustrated in Figure 6.3, credit can be a powerful anti-poverty tool. What is important is to provide credit to the *right* people – those who can benefit and have the required entrepreneurial skills – and not to those who risk increased misery.

There are basically three different microcredit methodologies: individual lending, solidarity group lending and village banking. In the first, a customer must present collateral or guarantors to get a loan directly from the MFI. In solidarity groups, four to ten persons guarantee each others' loans. In village banking, members of a community – usually 15 to 30 people – are trained in operating their own little 'bank', where they borrow capital from the MFI, which they then lend on to the members.

An important characteristic of a professional MFI is that it should become financially sustainable. Only then will it be able to service the customers in the long run. However, most MFIs, even the more professionally oriented, are still not sustainable. On average the annual operating costs in an MFI are 31 per cent of its average loan portfolio (Mersland and Strøm, 2009). In addition there is the cost of capital (often above ten per cent) and the cost of defaulters (often around two per cent). Thus, in order to keep financially afloat most MFIs need to charge an interest rate above 40 per cent if they are not to depend on support from donors.

Often DPOs advocate special loan conditions for their members. However, for MFIs struggling to keep afloat, the offering of loans on sponsored interest rates is simply impossible. Furthermore, by asking for reduced interest rates the DPOs create a barrier between them and the MFIs, thereby hindering a real integration and dialogue between equal partners. It is important to respect the fact that sustainability-oriented MFIs simply need to cover their costs. It is also important to note that even if a 40 per cent interest rate *per annum* may be considered high, MFIs' interest rates are normally much lower in comparison with the rates charged by other money lenders (Robinson, 2001). Since repayment time is often short, and the outcome from a business activity can in some cases be very high, paying a high interest rate can be a lesser problem than accessing the credit itself.

Studies have confirmed that the benefit of gaining access to credit is higher for those already in business, and have shown that the benefit increases over time (CGAP, 2003). This means that one should not expect a great benefit from the first loan. It is only after repeated loans that significant impact can be expected. This understanding is now incorporated into the practices of most professional providers of microcredit who, if repayment has been as scheduled, offer repeat and increasing loan opportunities to borrowers.

Credit for business purposes is what most have in mind when microcredit is being discussed. However, microcredit can also be used for housing, education, healthcare or consumption. Often poor people value credit for these purposes rather than for their businesses. The pivotal question asked by professional providers of loans is not whether a loan is for a business, but whether the potential client possesses the willingness and the capacity for repayment. If willingness and repayment capacity can be proven, there should be no problem in allowing disabled persons, as any other persons, the right to borrow to cover the needs they themselves consider to be most important.

Who should borrow money?

Capital is a necessary resource for self-employment but cannot stand alone in ensuring the sustainability of a business. A range of skills as well as access to other types of resources are necessary for the efficient use of capital. Success in self-employment depends on the opportunity and ability to access markets and to compete successfully. The main problem facing many persons with disabilities is often not the lack of capital, but the lack of skills and additional resources needed to be successful in business. The necessary skills can be divided into the following three groups.

- Life skills: personal aptitude, talent and motivation for business, as well as savings habits and willingness to make personal sacrifices in the short run to achieve gains in the long run.

- Technical and vocational skills: how to raise goats, how to mould pots, how to bake bread, how to weave carpets, etc.

- Business management skills: purchasing, marketing, organising, calculating, controlling, networking, etc.

Figure 6.4 presents a matrix to aid understanding of when microcredit may be considered useful for a poor person.

	High Level of access to skills **Low**	
High Level of access to microcredit **Low**	Successful entrepreneurs Role models for others	Access to credit may have negative impact
	Access to credit will often have immediate positive impact	Need input of both capital and non-capital resources

Figure 6.4: Market matrix for microcredit

As the matrix illustrates, only those persons with access to the necessary skills will benefit from accessing credit. So when a person does have the needed skills he or she should be provided credit, and if he or she already has access to credit, the person serves as a role model for others. However, as illustrated, if a person does not have the necessary self-esteem, business aptitude, vocational and business management skills to succeed in business, credit might well do more harm than good. The core of a business is not capital but skills and personal aptitude. It is therefore important to assess a person's level of skills before promoting credit as a developmental solution. The categorisation suggested in Figure 6.4 is thus an important exercise to carry out before determining the most appropriate type of intervention when wanting to improve the livelihoods of poor and disabled people.

The basics of insurance

Sometimes insurance can be the most appropriate way of accessing a lump sum of money when it is needed. Whenever people face death, accident, loss of crops, or a health problem they will always have a need for extra money. In these cases, insurance contracted beforehand may help to avoid economic stress.

During the past decade, micro-insurance has been put on the development agenda. It is obvious that poor people's need for life insurance, health insurance, crop insurance, etc. is enormous. Take, for example, crop insurance, where the assumption is more or less as follows.

Box 6.1 Crop insurance

Poverty is concentrated in rural areas, where agriculture is the main source of income. In sub-Saharan Africa, two thirds of the population are agriculturists living in rural areas (Todaro and Smith, 2006). The two factors most influencing the outcome of agricultural activities are the climate and the market prices on crops. Neither of these can be controlled by the farmers. Therefore, in order to invest more wisely in agriculture farmers need access

---

to insurance schemes such as rainfall insurance and guaranteed minimum prices on crops.

Few such insurance types are available – however, they do exist, for example in Malawi, where Opportunity International is partnering the World Bank to provide rainfall insurance to local farmers.[2]

Increasingly, MFIs offer life insurance attached to their loans. In these cases a loan will be completely written off if death occurs while repaying the loan. A few MFIs also offer disability insurance attached to their loans. In these cases the outstanding loan balance will be written off if the client becomes permanently disabled before the final repayment.

The need for designing and promoting disability insurance as a preventive mechanism against economic distress has generally still not entered the standard practice of livelihood interventions. With the increased emphasis on micro-insurance we consider that it is now time to get this important policy issue on the agenda. Economic misery is too often a consequence of becoming disabled. Making disability insurance widely available among the poor could be an important measure to modify economic distress when someone becomes disabled.

The basics of money transfer

With increased national and international migration and trade taking place at regional, national and international level, most people – even the very poor – are increasingly in need of systems where money can be transferred in a safe and convenient way at a reasonable cost. Today money transfers from guest workers account for three times the total foreign aid provided by OECD countries.[3] Unfortunately some of the money-transfer systems available are unsafe – for example, sending cash with friends or family members – or are costly, sometimes with charges of more than ten per cent of the amount transferred. However, increasingly more convenient and efficient money-transfer systems are becoming available. For example, in some countries, such as Kenya, it is today possible to send money via mobile phones.

Some people with disabilities cannot work and so depend on support from others. For them, access to an efficient money-transfer system that makes it easy to receive support can be very important indeed. As technology advances and it becomes easier to wire money to loved ones, we expect that those disabled persons who totally depend on the support of others will increasingly receive money from their families and friends in such ways. It will also become easier to organise public cash-transfer systems for targeted groups, for example some disabled people, and we expect to see more of such systems in the future (Gooding and Marriot, 2009).

The impact of accessing microfinance services

The promotion of microfinance has become an important development tool due to the likely positive impact on those who will then get access to financial services. It is obvious that savings and insurance provided by safe, convenient institutions at a reasonable price will have a positive impact on the users. It is also obvious that access to efficient money-transfer systems can be positive. However, some fear that a potential dependency culture will develop and so question the disincentive to work this might create (Mersland and Thøgersen, 2009). As money-transfer systems rapidly develop and cash-transfer schemes become more widespread, we consider it important that dedicated studies are carried out on how this new situation affects the livelihood and the empowerment of disabled persons.

The impact of accessing microcredit is widely discussed in the literature and is the research topic of most interest within microfinance (Littlefield et al., 2003). Generally speaking, most studies identify a positive impact from access to microcredit, with improvements in business stability or growth and in household economic welfare. However, these improvements are often not major, and frequently contracting credit can lead to increased misery for individuals and their families. It is therefore of the utmost importance that the prevailing socio-economic conditions and potential impact on the target group are carefully considered before initiating interventions that solely promote access to credit.

Lack of transparency is a serious problem in the microfinance industry. All too often there are hidden costs related to savings accounts or contracting a loan. Furthermore, microcredit and micro-insurance contracts can be difficult to understand, and the transfer of money is not always as convenient as claimed, with the costs involved often surpassing ten per cent of the amount transferred. There is therefore a considerable need for consumer education in this area. Similarly there is a need for more transparent providers of microfinance[4]. Finally, more 'truth in advertising' is needed. Microfinance is important and can contribute to development, but it is not a panacea; as we have repeatedly stressed in this chapter, in some cases microfinance, especially microcredit, can have negative impact on its customers.

There is one other effect of accessing microfinance that is seldom discussed in the literature. That is the effect on a person's self-esteem. Being trusted by a credit company or having been able to steadily save money can totally change a person's self-respect. For many disabled persons this is of absolute importance, as explained by Shahidul Haque in Social Assistance and Rehabilitation of the Physically Vulnerable in Bangladesh (SARPV):

> Credit is acceptance, hope, honour and confidence. It is not easy, rather much harder to attain acceptability, honour, trust and confidence from someone's counterpart. Someone has to be committed to achieve those. Credibility and credit go together. Credibility is the only factor to get credit. So, it goes to those who have credibility, who deserves it, who can possess it and above all who can uphold it.' (Shahidul Haque)[5]

We believe that access to credit and the accumulation of savings can indeed help to boost a disabled person's self-esteem. We thus welcome systematic project efforts as well as rigorous research to study the self-esteem effect from accessing microfinance.

The providers of microfinance

Providers of microfinance can broadly be divided into three groups – specialised providers, different types of savings and credit groups and credit components or revolving funds operated by non-specialised providers. In what follows we introduce each of the three groups and assess their opportunities and challenges in relation to persons with disabilities.

Specialised providers

Specialised providers are formal, legalised organisations whose core – and normally only – activity is to offer financial services to members and clients. Some specialise in microfinance, like MFIs, while others may offer microfinance alongside traditional financial services for other market segments. For example, Ecuador's largest bank, Banco de Pichincha, also offers microfinance through its Credife programme.

Being a specialised provider brings several benefits. When operations are concentrated and specialised, communication with customers, employees and other stakeholders becomes easier. This can reduce transaction and operational costs. CGAP (www.cgap.org) is a Bank attached centre that has been established in order to disseminate information to improve the professionalism and sustainability of the specialised providers.

Specialised providers of microfinance differ a lot in their ownership forms. They can be incorporated as NGOs, or be financial companies, banks or SACCOs. Some are small and serve only a few hundred customers, while others are large, reaching out to millions of clients (e.g. Grameen Bank). Together with the MFIs, in most markets SACCOs are the most important providers of microfinance; they are owned by their members and exist in thousands across all continents. Most SACCOs are small, servicing only a few hundred members in rural areas, but some serve thousands of members, including some in the cities.

In the NUDIPU study in Uganda referred to earlier, the respondents were asked where they kept their savings. The following table shows their answers.

Where do you save?	Numbers
SACCOs	28%
ROSCAs	21%
Commercial banks	16%
MFIs	13%
None	22%
Total	**100%**

Source: NUDIPU, 2009

This Urgandan survey underlines the fact that in addition to keeping the savings 'underneath the mattress' (22 per cent), disabled people, alongside other poor people, tend to prefer SACCOs and ROSCAs when entrusting their savings. There are basically two reasons for this: first, because MFIs and banks often concentrate their efforts in urban areas and not in rural areas where poor people tend to live and, second, because MFIs and banks often show little interest in reaching out to people who are just starting to get used to financial services.

Even if it is against the Consultative Group to Assist the Poor's (CGAP, 2004) recommendation, some MFIs are able to successfully combine the delivery of microfinance with other services like business training. For example, BRAC, a successful Bangladeshi MFI servicing millions of clients, refuses to specialise and continues to offer microfinance alongside training and different types of social services.

BRAC argues that since poverty is multidimensional, providing credit alone will not bring about much development for the poorest people (Halder, 2003). Many disabled persons need to improve their skills and knowledge in order to improve the outcome of their business ventures. The MFIs providing additional services alongside microfinance could thus potentially become important partners in improving the livelihood of disabled people. However, there are few MFIs that do not specialise, and several of those that provide additional services are not sustainable and too often deliver low-quality financial services (Lensink and Mersland, 2009). As a consequence, skills training and microfinance will normally need to be provided by separate organisations. Coordination between the different providers is therefore important.

Specialised providers aim to be financially sustainable. Thus, the pivotal question when offering credit is whether the potential clients possess the willingness and the capacity to repay a loan. All other arguments fail if this cannot be proven. Arguments such as 'MFIs "should" service disabled people because they are poor or because they have impairments' will normally not convince a professional MFI. Moreover, to reduce credit risk, specialised providers tend not to provide credit for start-ups, and the repayment capacity is normally calculated based on existing income streams before contracting a loan. Thus, in order to convince specialised providers that they should start servicing disabled people it is important to present this as a market opportunity. A shift in argument is needed: from presenting disabled people as 'needy' to presenting them as resourceful entrepreneurs.

Very few MFIs or other specialised providers are today consciously targeting disabled clients (Mersland et al., 2009; Handicap International, 2006). Nevertheless, most MFIs have some disabled clients among their customers, but normally fewer than one per cent (Handicap International, 2006). In a recent survey carried out by the Association of Microfinance Institutions of Uganda (AMFIU), 16 MFI branches were asked to report the number of disabled loan customers they had. The survey results showed a range from 0.24 per cent to 2.18 per cent of disabled customers; on average 0.68 per cent of the loan customers were disabled people (AMFIU, 2009).

The AMFIU (2009) study confirms a former study in Uganda, which found that 0.65 per cent of the clients of larger MFIs were disabled. However, in that study, reported in Mersland et al. (2009), it was also found that MFIs could be easily persuaded to take on more people with disabilities as customers. Thus, less than a year after having been informed and motivated in a short training session, the same MFIs now reported that one per cent of their customers were disabled people (Mersland *et al.*, 2009). The numbers are still small, but a 50 per cent increase (0.65 per cent to one per cent) is significant and demonstrates that changes are possible and not necessarily difficult. It is also important to keep in mind that one per cent of the client base in an MFI with thousands of clients adds up to several hundred people with disabilities being served. Thus, if low-cost information efforts are what it takes to persuade an MFI to increase its outreach to disabled people, it is essential that this is done. Nonetheless, even if every MFI goes on to have one per cent of its customers as disabled people, there is still a long way to go before all disabled people have access to microfinance.

Self-help savings and credit groups

The world's most commonly used financial systems for poor people are different types of groups, often referred to as ROSCAs, where the members regularly, often weekly or monthly, pool their savings or contributions and rotate these as grants or loans among members. The groups normally consist of 10 to 30 members and are organised by the members, either collectively, or by one or a few of those predominantly involved.

These groups have existed around the world for centuries, and have different names in different countries, like Merry Go Round in Kenya, Tontines in West Africa, Self-Help Groups in India and Cadenas in Ecuador. Many refer to the groups as ROSCAs, while others simply call them 'self-help groups' (SHGs).

These traditional schemes represent an efficient banking system at the community level, where members can easily save and periodically receive a lump sum of money (Bouman, 1995). In principle, a ROSCA is closed down when each member has received his or her pot of money. However, in practice many (perhaps most) ROSCAs continue opening new rotating rounds, and some accumulate the savings and offer them to members as loans instead of free contributions. These ROSCAs are sometimes referred to as accumulating savings and credit associations (ASCAs) (Bouman, 1995). Thus, many ROSCAs are kept intact for several years with the same or increased capital.

It is unlikely there are two identical ROSCA set-ups in the world. Nevertheless, there seem to be some fundamental conditions that make a ROSCA work over time.

- Social connectedness. This means that the members will normally be known to each other and belong to the same social strata, community, and social group (e.g. ethnic, religious, etc.). When the members are socially connected to each other it is more difficult for them to default on payments.

- Self-selection of members. The group as a whole or the leader(s) are the ones who decide who can join a ROSCA. If membership is imposed by others, such as donors or external agents, the group will weaken.

- Leadership. ROSCAs tend to have strong leaders who keep the group intact and are able to ensure that the members follow the rules.

Even if ROSCAs are popular they often encounter some common problems, like the following.

- Loss of savings. Many participants have experienced losses when participating in traditional ROSCAs. Before they receive their round of money the group simply disintegrates. An example from Kenya is as follows: 'The usual form of cheating is for a new member to come to a merry-go-round (the local name for a rosca), and ask for number 1 or 2 because they have an emergency ... And then, they stop contributing. (...) There are many cheaters like that, about half of the population! Some of them are well known, and still, some groups fail due to cheating.' (Anderson et al., 2003, p. 3).

- Elite capture. This is the situation when leaders of the ROSCA turn it into their personal business. If this is understood and responded to by the members from the beginning, it is not necessarily a problem, but too often leaders enrich themselves at the cost of members without the members' knowledge.

- Theft. Pure theft can happen either in the form of a person (normally a leader) who simply appropriates available cash, or by a member who deliberately stops contributing after having received his or her round of money.

- Inflexible savings and credit design. The savings and credit design in ROSCAs are generally inflexible and only fulfil the need of the participants to a minor degree.

- Exclusion of vulnerable members. Self-selection of members facilitates a continued practice of exclusion in the local communities. The more vulnerable, like people with disabilities, are often excluded from participating in ROSCAs.

Increasingly, donors are becoming aware of the traditional ROSCA systems. As a consequence the creation and mobilisation of self-help savings and credit groups is becoming more popular (Allen, 2006). The reasons for this are mainly that:

- such groups are based on savings

- such groups are driven and owned by the people themselves and make use of their own resources, both financially and socially

- such groups help develop both financial and social capital

- such groups can be cost efficient and can reach more rural areas and poorer target groups

- such groups use a flexible model and the groups can be used as platforms for the delivery of other development services

- donors believe that the weaknesses of the ROSCAs can be balanced with the help of proper training and the introduction of transparent leadership and money management systems.

When designing development programmes, donors and stakeholders often want to influence the makeup of savings and credit groups. Some, inspired by principles of equality and inclusion, would like to mix people from different social strata, ethnic groups, religions or disabilities. However, savings and credit groups need to balance a fine line when such values are introduced from the outside, and there is a considerable risk that the groups will end up having an externally driven design with a minimum chance of long-term survival. The internal cohesion of a credit and saving group is the primary element that can ensure its own sustainability, and efforts should be made to support the creation and development of groups that have strong bonds between the members.

For the enhancement of disabled persons' livelihoods the promotion of savings and credit groups can be of particular importance, since these schemes can allow for a more flexible and integrated approach, allowing outreach to vulnerable groups like disabled people. Compared with MFIs, the savings and credit group methodology can reach out to poorer target groups and help enhance social capital (Eggen and Mersland, 2007). For a savings and credit group to become sustainable it is of utmost importance that the money management, the leadership and the savings and loan operations are properly organised. Any other inputs to a group, like literacy or enterprise training, will be made in vain if the groups are not properly organised.

Programmes promoting savings and credit groups often have a credit component where the groups are provided with additional capital, either as loans to some of the members or as a loan directly to the group, which can be used to lend-on to members. These inputs give the members the possibility of accessing bigger loans and investing in larger business ventures. However, experience shows that access to capital from the outside creates a 'credit focus' in the groups, reducing the members' incentives to save, and often creating governance and ownership challenges. As a result, outside funded groups tend not to be sustainable (Murray and Rosenberg, 2006).

A major challenge for disabled persons is that community members decide on whom to include as members in a savings and credit group. This normally leads to the exclusion of people with disabilities if community awareness has not been raised on disability issues (Thomas, 2000). Particularly in donor-funded programmes for the promotion of savings and credit groups, it is important to include a conscious strategy on how to secure the inclusion of marginalised people in community initiatives. In this regard a recent initiative in Uganda is interesting. Here, with the help of the FAHU foundation in Denmark, the National Union of Disabled People of Uganda (NUDIPU) is partnering with CARE (a leading humanitarian organisation fighting global poverty) to influence implementing partners in charge of mobilising savings and credit groups in the SUSTAIN programme to ensure that disabled people are included as members.

Even if people with disabilities often tend to be excluded from participation, the ROSCAs continue to be the number one financial system for persons with disabilities in many (probably most) contexts. In the NUDIPU study in Uganda, 71 per cent of the respondents indicated that they were members of a ROSCA or a similar association (NUDIPU, 2009).

However, instead of integrating into regular community groups, people with disabilities often organise their own savings and credit groups. The reason for this is not only that they are excluded from other groups, but also because they feel more at ease and can reinforce their self-esteem and advocacy through such groups (Handicap International, 2006).

Credit components operated by non-specialised providers

Non-microfinance specialised NGOs, religious organisations, CBOs and DPOs often operate different types of revolving funds and credit components. For example, a Handicap International (2006) study revealed that 83 per cent of 58 surveyed DPOs operated their own credit scheme, wherein all of them had some sort of special loan conditions. Furthermore, they often tended to be less strict in client screening and enforcement of repayments.

The loans in this type of scheme are frequently offered in combination with vocational training and business skills training, and are often only provided once. Thus, these programmes are rarely sustainable. Of the 48 credit schemes supported by DPOs surveyed in the Handicap International study, none were sustainable (Handicap International, 2006).

There are several challenges related to credit schemes operated by non-specialised providers.

- Several studies have indicated that the impact from one loan only is limited. People need access to permanent financial services (CGAP, 2003).

- Operating loan services over time is difficult and requires professional management of a type that is normally different from managing a DPO.

- These programmes are often unable to select beneficiaries who have a true interest and talent for running their own businesses. Too often the selection of beneficiaries is based on friendship or membership, and not on business aptitude.

- The cost of operating such a programme is generally disproportionately high in relation to the outcome achieved. Seldom does such a programme reach more than a few hundred beneficiaries (Handicap International, 2006).

For these reasons, the provision of credit by non-specialised providers should, according to several observers, be discontinued (Murray and Rosenberg, 2006; Dyer, 2003). Others, however, argue that since savings and credit groups as well as specialised institutions tend to discriminate against disabled people there may still be a need for DPOs to provide credit to their members (Cramm and Finkenflugel, 2008).

In most cases we would disagree with the recommendation that a DPO start providing credit. Instead, we would advocate a linkage strategy where the DPO partners with a professional bank, SACCO or MFI. Such a partnership may bring along several benefits, like the following:

- a bank, MFI or SACCO may provide other types of financial services, like savings and money transfer, and not just credit

- the quality of service may be better

- the sustainability of service will in most cases be better

- repeated loan opportunities are available

- screening of potential clients is based on professional criteria to assess creditworthiness and potential entrepreneurship and not on friendship or membership

- potential conflicts within the DPO related to the ownership of funds is avoided

- disabled people are mainstreamed as customers of existing service providers, which is more in line with current disability policies and human rights approaches.

In order to gain access to the professional provider it is of utmost importance that the DPO understands the 'rules of the game' of an MFI. The first thing a professional MFI will (and should) ask is: 'What's in it for me?' Negotiating successful partnerships often requires in-depth knowledge of microfinance. In many cases a DPO will benefit from involving technical expertise in the negotiation.

Barriers excluding people with disabilities from accessing microfinance

So, why is it that people with disabilities tend to be excluded from microfinance? Building on Simanowitz (2001), Mersland et al. (2009) laid out five barriers, each of which has the potential to exclude access by people with disabilities to microfinance services. The barriers are:

- exclusion because of low self-esteem (sometimes referred to as 'self-exclusion')

- exclusion by other members

- exclusion by MFI staff

- exclusion by service design

- exclusion because of the disability itself (physical and/or informational exclusion).

We will look at each of these in a little more detail.

Exclusion because of low self-esteem

People with disabilities often experience exclusion and rejection. The accumulation of such repeated negative experiences produces secondary incapacities like lack of self-esteem, which often lead to self-exclusion from public and private services such as microfinance (Roeske, 2002). Furthermore, some persons with disabilities and their families may have the expectation of constantly receiving charity or special conditions (Thomas, 2000). Such an attitude is incompatible with sustainable MFIs, SACCOs or ROSCAs, and will naturally lead to exclusion from services and membership.

According to a Handicap International study (2006), as many as 53 per cent of MFIs considered low self-esteem to be the main barrier hindering disabled people in accessing their services. Mersland et al. (2009) also considered lack of self-esteem to be the main hindering factor.

Improving people' self-esteem is not easy and calls for innovative and integrated approaches. Some ideas and principles for stakeholders involved are as follows:

- providing the opportunity for learning by doing

- starting something small and manageable where a person can experience success

- integrating groups of both fellow disabled persons as well as participation in mixed groups with both disabled and non-disabled members

- learning skills needed to manage a business

- being familiarised with the existence/practices of MFIs through visits and information by them.

The NUDIPU (2009) study found that persons disabled at birth or during childhood were the poorest and the most excluded from accessing microfinance services. Thus, parents' upbringing of a disabled child is clearly very important. Learning to be independent and developing a sense of self-esteem happens mainly at home and during childhood.

Exclusion by other members

Self-help savings and credit groups, ROSCAs, etc. are based on self-selection of members. Moreover, most MFIs use different types of group methodologies for microcredit, like solidarity groups or village banks, where members themselves decide whom to include in the group. A core element in group methodologies is that all members are jointly liable for each individual's loan. The poorer and the more vulnerable community members therefore tend to be excluded from such groups by 'stronger' persons. There are also studies showing that poorer persons who do join a group have a shorter membership time than average (Montgomery, 1996). However, it is not only the level of vulnerability that decides whether or not to include a member: local stigmatisation or the perceived risk posed by persons with disabilities becoming members in groups also often discourages community members from including them.

The AMFIU (2009) study found that according the MFIs' staff they considered the group methodology to be the main hindering factor. Savings and credit groups cannot, however, have persons with disabilities imposed upon them as members, and nor can solidarity groups or village banks. Awareness raising of community and group members is needed, which requires work at policy levels as well as at the grassroots level. Furthermore, the identification of successful disabled persons can serve as role models both for fellow disabled persons and for community members.

Exclusion by staff

Due to attitudes and prejudices within society, the staff of an MFI, bank or SACCO will often deliberately or unconsciously exclude persons with disabilities. Personnel often lack the necessary experience and training to distinguish between a real and a perceived credit risk. Often a credit officer is not able to see through the disability to recognise the real abilities of a person with a disability. Furthermore, if an MFI practises any form of group methodology there is also evidence that 'staff pressure' triggers 'group pressure', leading to exclusion of poorer members (Montgomery, 1996). MFI staff, and particularly their credit officers, are therefore a core target group to be influenced. However, if such influence is to be effective, it must be backed by MFIs' top management.

Experience has shown that staff members *are* willing to be influenced. A general response when asked why they serve so few disabled customers is: 'We haven't thought of this' (Mersland, 2005). However, a major challenge is the time MFI staff have available in which to be influenced. Being an MFI manager or credit officer is very time-consuming and they are seldom willing to dedicate much time in order to be informed and influenced about disabled people's concerns. It is therefore important to find ways of influencing the staff that are not time-consuming. At the same time, one must expect to have to keep up the influencing efforts over time.

Motivating the MFI to identify existing and successful disabled customers can often be an effective way of gradually changing MFI staff's attitudes. Overall, it is important to present customers with disabilities as a potentially important market segment for the MFI. At the same time, providing more accessible services would also help the MFI to practise the double bottom line (achieving financial and social results) that is becoming increasingly important for MFI donors and investors. Partnering with DPOs and servicing more disabled people can thus help strengthen the MFI's financial results as well as its social results.

Exclusion by design

The design of the savings and credit services may create obstacles not only for disabled persons, but for vulnerable groups in general. Savings accounts, for example, often require an opening balance of US$10 or 20, amounts that can easily be one month's income for a person, and several dollars may be needed for the monthly cost of maintaining the account. Similarly, accessing credit may require up-front savings or financial endorsements that many disabled persons do not have access to. Moreover, the credit methodology is often standardised and inflexible, thereby hindering persons with disabilities from participating. For example, mobility challenges may make weekly repayments a greater obstacle for persons with disabilities. Also, since credit history in microcredit in many ways replaces formal collateral or guarantees, it becomes difficult for persons with disabilities to get started when most credit officers are not able to distinguish between the disability and personal skills and character for a disabled person who has not received credit before.

Since type of disability varies considerably and since the overall disability segment is, after all, quantitatively limited, it will seldom be cost-efficient for an MFI to develop specialised products for disabled clients. A better alternative is to develop products that are accessible and 'friendly' for vulnerable groups in general. In such efforts an MFI can benefit from including disabled clients in their consumer panels. If a product is found to be attractive for people with disabilities it will most probably be attractive for most vulnerable groups. Moreover, if an MFI can demonstrate its ability to include disabled customers, non-disabled potential customers will probably understand that they can also be included. After all, self-exclusion from services is probably the main reason why vulnerable groups in general do not access microfinance services.

Exclusion because of physical and informational barriers

An impairment in itself can be a major barrier to the access of offices or information. MFIs give information in both verbal and written form, which is of course inaccessible to many deaf or blind persons. Branches are located far away from people's homes, and to enter the premises stairs often have to be climbed and crowds have to be negotiated. However, these are all barriers that can be overcome, often at not too great a cost, and that can enable the creation of physical environments accessible to everyone.

An example from Uganda

The following table summarises how a project in Uganda has systematically tried to address exclusion mechanisms.

Exclusion mechanism	Relative importance as experienced in the project	Major activities in the project to reduce the barriers
Exclusion stemming from low self-esteem	Very high	Training of entrepreneurial persons with disabilities on the aspects of business, microfinance and savings. Bridge-building between disability and microfinance 'communities' and the active use of role models.
Exclusion by other members	High/moderate	Lobbying efforts in the government, etc. Radio and TV talk shows.
Exclusion by staff	High	Training of MFI staff, particularly credit officers, and the sensitisation of MFI top management. Bridge-building between disability and microfinance 'communities' and the active use of role models.
Exclusion by design	High/moderate	Promoting the idea of *not* developing special products for disabled clients, but to involve persons with disability in the design of new products tailored for the needs of vulnerable groups.
Exclusion because of physical and informational barriers	High/moderate	Motivating MFIs independently to make their premises more accessible and to carry out outreach efforts in the disabled community. Lobbying towards MFIs, donors and authorities to make sure that all new branches are made accessible.

Source: Mersland *et al.*, 2009

How microfinance could be made more effective for people with disabilities

As we have seen, in most cases ROSCAs of various kinds represent the most flexible financial system. Advocating the inclusion of people with disabilities in their membership can provide an entry-point for economically marginalised people to start saving and to receive initial credit. Membership of these groups can enable the development of the financial management culture that is essential in order to move away from a condition of poverty. Also, the promotion of grassroots financial groups, consisting primarily of people with disabilities, can be a sustainable strategy that allows people with similar challenges to get together and share positive experiences on their road to sustainable livelihoods. Once these groups have reached a good level of maturity and have been able to generate more important financial volumes, their members can be motivated to join similar mainstream groups or to connect with other services providers to get access to more complex and demanding financial services. ROSCAs can therefore be a good breeding ground for economically marginalised people to develop confidence in financial management and to provide initial capital for the establishment and expansion of microenterprises.

In recent years, pressure has been increasing from the donor community to demonstrate the fulfilment of the social mandate of the MFIs towards poverty alleviation. Once MFIs have reached good financial ratios and have achieved some sound sustainability in their markets, they are increasingly being pushed to perform well in their social mandate too. There is therefore fresh interest from MFIs in exploring new ways of increasing their outreach to more economically marginalised customers and vulnerable groups.

The inclusion of people with disabilities, a social group rarely tackled specifically by mainstream MFIs, can represent an untapped potential customer base that strengthens their social performance. Many MFIs have ventured, with NGOs and other specialised agencies, to broaden their customer base to people with disabilities by increasing the awareness of their staff on disability issues and improving the accessibility of their financial services. The benefits of these strategies are seen in their enhanced capacity to deal with a wider range of customers and in their more appealing social performance profile.

Recently conducted research (Handicap International, 2006) shows that, despite the great interest of DPOs in microfinance, current experience is characterised by poor sustainability ratios and marginal impact on the livelihood of their members. As non-specialised service providers, DPOs are in most cases badly equipped to manage the provision of microfinance to their membership. Evidence shows that better roles could be played by DPOs in facilitating access for their members to mainstream microfinance schemes, through support for raising awareness on disability and promoting equality of access with sensitive microfinance service providers and in monitoring social performance of existing microfinance providers.

Conclusions and unsolved puzzles

This chapter has presented the basics of microfinance and discussed the barriers hindering access by disabled people to microfinance services. In the text we have made several recommendations on how to increase disabled people's access to microfinance. We must, however, admit that the issue of microfinance and disability is still to a large extent an undiscovered research area, with many unsolved puzzles remaining. Clear guidelines and recommendations can therefore be difficult to put forward. Our main recommendation is therefore to continue and strengthen research efforts in order to understand better the issue of microfinance and disability. To stimulate debate and further research we present a list of questions that we believe are key to learning more about microfinance and disability.

Box 6.2 Key questions

1. To what degree are people with disabilities excluded from microfinance services? Do they actually tend to be, as we claim, more excluded than others?

---

2. How can MFIs, SACCOs and banks be influenced to take on more disabled persons as customers?

3. How can vocational training and access to microfinance be provided in partnerships between DPOs, MFIs and other actors? What would be the role of DPOs in such partnerships?

4. When are microgrants an alternative and how should microgrants be designed in order to secure the best possible entrepreneurial incentive for the person with disability involved?

5. How can DPOs and disabled people in general best be involved in the mobilisation of savings and credit groups, and how can such groups best combine disabled and non-disabled members?

Notes

1. The respondents in the survey have participated in business and microfinance trainings provided by the National Union of Disabled People of Uganda (NUDIPU). With the help of local NUDIPU members and public officials responsible for disability rehabilitation, all disabled persons with some kind of economic self-employment activity are invited to participate in the training.

2. http://www.opportunity.org/Page.aspx?pid=787 [Accessed 5 March 2010].

3. http://www.oecd.org/dataoecd/40/3/35389786.pdf [Accessed 5 March 2010].

4. http://www.mftransparency.org/ [Accessed 5 March 2010].

5. Shahidul Haque, http://www.sarpv.org [Accessed 15 August 2008].

References

Adams, D.W. and Fitchett, D.A. 1992. *Informal Finance in Low-income Countries.* Boulder, CO: Westview Press.

Allen, H. 2006. Village Savings and Loans Associations – sustainable and cost-effective rural finance. *Small Enterprise Development,* 17, 61–8.

Ambec, S. and Treich, N. 2007. ROSCAs as financial agreements to cope with self-control problems. *Journal of Development Economics,* 82, 120–37.

AMFIU 2009. *Microfinance and Disability – a Survey of MFI Staff.* Kampala, Uganda: AMFIU.

Anderson, S. and Baland, J.-M. 2002. The economics of ROSCAs and intrahousehold resource allocation. *The Quarterly Journal of Economics,* August, 33.

Anderson, S., Baland, J.-M. and Moene, K.O. 2003. *Sustainability and Organisational Design in Informal Groups: Some Evidence from Kenyan ROSCAs.* Vancouver, Canada: University of British Columbia.

Bouman, F.J.A. 1995. Rotating and accumulating savings and credit associations: A development perspective. *World Development,* 23, 371–84.

CGAP 2003. *Donor Brief No. 13, The Impact of Microfinance.* Washington, DC: CGAP.

Christen, R.P., Rosenberg, R. and Jayadeva, V. 2004. *Financial Institutions with a 'Double Bottom Line': Implications for the Future of Microfinance. Occasional Paper.* Washington, DC: CGAP.

Cramm, J.M. and Finkenflugel, H. 2008. Exclusion of disabled people from microcredit in Africa and Asia: A literature study. *Asia Pacific Disability Rehabilitation Journal,* 19.

Dyer, S. 2003. *The Inclusion of Disabled People in Mainstream Microfinance Programmes.* London: Leonard Cheshire International.

Eggen, Ø. and Mersland, R. 2007. *You Cannot Save Alone – Financial and Social Mobilisation in Savings and Credit Groups. NORAD Report.* Oslo, Norway: NORAD.

Gooding, K. and Marriot, A. 2009. Including persons with disabilities in social cash transfer programmes in developing countries. *Journal of International Development*, 21**,** 685–98.

Gugerty, M.K. 2007. You can't save alone: Commitment in rotating savings and credit associations in Kenya. *Economic Development and Cultural Change*, 55**,** 251.

Halder, S.R. 2003. Poverty outreach and BRAC's microfinance interventions: Programme impact and sustainability. *IDS Bulletin*, 34**,** 44–53.

Handicap International 2006. *Good Practices for the Economic Inclusion of People with Disabilities in Developing Countries.* Paris: Handicap International.

Helms, B. 2006. *Access for All.*, Washington, DC: CGAP.

Hirschland, M. 2005. *Savings Services for the Poor.* Bloomfield, IL: Kumarian Press.

Horne, H.O. 1947. *A History of Savings Banks.* London: Oxford University Press.

Hulme, D. 2000. Is microdebt good for poor people? A note on the dark side of microfinance. *Small Enterprise Development*, 11**,** 26–8.

Ledgerwood, J. 1999. *Microfinance Handbook.* Washington, DC: The World Bank.

Lensink, R. and Mersland, R. 2009. *Microfinance Plus.* Kristiansand, Norway: University of Agder.

Lewis, C. 2004. Microfinance from the point of view of women with disabilities: Lessons from Zambia and Zimbabwe. *Gender and Development*, 12**,** 28–39.

Littlefield, E., Murdoch, J. and Hashemi, S. 2003. *Is Microfinance an Effective Strategy to Reach the Millennium Development Goals? Focus Note 24.* Washington, DC: CGAP.

Mersland, R. 2005. *Microcredit for Self-employed Disabled Persons in Developing Countries.* Oslo, Norway: Atlas Alliance.

Mersland, R. forthcoming. The governance of non-profit microfinance institutions – lessons from history. *Journal of Management and Governance.*

Mersland, R., Bwire, F.N. and Mukasa, G. 2009. Access to mainstream microfinance services for persons with disabilities – lessons learned from Uganda. *Disability Studies Quarterly, 29.*

Mersland, R. and Strøm, R.Ø. 2009. Performance and governance in microfinance institutions. *Journal of Banking and Finance, 33,* 662–9.

Mersland, R. and Thøgersen, J. 2009. *Direct Cash Transfers to Stimulate Economic Growth in Developing Countries. Working Paper.* Kristiansand, Norway: University of Agder.

MIUSA 1998. *Loud, Proud and Prosperous.* Eugene, OR: Mobility International USA.

Montgomery, R. 1996. Disciplining or protecting the poor? Avoiding the social costs of peer pressure in micro-credit schemes. *Journal of International Development, 8,* 289–305.

Murray, J. and Rosenberg, R. 2006. Community-managed loan funds: which ones work? *Small Enterprise Development, 17.*

NUDIPU 2009. *Microfinance and Disability – a Survey of Economic Active Disabled People.* Kampala, Uganda: NUDIPU.

Robinson, M.S. 2001. *The Microfinance Revolution.* Washington, DC: The World Bank/Open Society Institute.

Roeske, H. 2002. *Disability and Poverty Reduction Strategies – How to ensure that access of persons with disabilities to decent and productive work is part of the PRSP process.* In: Discussion Paper pp. 1–23. Geneva: ILO.

Rutherford, S. 2000. *The Poor and Their Money.* Delhi, India: Oxford University Press.

Rønning, B.R. 1972. *Norsk Sparebankvesen inntil 1850.* Oslo, Norway: Gyldendal Norsk Forlag.

Simanowitz, A. 2001. Thematic report No. 4: Microfinance for the Poorest: A review of issues and ideas for contribution of Imp-Act. *Improving the Impact of Microfinance on Poverty.* Brighton, UK: Imp-Act.

Teck, A. 1968. *Mutual Savings Banks and Savings and Loan Associations: Aspects of Growth.* New York: Columbia University Press.

Thomas, M. 2000. Feasibility of integrating people with disabilities in savings and credit programmes in Bangladesh. *Asia Pacific Disability Rehabilitation Journal*, 11.

Todaro, M.P. and Smith, S.C. 2006. *Economic Development.* Harlow, UK: Pearson – Addison Wesley.

Tucker, D.M. 1991. *The Decline of Thrift in America – Our Cultural Shift from Saving to Spending.* New York: Praeger.

UN 1993. *85th Plenary Meeting of the UN. Standard Rules on the Equalisation of Opportunities for Persons with Disabilities (A/RES/48/96).* New York: United Nations.

UN 2006. *Building Inclusive Financial Sectors for Development.* New York: United Nations.

UN 2008. *Convention on the Rights of Persons with Disabilities.* New York: United Nations.

Yunus, M. 2003. Halving poverty by 2015 – we can actually make it happen. *The Round Table*, 363.

Self-employment is a viable option for people with disabilities
Photo: Jenny Matthews/Leonard Cheshire Disability

Chapter 7

Self-employment for People with Disabilities

Bev Moodie

Summary

The focus of this chapter is on self-employment for people with a disability. It argues that if they are properly encouraged and supported and given the right tools, people with a disability can and should become self-employed. The author starts by discussing the context in South Africa. She then offers some case studies of people who have succeeded in becoming self-employed as well as some who have not, and in the next section she draws a number of lessons that can be learnt from the case studies. The following section is devoted to an examination of strategies by which people with a disability can become self-employed. She starts by discussing Die Werkswinkel (The Workshop) in Knysna, Cape Province, outlining ways in which people can transform themselves from being workers to contractors and independent businesspeople. She then considers different kinds of skills and resources that they need to succeed. In her conclusion she points to the overall benefits that self-employment can bring to the community and to people with disability themselves, including increased earnings, greater self-confidence and self-esteem, wider social relationships and inclusion in the community.

Introduction

Box 7.1 Case studies of entrepreneurs with a disability

Randall Scholtz is an entrepreneur who suffers from epilepsy. He has built up his consultancy selling funeral policies and is much loved and trusted by his clients.

Patrick Saayman has a disability, is self-employed and an athlete. Patrick repairs shoes and makes leather products at home. The income generated from this business supports his family of five.

Tamsanqua Stimela is self-employed, fixing appliances from his home in Nekkies, Knysna. His home-based business supplements his disability grant.

Bart Muller is a self-employed bookkeeper for many small business clients. His condition, known as Guillan Barre syndrome, changed his life, but his business at home has enhanced it in many ways.

Tanya Gardy, who has cerebral palsy quadriplegia, has strived to overcome her severe disability. She has offered her services as a counsellor to others with disabilities, which would allow her to work within the confines of her disability and share her experiences and her wisdom.

Their stories, success and challenges, shared in this chapter, illustrate the meaning of 'entrepreneur', 'self-employment' and disability.

This chapter is built around case studies and the stories of the people with disabilities introduced in Box 7.1. Some have already become self-employed, while others have tried to do so but not yet succeeded. It describes their successes and difficulties and discusses the obstacles they face, the solutions they found and, most importantly, the impact of self-employment for people with disabilities with regard to financial prosperity, friendships and social inclusion.

Setting the scene

To understand this chapter you need to understand the context surrounding business development, self-employment and people with disabilities in South Africa. People with disabilities can apply to the state for a disability pension of R1080.00 per month. However, some are excluded from this pension if their condition is not considered to be severe enough.

Developing small businesses and the second economy (as it is called) is a goal of the South African government through a government agency called the Small Enterprise Development Agency (seda), which has been set up specifically to help develop small businesses. Seda provides information and some financial assistance with business development services, and also facilitates training and mentorship. The emphasis is on developing business plans and business skills rather than capabilities.

Finance for small business start-ups is very difficult to acquire, even though seda and government lending schemes have been put in place for this purpose. Repayment of small business loans has been poor in South Africa and has, in the past, even contributed to the collapse of a bank. Although there are many different funds and finance schemes for assisting new businesses, start-up capital is largely inaccessible, especially for the poor who have no assets, credit history or bank accounts. This is an even greater problem for people with disabilities.

Many local non-governmental organisations work with poor and unemployed people, and sometimes with people with disabilities, teaching the various skills that could be useful for self-employment. These focus more specifically on hard skills training than on the business development of the person wanting to become self-employed. The government has also set up many social development projects in which community groups are given tools, equipment and buildings and taught skills such as making furniture, bricks and clothing, or growing vegetables as a community business venture. Many of these have collapsed because the participants had little or no business or financial understanding and did not feel any ownership of the venture. They did not choose the business for themselves: it was chosen for them. Once the money runs out, the people in the project leave. Thus, for the most part business development in South Africa is generally splintered, complicated and uncoordinated. Each organisation focuses on its own endeavours, isolated from other organisations and the realities of the business world.

Box 7.2 People with disabilities can become entrepreneurs

An entrepreneur is someone who undertakes an enterprise or business with the chance of making a profit or a loss. This definition describes the self-employed and the process of self-employment. In business and self-employment no one is favoured. People do not have to be well educated, able-bodied or rich to start a business. Although it may be easier for able-bodied people and those with capital to start up a business, its success depends on the innovation and efforts of the business owner – the entrepreneur.

There are many examples of people with disabilities going into business. One of South Africa's greatest entrepreneurs was the late Tony Factor, who pioneered a discounted furniture industry. Tony was dyslexic and struggled to read and write. Learning disabilities may not fall into the same category as physical disability, but people who have them are often considered as being disabled, both by themselves and by others.

My discussion includes my own observations from experiences gained over 15 years of helping people, both with and without disabilities, to tap into their entrepreneurial potential and become self-employed, noting that there are more similarities than differences between the two groups. I believe that we all have some entrepreneurial flair (see Box 7.2). We often tap into this natural resource only when we are faced with adversity in some form or another. This adversity could be an accident that leaves us with a disability, or it could be finding ourselves without a job and unable to find one, which motivates us to start our own enterprise.

When we seek ways and means of earning an income through self-employment we need to look at what we have, rather than what we do not have. People in poverty, especially in South Africa, focus instead on what they do not have and therefore cannot do: their lack of money, education or opportunities. This is also true of people with disabilities: they see their physical disability as a barrier and what they cannot do becomes the all-consuming focus of their lives. But there are no boundaries for business, self-employment and entrepreneurship and they are available to anyone who is prepared to reach out to them.

Before we start, we face questions such as 'What can I do to earn money? Where do I start?', with all their accompanying doubts and fears. Fear of change and the unknown is common when starting something new, together with fear of failure and of the ridicule or rejection it may bring. This fear is shared by everyone who starts his or her own business. If you identify the areas in which you can work and would like to work, your business is more likely to succeed. It will also help to conquer your fears and open up opportunities in the marketplace, within any limitations you may have. This works for everyone, including people with disabilities.

Case studies: Trying and succeeding

Randall Scholtz

Randall's story, shared in the telling by his wife, Johanna, aptly describes the difficulties, pain, triumphs and joys of self-employment. Randall developed epilepsy at the age of three months and was raised by his grandmother. No one treated him differently and he was given no favours because of his disability. When Randall was nine years old, his grandmother died and he had to live with an aunt. Life was hard.

Randall and Johanna met while they were still at school and were married five years later. Johanna had never been told that Randall had epilepsy, as no one ever spoke of it. She first found out what it meant when he had a seizure three months after their marriage. A few years later Randall's seizures forced him to stop work and Johanna lost her job. Life for them

Self-employment supported Randall's self-esteem. Photo: Bev Moodie

became a real struggle, as they now had three young children. 'Randall had given up on himself and was not the loving, caring man I married', says Johanna, who admitted that she was thinking of moving out at this time, as this was not the life she had chosen.

It was through a support group started by Epilepsy South Africa that Randall and Johanna were first able to talk about his condition and meet others in the same situation. Randall was also invited to join Business Outreach's entrepreneurial programme, after which he decided to sell funeral policies. He chose that business because he had skill and experience in sales and he loved people.

Although Randall sells funeral policies, earning commission from a parent company, he is self-employed and has made this business his own. He has his own business cards and sets his own standards and business practices for himself and his clients. He fights on his clients' behalf when his company tries to put up premiums. He is open with his clients about his epilepsy, explaining that if he cannot turn up at the scheduled time to collect their premiums, it will be because he is sick and cannot get there. 'In fact', said Johanna, 'one weekend when Randall couldn't get out, he made more money than usual because all his customers came to pay their premiums at his home and to see how he was'.

In being honest and open about his epilepsy in his work, Randall has also opened up the subject of epilepsy to many who did not know what it meant, removing the fears and prejudices that so often surround the condition. Nowadays he is working too much and will have to cut back a little because he is starting to have more seizures than usual. But being self-employed allows him to do this. The business lessons he has learned are simple: 'Recognise the skills that you have. Love what you do, because it empowers people. Keep your values. Be loyal to your customers and they will trust you. Keep your promise and be professional. Go that extra mile.'

Randall notes that there are always problems in business. 'The customer is very difficult and will often let you down, but I never let it get me down. I kept following up and people have come to trust me. I keep my promise and I am loyal to all my customers. I was lucky in that I wasn't treated differently because of my disability. The hardships of my youth have made me tough. I'm proud of my business and have made it my own.'

Johanna concludes, 'We are both so proud. Two of our three children were able to get bursaries and are now finishing university or working overseas. We own our own house and although it's just a little house, it's all ours.'

Patrick Saayman

Faced with adversity and an unknown future, Patrick Saayman began his business by working with what he had. Patrick was a skilled artisan and bricklayer who became disabled as a result of an accident. During rehabilitation he was taught leatherwork, which he enjoyed. Facing poverty and an uncertain future, now as a man with a disability, Patrick started to repair shoes from home. His business has grown steadily and he now also produces quality leather products such as cellphone cases, glasses cases, wallets and book covers, which he also sells at craft markets. Through direct exposure to his customers, Patrick has learnt valuable business lessons that have helped him become more innovative with his products and increase his sales. It is his business that keeps his family of five above the poverty line and has contributed to their quality of life.

Bart Muller

Bart Muller, too, fell back on a skill he had before he contracted Guillan Barre syndrome. Bart was an accountant. He found himself in business when small local businesses asked for help with bookkeeping. His client base has grown since then. Being self-employed as a disabled person gives Bart the freedom to work at his own pace, within the boundaries and limitations imposed by his disability. It also exposes him to clients and people with whom he would not normally come into contact and so keeps him in touch with life.

Tamsanqua Stimela

Tamsanqua used to be a taxi driver until he was injured in an accident six years ago and lost the use of his legs. He had always known how to fix appliances so he started doing this from home. His work comes to him through word of mouth; his customers bring him their kettles, microwaves and other electrical appliances and he fixes them for a fee. His wife works only one day a week and he has a 15-year-old child at school. Tamsanqua is able to support his family from his disability grant, supplemented with the income from his small business. He is still the breadwinner of the family.

Should the grant be taken away, he could manage on his income from his small business. He would have to take on more customers and work, but the family would be able to live. Because he deals with customers daily, he is very much part of his local community and has many friends. If he did not have this work, he would spend his day (in his words) in 'a very dark place'. The job has broadened his expectations of the future and improved his family's prosperity and quality of life.

Disability did not stop Tamsanqua from supporting his family
Photo: Bev Moodie

These stories are from four people with disabilities who have succeeded as self-employed entrepreneurs. The pattern of their journey into self-employment is shared by others who have become self-employed. They have to overcome their fears when faced with a new beginning and also find something they can do that will sell in the marketplace. They need to find innovative ways to make their product or service different and attractive and to find ways of dealing with difficult customers.

They also experience common business problems, such as transport. Most do not have their own so they have to find private transport, relying on taxis or friends to buy the materials or spare parts they need in their business. Having materials and goods delivered is not always an option when the quantities needed do not support the expense of delivery. Being self-employed puts everyone on an equal footing.

Case studies: Trying and giving up

Jean-Pierre Lingervelder and Jannie Smit

Jean-Pierre Lingervelder and his friend Johannes Smit (Jannie) explored the possibility of starting a web-designing business, as both had an aptitude for computers. They explored a franchised web-design opportunity that would have provided them with a successful programme, business recipe and income opportunities.

Jean-Pierre and Jannie are younger than Randall, Patrick, Tamsanqua and Bart, live at home with their parents and have no families of their own. The web-design business venture did not work out for them. The sophistication of the franchise business and agreement were quite complicated and the terms were binding. The cost of the franchise was high. Neither Jean-Pierre nor Jannie had had much experience in the formal workplace and the work was, they admitted, too sophisticated for them. Jean-Pierre's comment perhaps expresses their experience in a nutshell: 'Business is like a shark tank and we were the T-bone steak'.

Tanya Gardy

Tanya Gardy has cerebral palsy quadriplegia, a severe physical disability. Tanya's skill lies in translating English and Afrikaans and she has a talent for writing, especially about disabilities and the world of the disabled. This is an exciting opportunity to earn an income by providing a very marketable service. She has written a number of articles in local newspapers about being disabled. A friend helped her to design a website where she offers a counselling service to people with disabilities, among others. Tanya has completed school and undertaken a number of courses, never accepting her disability as a limiting factor, but seeing it as one that requires a different attitude and approach. She has had a few enquiries and calls for advice from the website, which she has responded to mainly using e-mail and without charging.

Tanya is cared for by her mother and lives at home. She is currently looking for a place with care and support where she can live as independently as possible and has found such a community in Riversdale. This is a commune for people with disabilities who live together with caregivers and contribute to the communal home, each with their own skills or talents and within the limitations imposed by their disabilities, thus contributing to the income and fund-raising initiatives of the home. Her main challenges are not her physical limitations, disability, or lack of confidence, but her lack of exposure to and experience in the marketplace.

Lessons from the case studies

Necessity and previous work experience contribute to success in becoming self-employed

Necessity is the mother of invention and a motivating factor when it comes to self-employment. Having to contribute to the family's income certainly introduces pressure and urgency into the equation. Amongst those who have shared their stories and experiences, age and previous experience seem to be relevant factors. Patrick, Randall, Bart and Tamsanqua had previous work or business experience. The younger people who are cared for by their parents remain in a safe place and have no reason to earn income for themselves, although it would benefit them in a number of other ways. They acknowledged their lack of exposure to and experience in the marketplace.

A social worker at Die Werkswinkel mentioned that those born with disabilities or disabled at a very early age seem to fare better than those who become disabled when they are adults. She added that it takes time to come to terms with the loss of a limb or the use of one's body. This could explain Jannie Smit's difficulties with finding employment. Jannie used to be a stuntman and although he has been in a wheelchair for more than 14 years after breaking his back as a result of a fall, he is still a stuntman at heart and nothing quite measures up to the excitement and fulfilment of that experience.

Developing and recognising appropriate skills for self-employment

From a self-employment perspective Jean-Pierre made an apt comment: 'We don't see our skills as a tool which we can use now that we've become disabled. And it's important not to limit ourselves.' And this is true for anyone going into self-employment. The tools we can use to become self-employed are within us. They are our skills, talents and experiences. Most entrepreneurs start their own businesses by formulating and developing a business idea by matching their abilities to an opportunity in the marketplace, or by spotting an opportunity in the marketplace and filling that gap, or even by finding someone else who could fill the gap and positioning themselves within the supply and demand process. An example would be noticing someone with skills and equipment (brickmaking), identifying a need in the market for that product (bricks) and facilitating a sale as the marketer or broker. This has been done and it requires very little in the way of capital resources.

Entrepreneurship is about doing things differently. Instead of buying space, equipment or tools, we could share or borrow from someone who has them. One person with transport can collect and deliver materials and goods for a business that does not have transport. This also provides someone else with an opportunity. This strategy would work well for people with disabilities, who may need support in different ways. In business it is important to know and work with our strengths, while being aware of our limitations.

Business is a hard taskmaster but it gives the business owner flexibility in how and where the product or service is produced, depending on the nature of the product. In this way, self-employment suits people with disabilities. It allows them to work at their own pace, at home, within their limitations. Tanya needs only a computer and her talent to write articles. But she needs confidence in her ability, to persuade other people to buy her articles and to believe that people will pay for them. Tanya is focusing on counselling, when writing would probably be a better option.

Those who have succeeded in becoming self-employed have fallen back on what they know and love. They have also had to support their own families and been supported by them in their business ventures – not with money, but with acceptance and expectations. They all admit it is hard work, and that the customer can be very difficult, but doing business has given them confidence in themselves and won the respect of their families, friends and their local communities (society). This is a positive cycle of effort and reward.

Patrick and Randall learned new skills that helped them to find work. Patrick was taught leatherwork after his accident. Randall was helped through an entrepreneurial skills process that built his confidence and helped him examine his resources, focusing on the skills and experience he had that could help him earn money. This process takes time and effort. However, attitude and confidence play by far the biggest role in becoming an entrepreneur and venturing out into one's own business, no matter how big or small. And this is true for everyone.

Facing rejection in self-employment

Self-employed people have to interact with others to sell their products or services. Interaction with clients also brings the businessperson face to face with the reality that a customer may not buy the product or service – for no other reason than it does not satisfy their needs or wants, or for personal reasons that have nothing to do with the product, service or supplier. Every self-employed person has to face rejection at some time or other. Their products have to be of good quality and competitive in the marketplace. Customers do not buy products because they feel sorry for the person who made them. This is true for all who go into business.

Perhaps people with disabilities are too sensitive to rejection? Jean-Pierre agreed: 'We scare off too easily and fear rejection and pity, instead of actually being rejected'. Edward Qakatayo, a skills and business trainer working at the Efata School for the Blind and Deaf in Mthata in the Eastern Cape, has observed that people with disabilities are spoilt and pampered by their families: 'Because they receive a grant from the government for their disabilities, they believe they must get something for whatever they do'. Edward Pedro, manager of Die Werkswinkel in Knysna, Cape Province, also agreed that the people with disabilities with whom he works are 'soft' and 'scared off easily'. He puts this down to the fact the Die Werkswinkel is a comfort zone for those working within its environment. They are not stretched personally, not exposed to the marketplace and not expected to take responsibility.

Johanna Scholtz, like Randall a member of the Epilepsy South Africa support group, commented that families can overprotect a person with a disability. 'It's not society that shuns them but the family that overprotects them and makes them feel they are not worthy, cannot contribute and believe they're different. It's not about being cruel to the person with disabilities, but about not pampering them. And building up their confidence and self-esteem by allowing them to do it themselves and be part of society.'

Facing difficulties and obstacles

People with disabilities have to deal with enormous frustration just getting around in an able-bodied world. Buildings do not have lifts, there are no ramps for wheelchairs and door handles are too high. And working with a disabled body sometimes takes a great deal of energy, just as being self-employed does. Two of the greatest obstacles in making a new beginning and creating our own business are fear and remaining stuck in our comfort zones. This is especially so for people with disabilities and those living in poverty. Elrich Komsa is a young man who became disabled in an accident nine years ago. He started to repair appliances as a small business very successfully from home for many years afterwards, but then stopped three years ago: 'I guess I just

Becoming self-employed requires confidence and determination
Photo: Fran Black/Leonard Cheshire Disability

became lazy', he says. Money is scarce and life is hard. Elrich receives a disability grant and lives with his mother and family in very poor circumstances. He admits that fixing appliances again would bring in extra money, ease his level of poverty and enable him to become more independent. But poverty seems to have become Elrich's comfort zone. Poverty is not only a situation or a potential destination, it is also an attitude. Elrich's disability grant provides him with the means to survive, but not much more. Lack of confidence, low self-esteem, lack of faith in their abilities and the failure to recognise that that they can contribute (albeit in a small, or different way) is another big obstacle for people with disabilities. It is a widespread attitude among the poor and under-educated in South Africa.

275

People with disabilities have limitations – but we all do in some way or another. And society's attitude to people with disabilities is difficult to accept. However, the greatest obstacle facing people with disabilities is the limitations they place on themselves, or those placed on them by their families who over-protect them. Even people whose disabilities place limitations on their activities, like Tanya Gardy, can learn to look at their situation differently and keep striving to contribute in whatever way possible.

Attaining self-employment through sheltered employment

Homes, centres and workshops that support people with disabilities, helping people to develop new skills and then providing them with sheltered employment, present an unrecognised opportunity for self-employment by encouraging, promoting and supporting it. One such place that offers new skills training and selling good quality products on the open market is Die Werkswinkel.

Die Werkswinkel opened in 1993 to help people with disabilities develop skills that would make them more employable in the open market. The idea was that once the skill had been learned and perfected the person would move on. However, this failed to happen. Some were placed in employment but most stayed and ten years later remain at Die Werkswinkel, partly because of their lack of education and partly because of the job market's attitude to employing people with disabilities.

In 1994 Die Werkswinkel started teaching people with disabilities how to make wooden products, later producing and selling wooden toys and bird feeders in response to market demand. Later a sewing department was added and tablecloths, aprons and table placemats were produced and sold through school fêtes. Die Werkswinkel started selling its products from a display table in front of a large retail outlet. Then Rotary helped them buy a wooden hut, which served as a shop, and was placed on the pavement in the main street of the town, surrounded by local craftspeople.

For about ten years the products made and sold by Die Werkswinkel earned good money and contributed to its upkeep. However, Knysna has since grown and the environment around Die Werkswinkel's shop has changed. This has resulted in a dramatic drop in the sales of their goods. The income from the goods sold at the shop now contributes only ten per cent of their total income.

Apart from the wooden and sewn products, Die Werkswinkel also undertakes contracts to restore furniture and brass items. A local supplier has contracted Die Werkswinkel to make packaging boxes and it also produces pauper coffins for the Knysna Municipality on contract. Contracting is definitely the way forward, says Edwin Pedro, the manager of Die Werkswinkel. 'We need to move away from making products and undertake more contract work. This would improve our income and broaden our opportunities.'

From sheltered employment to self-employment

People working in sheltered employment sometimes become complacent, comfortable and, in some ways, lacking motivation. Sheltered employment does not encourage people to move on to the open marketplace, a challenge not only because of their disabilities but also because of their lack of education. Nearly everyone at Die Werkswinkel has at best only a primary school education. Yet many homes supporting people with disabilities in South Africa, such as Epilepsy South Africa, which also has workshops and sells products on the open market, have to find ways to move the stronger individuals out of their protected employment to make room for weaker ones.

Currently, those working in Die Werkswinkel are paid a very small daily wage, depending on their ability and place in the process line. This income subsidises their disability grants. This could improve if Die Werkswinkel contracted the workers and paid them for all the saleable items they complete. Moves are under way for this to happen. This would not only improve the income of the worker; it would also provide a good stepping stone to greater independence. Workers could also be encouraged (and guided) to provide employment for less able workers within their business unit. If successful, this could encourage self-employment, bring with it a greater level of self-reliance for the person with disabilities and create exposure to the realities of the business world. The same approach could be tried out in similar homes.

Supporting self-employment in sheltered employment

First, there needs to be a change of thought and approach from social development to an emphasis on business development and self-employment in homes and centres for people with disabilities. Management needs to be comfortable with the approach, and the paradigm shift has to come from the top.

Second, the people involved (including management) need to be encouraged and educated in business and realise the benefits of self-employment in the production and sales process. There is no motivation to change unless the benefits are made explicit. Similarly, the costing structure needs to ensure that all will benefit financially from the change. All of this is directly related to the quality and sales of the product or service offered. For centres such as Die Werkswinkel, many of the elements are already in place, the most important of which is the market. What remains to be changed is the workers themselves: they need to become more business-like and focused on self-employment, and the costing structure needs to adjusted in tandem with this. Once this system is in place, links can be formed as part of the business development process to provide added-value services that supplement those lacking or needed by people with disabilities, such as marketing, deliveries and administration, which could become business opportunities in themselves.

Supporting the business development of people with disabilities

Supporting the business development of people with disabilities is no different from doing the same thing for able people. There may, however, be more opportunities for linkages among the former group, because if a person with a disability cannot do an activity, such as marketing, this provides an opportunity for someone else who can. Able-bodied people could probably do all the functions and activities themselves. The first step in the process, however, is to help people with disabilities realise that they can contribute and help them find a skill or a talent they can use to develop a product or service. People with a disability are not different, although they may perhaps have different limitations. By far the greatest support mechanism for any self-employed person, especially those starting up, is encouragement and more encouragement, as well as recognising and acknowledging small successes. The Business Outreach Project is a case in point.

The Business Outreach Project

The Business Outreach Project is a support network that emerged spontaneously from a business bridging project that I piloted under Business Outreach recently with the local municipality in Knysna. The business bridging programme starts with an entrepreneurial capacity-building and skills course, where participants discover and tap into their entrepreneurial abilities and develop a business idea. After this the graduates join the Business Outreach Project.

The Business Outreach Project brings the graduates together once a month to share their experiences, challenges and successes. Some businesses may not have got off the ground yet, while others have may already have customers. They motivate and guide each other with their experiences. Friendships and links (encouraged in the training programme) are formed here. For example, Hugh Lawrence has a car and Elmarie Jonas (Lungi's Laundry) needs someone to collect and deliver laundry. In this way Hugh has a business opportunity in collecting and delivering laundry for Elmarie, fulfilling the needs of a fellow emerging entrepreneur and earning income himself.

Along the way the network invites existing business owners from mainstream business to come along to meetings. For example, a local interior design shop has asked Katy Janklaas to make one of her ceramic pots to a specific design for one of their clients. All business owners who attend the network meetings are impressed and inspired by the activities of the emerging entrepreneurs and many share similar business challenges. The *Network News* is published every three months, sharing stories, highlighting the successes and challenges of the emerging entrepreneurs, and relating the experiences of existing business owners attending the meetings. One of these is Edwin Pedro, the manager of Die Werkswinkel, who is disabled.

Business development takes time. Some of the emerging entrepreneurs coming through the business bridging programme have taken 18 months and needed to make some adjustments to their business idea to get it off the ground. None has been able to access start-up finance but this has not stopped them.

Market research

Focusing a product or service and packaging it for the market is vital to the success of the business, and this is where market research is important. Market research can be very complicated, extensive and expensive and there are companies that do this professionally. However from a small business point of view the basics of market research suffice. Small business owners must do it themselves to get a feel for the marketplace. Before venturing into the marketplace to do market research, we need to be very clear about the nature of the product or service that is being offered as well as the kind of customers who would buy this particular product or service.

A sample of the product then needs to be tested in the market by showing it to people and asking their opinion. If a service is being developed the businessperson needs to ask around and find out if there is a need for that particular kind of service and to be open to what the customer has to say, not fearful of it.

Patrick Saayman noticed from the samples he made that many customers did not understand how his leather cases and covers could be used. He then started to put the name on the case or book to indicate its use, for example, Bible cover, cellphone case. This improved the sale of his products. This market research and market testing should continue throughout the lifespan of the business, as the market changes all the time and businesspeople should adjust their products and services to meet this need. Market research allows a business to discover clients' needs and wants. They may also find that while they expected one kind of customer, they attract a different kind. Market research also allows a business to find out what type of customer would buy its products or services.

Being aware of competition in the market place is also of paramount importance. It can be learned through asking: Who are my competitors? Where are they? What do they offer? How are they servicing their customers? And how am I different? In this way a business avoids making hundreds of products that a customer does not want and will not buy. This is often a problem for community skills development programmes, where many products are made to develop skills, without focusing first on what kind of products would sell. Thus a lot of money is locked up in finished products that do not sell, demotivating the people who were taught to make them.

Partnerships

The value of partnerships can never be underestimated. Partnerships have a vital role to play in business development, especially in helping people with disabilities to become self-employed. In a partnership, each partner contributes. Usually the contribution is a financial one so that partners share the cost of setting up the business venture, or skills. A partnership is a binding relationship to produce or achieve something together. Partners operate under the name of the business or the venture.

In any partnership, partners' roles or responsibilities will differ because each partner has different skills and talents. If both partners have similar skills, they need to find different responsibilities and activities, otherwise they will get in each other's way, which eventually causes friction, discord and the breakdown of the partnership. Partnerships are invaluable in business development, where one partner may provide the business skills, another a mentoring programme and the third microfinancing. In this way they all bring their own expertise to the table and provide an all-encompassing service with a focused outcome, reducing effort and costs and increasing impact. In this instance they would be called project partners.

It is also possible for centres, homes and workshops providing sheltered employment or self-employment opportunities to become partners in a specific situation, sharing skills, resources and expertise. This can be achieved in setting up a self-employment programme as a separate venture that can be supported by all, and in the sharing of experiences or resources. In this way each adds value to the process in some way. Partnerships, however, require people to work together for a common goal or cause, and this is often where things come unstuck, as personal and hidden agendas may cause confusion and conflict.

Linkages

Linkages are not necessarily the same as partnerships, in that the one party is not bound to the other, but merely provides an added-value service or product to the end process of delivering that service or product, such as the case of Hugh Lawrence's transport service to Lungi's Laundry. Lungi's Laundry is Hugh's client, not his partner. Another example is a link between business owners and emerging entrepreneurs in the Business Outreach Project. This enables them to meet and learn more about each other and opens up opportunities for all as individual operators. The added-value supply chain in business opens up many opportunities. It enables entrepreneurs to focus on their core business and provide opportunities for others to support or add value to them.

Conclusions

Self-employed people with disabilities can make a difference

Randall is known far and wide in his community. Through his business Randall has exposed the community in a positive way to epilepsy. Likewise Patrick is also contributing to destroying the myths surrounding people with disabilities and in wheelchairs. He is outgoing, strong and confident and produces good products that sell, competing equally in the marketplace. In this way he shows society that although he has disabilities and is in a wheelchair, this has not stopped him from living life to the full.

The benefits of self-employment for people with disabilities

The benefits and rewards for the effort of becoming self-employed are numerous. Most do not earn a lot of money, but what they do earn keeps the family above the poverty line and much more. Patrick notes that the money he earns from his business puts food on the table. But more importantly, contributing to the family's income in this way has given him a place and respect in the family and his community. Patrick also sells his products at craft markets (something that is difficult for many people), which has built his confidence even further. Having his own business has exposed him to a broader variety of people than would be case if he were sitting at home.

Bart agrees with this view. Becoming disabled forced him to look at other ways of making a living, which is how he learned how to work on a computer. The money he earns from his business enables him and his wife to eat at a restaurant occasionally and even go on holiday, adding to their quality of life. Edwin agrees: 'If these [people with disabilities] were not at Die Werkwinkel each day they would be melting away at home, depressed and hidden from society. Being part of Die Werkswinkel has improved their self-esteem, given them an opportunity to get up in the morning, contribute to the economy, albeit indirectly, and increased their confidence and quality of life.'

Randall does not earn a lot of money, but the income from his business venture reduces his dependence on his disability grant. His business has also given him self-respect and self-esteem and improved the quality of life for his family. As Johanna Scholtz said: 'It's not about the money. It's about self-respect and having a reason for getting up in the morning and about making a difference'.

The world of business has no favourites. All self-employed people are on the same footing and face similar business lessons and challenges. There are opportunities for everyone. You do not have to be well educated, rich or able-bodied to succeed but you do need a skill or a talent and to find a way to use it to make money. It is also important to love what you do.

Being self-employed gives people flexibility. It has brought prosperity, self-respect and self-esteem to some people with disabilities. It has included them in society, provided them with friendships and broadened their experiences and expectations. They have become exposed in positive ways to society and in the process the myths, fears, suspicions and misconceptions about disabilities and conditions such as epilepsy are being dispelled.

Yet there are situations in business that are more difficult for people with disabilities. Facing rejection is one of them. One of the limiting factors for people with disabilities is their lack of experience and exposure to the marketplace. Another may be that families overprotect them and make them feel they cannot contribute. Business demands that we believe in ourselves and the product or service we are supplying. It is this self-confidence and self-belief that keep us going in the tough business environment.

Poverty is as much a comfort zone and an attitude, as a situation and potential destination. Disability grants support the comfort zone. People receiving grants can survive, albeit at a subsistence level. But becoming self-employed and becoming disabled later in our life are strangely similar. Both need time for adjustment. Going into business brings us face to face with new circumstances with which we have to come to terms and accept. Likewise, when we become disabled as adults it also takes time to come to terms with and accept our new reality and circumstances.

It may be unproductive to accept one's circumstances passively if this does not allow room for growth and improvement. It takes time, skill and a different approach to help people, especially those trapped in poverty and with disabilities, to realise and tap into their entrepreneurial potential. Self-employment provides good opportunities both for those with disabilities and those who are poor to lift themselves up and contribute to the well-being of themselves, their family, their community and their society. Helping people with disabilities to become self-employed is perhaps the best gift anyone could give and doing so should become an integral part of every rehabilitation and skills development programme.

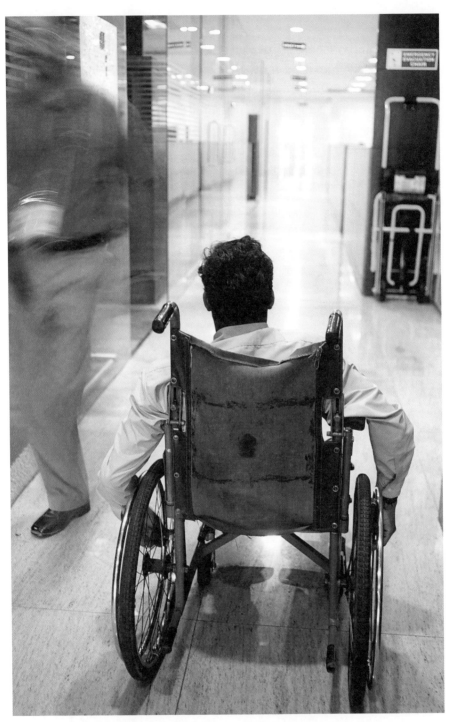

Stereotypes of disability and employment can be overcome
Photo: Gideon Mendel/Leonard Cheshire Disability

Chapter 8

Waged Employment

Javed Abidi

Summary

The *Concise Oxford Dictionary* defines 'waged employment' as 'regular paid employment'. The objective of this chapter from my point of view is to be able to understand why disabled people don't find employment, as in a regular job, and also, perhaps, what can be done to change that situation.

When I was asked to write this chapter on 'Waged Employment'. I felt privileged but I did caution the editors that being a disabled activist, it would be impossible for me to write a 'bookish' chapter. I am grateful to them for having given me the liberty to address the issue as I see it. I have tried to tell you my story and that of my country. I believe that, by and large, the issues are the same across the world: disability, prejudice, stereotypes, self-created barriers, insensitivity, poor leadership, lack of unity amongst disabled people themselves and so on. If the issues are the same, then I guess the remedy will also be similar. We have to adopt a rights-based approach and then stick to it. We have to question the basics. The status quo has to be changed.

This is the story of prejudice and perception. This is the story of stereotyping millions and millions of young disabled people, of first giving them a label and then short-changing their lives.

Introduction

Let me begin this chapter by telling you my story. I was born in 1965 in an average Indian town, Aligarh in Uttar Pradesh – not too small a city but not a metropolis either. My father used to teach at the university there, my mother was a housewife and we were three siblings: me first, then my younger sister, and then my younger brother. Economically, we would be labelled as middle class, I guess. My father earned enough to give us a decent life and a convent education. I had a congenital disability and this brought with it certain additional expenditures. My father gave tuition in the evening to earn the necessary extra money.

I finished high school in 1980. This was an era when just about every young boy or girl in India wanted to be either a doctor or an engineer. My father wanted me to be a doctor, but I hated biology, zoology and everything else that was compulsory to learn in order to even think of heading in that direction. One fine day, I quietly rebelled, and dropped out of the pre-medical course in which I was enrolled. My father came to know of this after about two or three months. He was heartbroken and, indeed, very, very angry. Worse, he lost all hope in me.

The next thing on his agenda was to set up a printing press for me! A small one, in a rented garage next door, where I could actually visualise poor little me, confined in my wheelchair, sitting at the reception of the garage-level printing press. However, Lady Luck had other plans. My father had taken long-term leave from his university job and moved to Delhi. There he became involved in politics and the famous Mrs Indira Gandhi appointed him a Joint Secretary in the Congress Party. He suddenly made many new friends in Delhi, one of whom was an American. This gentleman went on to become a family friend and motivated me to go to America, not so much for 'further education' as for 'exposure'. 'It is a totally different place. You will learn so much there. It will do you a lot of good.' He assured and reassured me.

To cut a long story short, in 1985, finally, I did manage to go to the US with no great aim or ambition in mind. In those years, many young Indian people went to the US to follow courses in computer science, engineering, medicine or some such high educational goal. After dropping pre-medical, I had enrolled myself in a bachelor's course with English literature as my main subject. And the only reason I chose English literature as my core subject was because it happened to be my father's subject; that's what he taught when he worked for the university. And so, practically from the time I was born, and thanks to my father giving tuition at home, I had no choice but to listen and listen and listen to Shakespeare and Milton and other such great souls, day after day and year after year. The adolescent logic was pretty simple: by taking English, I could do the least possible study and yet get a university degree!

However, going to the US changed all that. I had to find myself a better goal! From 1981 to 1985, while not doing pre-medical and while pretending to do a bachelor's of English, I had sort of discovered myself. (Funnily enough, I didn't realise it then; the realisation occurred some years later.) In those years, I was the most regular in going to the university but hardly ever attended any classes! On campus, my favourite destination was a place called the General Education Centre. There were two clubs of which I became a member and later, an office bearer – the Great Book Club and the Literary Club. It was in those formative years that I discovered that I had a flair for writing. We even brought out a rag-magazine called *Verve*. It was, and still remains, very close to my heart.

While in the US, at Wright State University in Dayton, Ohio, I first dabbled a little with management courses, then with law courses. And then, one day, as if a light bulb had been switched on, I found my goal – I decided to be a journalist.

In 1989, I graduated *summa cum laude* and, in September that year, I decided it was time to head back home. My entire family had moved to Delhi by then and I looked forward to being with them. Almost all my friends had also finished their various degrees and had moved to Delhi. So, Delhi was the place to be: Delhi, the capital of India – the capital of modern India, I should add.

I was, therefore, pretty surprised and taken aback when almost all of them, family as well as friends, opposed the idea of my returning home. They told me that I was 'lucky' to have got to the US. Life there would be 'easy' and returning to India would be 'foolish'. Living here as a disabled person, especially as a wheelchair user, would be 'difficult'. My father added gravely that it would be 'suicidal' if I made the 'mistake' of returning home to India.

However, when you are that young (I was 24) you have your own ideas. I was not even convinced that there was a risk. I thought that they were all being too fussy and over-protective. Why would I have a problem? And so what if I was disabled? After all, I was a qualified journalist, with a fat American degree, and *summa cum laude* at that! I had visions of my own. Editors will queue up outside my house and the best publication would want to take me in. I certainly had my head in the clouds.

How utterly wrong I was! Months went by and I remained jobless. Forget the best publication; not even a city-based small-time magazine was willing to hire me as a paid employee. I went from office to office and met editor after editor. They all were suitably sympathetic. They all patted me on the back. They all told me how brave I was, how courageous I was. Some even complimented me on my *summa cum laude* and told me how intelligent I was! But ...

The word 'But' and the three dots that follow it summarise and explain not just my story but the story of just about every disabled Indian young man or woman. And not just Indians; I guess this is not simply the story of Asia or Asia-Pacific but just about the whole globe. America after the Americans with Disabilities Act (ADA) may perhaps be an exception but even then, I am not all that sure.

This is the story of prejudice and perception. This is the story of stereotyping millions and millions of young disabled people, of first giving them a label and then short-changing their lives.

Only a rights-based model of disability will lead to employment
Photo: Gideon Mendel/Leonard Cheshire Disability

The disabled and employment

The *Concise Oxford Dictionary* defines 'waged employment' as 'regular paid employment'. The objective of this chapter from my point of view is to be able to understand why disabled people don't find employment, as in a regular job, and also perhaps what can be done to change that situation.

Like most other countries and societies, India also adopted the 'Charity Model' vis-à-vis its disabled population. When India gained independence, some charities already existed. With the passage of time, a new term evolved – NGOs, which stands for non-governmental organisations. A whole lot of people – parents, families, friends, well-wishers, professionals, etc. – stepped in supposedly to fill a void: to care for India's disabled by feeding them and clothing them and, in certain cases, by teaching them vocational skills like cane-weaving, candle-making, and so on.

Some wise people thought of setting up special schools and, thus, blind schools, schools for the deaf and spastic societies were established. Segregation was firmly set in, by none other than those who claimed to love their disabled child, ward or friend. In saying this, my intention is not to insult these people but to question seriously their so-called 'vision' – their decision-making capacity.

291

The net result of this was that while India progressed, the lot of the disabled continued to suffer. They had no schools to go to. The setting up of these 'special' schools created a perception that disabled boys and girls could *only* go to these very special hell-holes created especially for them, and therefore, average/regular schools and their principals had every right to turn down the admission of disabled children. 'Oh, you are blind, please go to a blind school'; 'Oh, you are deaf, now please find yourself a deaf school', and so on. And where on the map of India were these very special schools? One could think ironically that the reason these so-called schools were so very special, was because there were so very few of them! Only the metropolitan cities and a few big towns had them. In fact, 99.99 per cent of India did not have any semblance of a school for its disabled children.

And because the mainstream, regular schools did not have to cater to disabled children, they thereby became unequipped for them. Even at the time of writing this chapter, in 21st-century India, 99.99 per cent of our schools are completely inaccessible for disabled children.

The organisation that I now work with, the National Centre for Promotion of Employment for Disabled People (NCPEDP), conducted an All-India Survey of universities and selected schools and colleges in 2003 with the following results.

- In schools as well as colleges, a mere 0.5 per cent of the student population comprised those with disabilities.

- At university level, only about 0.1 per cent of the students were found to be those with disabilities.

- Out of 319 schools that were surveyed, only 55 schools had any disabled students enrolled.

- Out of these 55 schools, there were only 19 that had students with visual impairments and none provided books in Braille.

- Also, 24 schools had students with hearing impairment and none of them had sign language interpreters.

- Out of the 55 schools, only 18 employed special educators and only 12 provided any kind of training to teachers for working with disabled students.

If disabled children cannot attend school, they cannot even begin to consider the question of going to a college or a university. And if they are not decently educated or skilled, how can they even consider the question of finding a job?

Access and attitudes

Aside from education, the other two major reasons why disabled people are not in waged employment are access and attitudes.

Here, I would like to proffer a theory of my own. Let us imagine a scenario whereby, after Independence, India opted for a development-based approach vis-à-vis its disabled people. Imagine that our parents and professionals and whoever else had formed a delegation and met Pandit Jawaharlal Nehru (India's first prime minister, and an extremely well-educated, polished, forward-looking, visionary gentleman and true leader), and had told him to direct his government to make the necessary arrangements to enable disabled children to study alongside their non-disabled counterparts in regular, mainstream schools. I wonder what his response would have been. But all we can do is lament that this didn't happen, and move on!

The damage that has been caused is irreversible. And the disability sector has no one else to blame for the situation today other than ourselves: we, the parents; we, the professionals; and we, the opportunists.

The damage is grave. An entire generation – perhaps even two generations – of people with disabilities were converted into an invisible minority. Since they could not study, they did not get jobs. Since they could not achieve economic independence, they did not even have a voice of their own. They were forever dependent and thus also formed a societal mindset. Disabled people were branded 'handicapped'.

Models of waged employment

When it comes to waged employment the world over, there are, broadly speaking, three popular models that have been experimented with.

1. *The Quota System:* The countries that adopt this system fix a particular percentage of jobs, say from 0.5 per cent to 10 per cent, that an employer has to give to disabled people – i.e. employers are obliged to hire that many disabled people. In some countries, this quota applies only to the public sector. In other countries, it applies to the private sector too.

2. *The Reward and Punishment System:* This is also called the 'Grant and Levy mechanism'. Here, a country fixes a quota that is compulsory for employers to follow. If they fulfil the quota, well and good. If not, a 'punishment tax' is levied on them and the money thus collected is then disbursed in the form of grants to the 'good' role-model companies to meet costs that they may have incurred in making their workplace accessible and disabled-friendly. Japan is a good example of this particular system.

3. *The Rewards Only System:* This is also known as the 'Incentives-based model'. Under this, a country fixes a huge target quota but this not mandatory. It is entirely up to the employer to try and achieve that targeted quota and, if it does so, the employer is rewarded in a fairly substantive way. China is a good example of this system, to the extent that they claim that 70 per cent of their disabled men and women are employed.

However, in all the above models, there is a certain patronage involved as all three arise from a certain charity-based outlook. Without doubt, each contains an element of sympathy, a sense of protectionism.

The USA is a rare exception. Their approach to employment is firmly rights-based. The state guarantees you non-discrimination and therefore, if you are qualified and/or skilled, you have to be treated on a par with the other non-disabled job seekers. And, if there is, God forbid, even a hint of any kind of discrimination, to the extent of a non-disabled job seeker being preferred over a disabled one, more often than not this leads to multi-million-dollar lawsuits. Employers, therefore, prefer to err on the side of caution to avoid being slapped with huge punishments and fines.

Lastly, there is the theory of 'positive discrimination' as well. I am not aware of any country having adopted this either as a law or as a policy but employers do practise this model and those employers can range from small companies to large corporations, as we will see in some case studies that follow.

Disability employment in India

As far as regular jobs are concerned, India hardly had a policy, let alone a law, until 1977 – three decades after the nation's independence! In any country's history, normally these first few decades are formative years. In our case, they were by and large wiped out.

Finally in 1977, the government came out with a policy that mandated a three per cent reservation in public sector jobs for those with disabilities. However, this was only in the 'C' and 'D' categories! In India, governmental jobs are classified as Class I, II, III and IV and also labelled as Category 'A', 'B', 'C' and 'D'. As is probably obvious, the reservation/quota applied only to the two lower categories. Indirectly, the government was saying that if you are disabled, you can be an office messenger (called a 'peon' in India) or, at best, a clerk. Don't dare dream of being an officer, not even a Grade B junior officer. And if the intentions were not in fact as stark as this then certainly the government's mind was being controlled and guided by the stereotypes of the time. A disabled person can do this, this and this and cannot do the rest: gross discrimination, indeed.

This policy should, in fact, have been rejected. Protests should have been held. But what happened was that there was not a whimper. The troika of parents, professionals and opportunists kept silent. Not much changed and yet the NGOs concerned with disability seemed content.

After all, their grants were flowing in. Vast tracts of land at prime locations in Delhi, Mumbai, Kolkata and Chennai were allocated to them. Large buildings were built. And some of them were even given India's highest civilian honours.

In the process, these people coolly forgot all about the disabled! The very people whom they were supposedly empowering were set aside; their voices were never heard. The troika operated on the premise that they had all the answers. An excellent example of this mindset is a prestigious and famous NGO building in the heart of Delhi. The entire complex is barrier-free, except the topmost floor, which is meant for the organisation's trustees and executives.

In 1998 NCPEDP published a Research Study, entitled *Role of NGOs vis-à-vis the Employment Scenario in India with reference to People with Disabilities*. The study was conducted on the top 150 NGOs operating in India. As many as 119 responded, and listed below are some key findings.

- The dismal role played by disabled people in the decision making of the respondent NGOs. Only 22.07 per cent of the Executive Body were disabled people. The administrative structure was dominated by 'non-disabled males'.

- Over a period of two years, only 1,377 disabled people were placed in jobs by the collective of the 119 top-notch respondent NGOs.

- Even these so-called 'placements' looked truly bogus when we learned that 90 per cent of the people placed earned below Rs 2000/- per month – which amounts at current rates to approximately £30 in the UK or about US$45–50.

- Only a handful of NGOs provided training in industry-related skills. The majority provided 'training' in skills like art and craft, making stationery items, etc.

Box 8.1 Case studies in disability employment

The Disability Act of 1995 was the first legislation on disability that India saw. It provides a three per cent reservation for people with disabilities – one per cent each for hearing impaired, visually impaired and orthopaedically impaired people in government jobs. Though reservation may seem to be against the very tenets of a rights-based approach towards disability, there is a strong feeling in India that without reservation, a level playing field cannot be achieved. Three people who gained employment through the reservation system speak about their experiences.

Anjali Arora is 36 years old, currently employed as a Law Officer with the Airports Authority of India. She holds a BA and LLB degree and is also pursuing an MBA. She is visually impaired.

She started her private practice as an Advocate in the Supreme Court of India. She did not do too well as potential clients focused more on her blindness and less on her capabilities as a brilliant lawyer. Later, she worked for some time with a human rights NGO.

Despite all her qualifications, Anjali found it difficult to find suitable employment. The reason, she cites, was because of discriminatory employment practices.

Although not a great champion of the three per cent quota for people with disabilities in government jobs, she feels that reservation did help her find a decent job. 'There is tremendous resistance towards hiring people with disabilities. Therefore, I feel that quota is necessary as it provides some protection for educated, qualified and talented disabled people.'

Another advocate of the three per cent reservation for disabled people in government jobs is Raja Mahendra Pratap. He is 35 years old and a quadriplegic (double amputation of upper and lower limbs) and is currently employed with Oil and Natural Gas

Corporation (ONGC). His experience with finding employment in the private sector was very humiliating.

'During my campus placements, I was called for an interview by a company. A day or two days before interview, the recruiter saw me. My name was deleted from the list of candidates called for interviews when the recruiter saw my physical condition though she was well aware that my disability will not affect my work at the job that I had applied for. Thus, I was rejected by the company even before the interview', he says.

'And in other interviews, none of them lasted for more than five minutes as the recruiters formed opinion within that time that I will be not be able to deliver goods just because I do not have hands and legs. They were assessing my suitability to the job from the prism of my physical disability but not my functional ability. This reflects their stereotypical mindsets', he feels.

It should be mentioned here that in spite of the severe nature of Raja's disability, he is fully self-reliant in every way.

It took Raja three years after he had finished his studies to find a job. According to him, quotas are necessary for disabled people to find suitable employment as the mindsets of India employers are yet to change.

The downside to reservation, Raja feels, is that unlike in other reserved categories (based on caste or tribe, etc.), disability is visible. So while other reserved category candidates may remain anonymous, people perceive that a disabled person obtained the job only because of the quota system, even if he or she got it purely on merit.

Raja is more than happy to be working in a government job, unlike the current trend of vying for private sector employment.

'Pay is not the only criterion while opting for a job', he says. 'And I did try for a job in the private sector but no private sector company will be comfortable employing a disabled person, especially a severely disabled person like me who at first sight appears to be dependent even for daily chores.'

Because of his inability to secure a job in the private sector, Raja had to think of a job in the government sector and quota helped him in that.

'I am fortunate to secure a job in India's No.1 Public Sector Undertaking finally', he sums up.

Sreetha Narayanan, 38 years old, is a hearing and speech impaired person. She works as a Junior Attendant in the National Thermal Power Corporation (NTPC). She had earlier worked in a private firm but was unhappy with her job. She noticed that her employer found it difficult to trust her with work as communication seemed to be a problem. There was also no job security. Once she quit her job in the private firm, she had to wait for nine years before she finally got into NTPC.

She feels that had it not been for the three per cent quota, she would not have been able to get the job. Moreover, she highly appreciates the practice at NTPC of dividing the one per cent reservation meant for deaf people equally among hearing and speech impaired people and hearing impaired people. Sreetha feels that this practice should be adopted by all government organisations as otherwise the one per cent meant for deaf people is simply filled up by hearing impaired people who can speak. This is a covert way of ensuring that only mild to moderately disabled people are employed under the quota system. One major disadvantage she finds with the quota system is that, even if a disabled candidate is eligible to be considered in the general merit list, he or she will be put under the reserved category.

However, she strongly feels that had the reservation system not been there in India, disabled candidates would not have had the opportunity to compete on a platform suitable to their abilities.

As you may have realised by now, there was a wide gulf between India's so-called disability sector (read NGOs) and India's 70 million disabled people.

The injustice meted out in 1977 was to remain unchallenged for another two decades. It was not until 1996 that the situation was rectified with the enactment of India's first law on disability, The Disability Act – on which I will elaborate further later.

The empowerment of disabled people in India

In December of 1991 India witnessed a huge tragedy. Former Prime Minister Rajiv Gandhi was assassinated. In order to celebrate his life and achievements, his family and friends set up the Rajiv Gandhi Foundation (RGF). It was decided that the organisation would focus its energy and resources on five core areas of work and the empowerment of disabled people was one such core area.

In April 1992 I took over as the Programme Officer in charge of RGF's Disability Unit. I must admit that even though I accepted the job offer, I did so with extreme hesitation, for two reasons. First, my passion for journalism: I had worked so hard for it and it wasn't easy to just abandon it. However, I was able to overcome this hesitation by one simple piece of logic. One fewer journalist would not harm or impact the world of Indian journalism, whereas one more person joining the disability sector might add to its strength.

My second problem was that I didn't actually know much about disability except, of course, my own. I had barely any knowledge of issues con-cerning blind or hearing impaired people. I most certainly had not even heard of words like autism, haemophilia or even cerebral palsy. I was seriously worried that I would fail, but the offer was far too tempting. By a sheer quirk of fate, I had been offered India's biggest disability platform. I had the conviction that if I made good use of the opportunity, I could bring about a change and therefore I decided to quit journalism and join the world of disability affairs.

Almost immediately after joining RGF in 1992, I was able to identify two huge voids plaguing the disabled community – one, the absence of any law guaranteeing them their basic rights; and two, the lack of unity among disabled people. 'Cross-disability' was a term with which India was not even familiar.

Thanks to RGF's platform, I was able to travel all over the country. And while this did give me the chance to see all the crooks up close, I did also meet some very committed people. Several of them were here in Delhi itself. We decided to network and thus formed the Disabled Rights Group (DRG), India's first cross-disability advocacy group. We also then began aggressive lobbying for the drafting and passage of a law to protect the rights of people with disabilities.

DRG was formed in 1993. By early 1994, we had catalysed the drafting of India's first law on disability. In 1995, the draft was made public and was widely debated. As if by a miracle, the law entitled 'The Persons with Disabilities (Equal Opportunities, Protection of Rights and Full Participation) Act, 1995' was passed by both the Houses of Parliament in a single day that December. I was in the Visitors' Gallery of the Upper House observing the proceedings and could hardly contain my tears.

The law was ground breaking for at least two reasons. First and foremost, the three per cent reservation in government jobs was extended to the 'A' and 'B' categories as well. Disabled people in India could now aspire to become officers! This was a huge paradigm shift. More than anything else, this reflected the nation's new mindset – its changing mood. India was no longer condemning disabled people to be merely peons and clerks. India was saying that if you have it in you then, yes, you can be an officer as well.

The second good thing that happened, thanks to this law, was that there also started to be a focus on the private sector. Even though India's lawmakers did not slap the quota on the corporate world they did put in Section 41, which promised 'incentives' to those companies who ensured that five per cent or more of their workforce comprised people with disabilities.

I am firmly of the view that any kind of a textbook discussion or a conference/seminar debate on the issue of employment, particularly waged employment, is meaningless without an adequate and sincere discourse on education and access. In that sense, India's 1995 law was also pretty comprehensive.

The stage was now set. The foundation had been laid. What was required now was for disabled people and their genuine well-wishers to ensure that the law was implemented – that it did not simply remain on paper.

While a lot of energy was focused on ensuring that the law was drafted and passed, equal, if not greater, attention was given to networking with disabled people and right-minded NGOs all over the country. The mantra was 'cross-disability'. A new culture was being created. A certain new identity was being shaped, that of us as 'disabled Indians'. The message was quite simple, and yet fairly stark: we are citizens too. This country belongs as much to us as it belongs to 'non-disabled' Indians!

Employment opportunities for disabled people

During 1995–6, another significant development happened: NCPEDP was born (this being, as mentioned earlier, the organisation for which I currently work).

By the mid-1990s, the winds of liberalisation were sweeping India. The Indian economy, which up until now had been based on a socialist model, was suddenly opened up to market forces. Foreign companies and multinationals of all shades and colours started queuing up. They were hugely attracted to India's vast pool of one billion consumers. As more and more companies entered India or were created, the private sector boomed. The resulting pressure saw to it that the public sector started shrinking.

These developments on the economic front, in turn, affected the employability of disabled people. As documented earlier, the three per cent quota applied only to government jobs and the public sector companies.

How much they heeded the quota and how many disabled people were actually given employment is a different matter altogether. The ugly truth had yet to be discovered.

The private sector was under no obligation whatsoever. No quota or reservation applied to them. No anti-discrimination law prevented them from grossly abusing their powers. There was little awareness and hardly any sensitivity.

It was at some time during 1995 that I was involved with founding a permanent organisation that would focus exclusively on employment opportunities for disabled people, especially in the corporate world. The NCPEDP was finally set up in 1996 and became operational on 1 July. Later that year, I took over as NCPEDP's new Executive Director.

India has two large Chambers of Commerce, the Confederation of Indian Industry (CII) and the Federation of Indian Chambers of Commerce and Industry (FICCI). One of the first things that I did after taking over as NCPEDP's Executive Director was to write to them and to seek an appointment with one of their officers.

My colleague who followed up on my two letters told me later on that when she contacted the concerned officers, at *both* places they thought that we were approaching them to seek a donation! Such was the state of affairs – so deeply rooted was the charity mindset.

What is sad, however, is that even after clarification was given that we were not seeking a donation but, instead, a dialogue on how to catalyse employment opportunities for disabled people, they still kept bouncing us off.

After sustained pressure over a few months, we did eventually meet the CII leadership. They proudly shared with us their Social Charter. In one glance, I could see that it mentioned just about all social causes – environment, HIV/AIDS, women's empowerment, child labour. However, there was no mention of disability and FICCI's Amit Mitra continued to avoid us.

By early 1999, we lost patience and decided to confront the industry. Not by way of rallies and demonstrations but by showing them a mirror. They had no clue what was going to hit them. Even they didn't know that the truth was so ugly.

Survey of top companies

In India, the financial year ends on 31 March. Soon thereafter all the business magazines publish some sort of a list of the top 100 companies. We narrowed down on a credible publication, *Business India*. We decided to send a short – a very, very short – questionnaire to their list of 'Super 100'. Our logic was: if you are one of the top 100 Indian companies, then let's see how aware and/or how sensitive you are to the 'cause' of employing people with disabilities. Such an effort had never been made in India before. The data about to be collected would be invaluable. It would also serve as a baseline.

Thanks to the hard work put in by my colleagues, we got as many as 70 responses. Now no one could question the veracity and the credibility of our data. Each response was signed, stamped and sealed by the concerned company. The results were as follows.

Total number of companies who responded to the questionnaire:	70
Public sector companies who responded: (Out of 23; response rate: 86.96%)	20
Private sector companies who responded: (Out of 63; response rate: 63.49%)	40
Multinational companies who responded: (Out of 14; response rate: 71.43%)	10

Total number of employees in the respondent companies:	796,363
Total number of employees with disabilities in the respondent companies:	3,160
Percentage of employees with disabilities in the respondent companies:	0.40%
Percentage of employees with disabilities in the public sector:	0.54%
Percentage of employees with disabilities in the private sector:	0.28%
Percentage of employees with disabilities in the multinationals:	0.05%

Findings

The results of our questionnaire clearly showed a rather dismal trend in terms of the current employment practices in the corporate sector with regard to people with disabilities. The government's apathetic attitude was amply reflected in the miniscule percentage of disabled employees even in the public sector organisations – who arguably have a larger workforce and for whom it is mandatory to have three per cent reservation for disabled persons. Other important findings included the following.

1. *Out of the 70 respondent companies, 20 companies did not employ any disabled person at all!* These include such big name companies as Castrol India Ltd with a workforce of 1,300; Colgate Palmolive (India) Ltd with a workforce of 1,300; EID Parry India Ltd with a workforce of

1,500; Eveready Industries India Ltd with a workforce of 4,700; and The Bombay Dyeing and Manufacturing Co. Ltd with a workforce of 10,000.

2. *The average percentage of employees with disabilities in the respondent companies was found to be a dismal 0.40 per cent.*

3. *Out of the 70 respondent companies, only 10 were found to have one per cent or above disabled employees.*

4. *In the majority of the respondent companies (40 out of 70), the percentage of the disabled workforce ranged between 0.01 per cent and 0.99 per cent.* Percentages sometimes do not reveal the entire truth. A close study of the table below will expose how sad the situation really is:

Company Name	Total Workforce	Disabled Employees	
		Number	Percentage
TISCO	60,205	6	0.01%
Hindustan Lever	40,000	4	0.01%
Indian Hotels Co.	13,000	2	0.01%
Mahindra & Mahindra	16,000	16	0.10%
Century Textiles & Industries	10,659	14	0.13%
Glaxo India	4,296	7	0.16%
Escorts	10,900	49	0.45%
Bajaj Auto	9,611	46	0.48%
Hero Honda Motors	3,055	17	0.56%
MRF	8,500	72	0.85%

5. It is disheartening to note that *there is no company among the Super 100 where even two per cent of the workforce comprises disabled persons.* In 1977 itself, the government fixed a quota of three per cent for disabled people in the public sector. The Disability Act 1995 guarantees incentives to both public and private sector employers, provided their workforce is composed of at least five per cent disabled people. Forget five per cent – even if our dream target is three per cent, we still have a long way to go!

This study and its results sent shockwaves everywhere. The media picked it up in a big way, including business newspapers, magazines and broadcasting channels. The Indian corporate sector was out there naked! It hurt them even more because it was the cream of the industry that was being exposed.

But somewhere, in between all this, even the government and the NGOs were red faced. India gained independence in 1947. This study was conducted in 1999, a full 50 years later. Was 0.4 per cent all that we had been able to achieve? It was a collective failure. As always, there was only one loser – the disabled person. Millions and millions of them remained jobless and, as a result, dependent.

Attacking the root causes of the problem

NCPEDP decided to confront this challenge head on and go down to the root cause of the issue. We decided that we cannot just look at the issue of 'employment'. We will also work passionately on the issues of 'access' and 'education'. We realised that in order to gain any genuine success in these three major areas, we needed to change laws and policies. So, 'legislation' became our fourth area of work. And finally, to facilitate work in all these four areas and catalyse it, we also needed to focus on 'awareness'.

With these five core areas defined, NCPEDP set out to work! And work, we did. Presented below is a summarised report of our work over the past ten years (1999–2009).

We identified all the concerned 'nodal' organisations (or 'apex' organisations as some refer to them): for example, the Central Board of Secondary Education (CBSE) to whom most of our schools are affiliated; the University Grants Commission (UGC) under whom all our 300+ universities fall; similarly, the Council of Architecture (CoA), the Indian Institute of Architects (IIA) and the National Institute of Design (NID). As far as employment per se is concerned, we were already engaging with CII and FICCI. However, for them we increased the flame of the burner a little bit: just enough to make them squirm, or at least not be able to ignore us any longer.

Under our 'awareness' domain, we decided to set up the Helen Keller Awards. The idea was to identify and honour those rare individuals and private sector companies who were already working towards ensuring equal opportunities for people with disabilities at their workplace – to bring them forward before society as role models. To say: 'Look, if they can do it, then why can't you?' To remove cobwebs from the minds of policy makers and decision makers as to what disabled people 'can do' or 'can't do'! Therefore, we also set out a category to acknowledge those disabled people who did not allow their disability to become a handicap and were therefore a role model for just about everyone.

Good practice in industry

Let me first give you the example of a few small employers who demonstrate good practice. Microsign Products employs 54 people, of whom 27 are disabled. Balloons, an export house that manufactures garments and home furnishings, employs 50 disabled people, including people with mild learning disabilities. Infar, a pharmaceutical company, employs 18 disabled people. Jyoti Limited, an engineering company, has 42 disabled people including blind people. Sakthi Masalas employs 103 disabled people including 8 people with mental disabilities.

Among larger companies, India's watch manufacturer Titan has a workforce of 169 disabled employees. Tata Tea has 320 disabled workers. The hotel industry opened its door, with ITC Hotel Windsor employing

Many Indian businesses now employ people with disabilities
Photos: Gideon Mendel/Leonard Cheshire Disability

10 disabled persons. The IT sector has also done very well, with corporations like Infosys and IBM India employing a large number of people with disabilities. One nominee that got an award was Reuters India, which truly overjoyed me. Reuters is a well-known global information company that runs the famous wire service as well as supplying news and articles to newspapers and magazines. In India, they now employ 45 disabled journalists!

Then there is Mphasis with 327; Pepsico India with 258; ITC Welcomgroup with 135; Vindhya E-Infomedia with 81; Godrej & Boyce with 60 disabled people, and so on.

Role models

I reserve the greatest admiration for 'role model' disabled people. My friend, Garimella Subramaniam, is totally blind but that didn't stop him from setting the London School of Economics ablaze! He is now a Senior Editor with *The Hindu*, one of the largest and most respected Indian newspapers.

A wheelchair user, 57-year-old Dr A.K. Banerjee is the Chairperson of the Recruitment Board at Shipbuilders and Engineers Ltd, and 51-year-old K. Ramakrishna, who is visually impaired, is General Manager with the Industrial Development Bank of India (IDBI). Atul Desai lost the use of both his legs due to polio at the age of two. He walks on crutches with great difficulty and heads three highly successful architectural firms that employ 35 non-disabled professionals! Another severely disabled man, Subhash Dhavale, had infantile paralysis at the age of four. Qualified as a Chartered Accountant, he obtained degrees in Law and Management and went on to become the Chief Operating Officer of ICICI Securities and Finance Company. Visually impaired Harish Kotian is Manager in the Department of Information Technology in the Reserve Bank of India, while visually impaired Nafisa Buhariwalla is Senior Manager, Human Resources Department, of the Central Bank of India.

I guess I could go on and on. With each example, my heart swells with pride.

The Corporate Code on Disability

The CII, mentioned earlier, is India's largest business chamber, with over 7,500 member companies. In 2006, they finally unveiled their 'Corporate Code on Disability'. It was a remarkable development and clear paradigm shift. The Code is reproduced below.

Box 8.2 CII – Corporate Code on Disability

It is being increasingly realised that people with disabilities can make [a] valuable contribution to businesses and to the national economy. Studies have shown that disabled people are capable, reliable employees, who often stay in the job longer than other employees. They contribute to productivity, to staff morale and to team spirit in the workplace as a whole.

Having a policy on disability in the workplace will enable companies to be recognised as companies with social commitment. In line with this, we list here a set of standards for voluntary adoption. This is intended to assist employers in developing such a policy.

1. The company may have a formal disability policy to ensure equal opportunities by offering employment for people with disabilities at par with others on the basis of their skills and ability to perform the job. The disabilities may be defined as per the Persons with Disabilities (Equal Opportunities, Protection of Rights & Full Participation) Act, 1995.

2. The company may work with relevant employment services in matching jobseekers with disabilities to jobs suited to their ability, work capacity and interest.

–   The company may state in their job advertisements that they are 'Equal Opportunity Employers' to encourage disabled people to apply for jobs.

3. The company will not discriminate against people with disabilities and endeavour to provide equal opportunities for promotion, transfer, career development and training, and proactively encourage them to fulfil their potential.

–   The company will encourage all disabled employees to discuss specific needs with their supervisors, or members of the HR team.

4. The company will provide access, if not already there and make appropriate adjustments to the workplace and/or employment arrangements in order to enable people with disabilities as required in the fulfilment of their roles.

–   The company will provide a working environment in which all of its employees are treated with dignity and respect.

5. Every reasonable effort will be made to enable employees who become disabled while employed, by providing them alternative suitable employment within the organisation.

6. The company will raise awareness of its employees on the range of issues that affect people with disabilities.

7. The company will train and educate managers on the meaning of disabilities, the company's policy and their responsibility to ensure enforcement.

8. The company will act as advocates for the promotion of employment opportunities for disabled persons.

9. The company may also sub-contract/outsource activities to disabled people/groups.

In February 2008, the government of India reciprocated by unveiling a ground-breaking Incentives Policy with an outlay of Rs18,000 million over a five-year period (2007–12); India's XIth Five Year Plan. That's a lot of money even in US dollars – it works out to roughly US$360 million!

The government's circular stated, 'To promote employment of persons with disabilities in the expanding private sector, it has been decided that incentives be provided to the private sector.'

It is hoped that this scheme will catalyse the creation of at least 100,000 jobs per annum – a tall order, indeed. However, even if 50 per cent of that was to be achieved, a very significant number of disabled people would benefit.

Government jobs and the law

As far as jobs in the government itself are concerned, the disabled people of India have the backing of the law. They have become aware of their rights and are now demanding them and, where needed, fighting for them. From simple advocacy to public demonstrations and hunger strikes, to thousands and thousands of court cases, it is all happening here in the world's largest democracy. The language of charity and pity is slowly being erased and the 70 million disabled people of India are now talking a different language – that of rights and equal opportunities. To understand this transformation, especially in the government, a little better, I will tell you one last story – that of India's première Civil Service.

Box 8.3 Civil Service case study

Our Disability Act was passed by Parliament in December of 1995. It was enacted on 7 February, 1996. It firmly mandated three per cent reservation in all government jobs and obviously that applied to our Civil Services too. But our mighty babus (the Indian word for bureaucrats) were prejudiced and caught in the cobwebs of the 'glorious' past. You will remember that from 1977 to 1996 the mindset was that disabled people could only be peons and clerks; that they could be recruited in only 'C' category and 'D' category posts and that they could not even apply for the jobs under the so-called 'A' and 'B' categories! And then, of course, the law was passed and things changed. Parliament mandated that disabled people could aspire to and apply for the higher category jobs also.

But here, we are not discussing laws and policies and guide-lines. We are discussing mindsets! And these are the most difficult to change.

For a full five years, the Indian bureaucracy ensured that not one single disabled person could get into any of India's 20-plus élite Civil Services. From 1996 to 2000, not one disabled young man or woman was recruited.

In the end, it was hard-headed advocacy, bordering on activism, coupled with a few court cases that finally pushed the doors open. In 2001, against a quota of 12, only 7 disabled people were taken in. During this period I realised that the term 'red tape' uses that colour because it is ruthless and brutal.

They said that while disabled people can be taken into the Civil Services, they would be eligible for only some Civil Services and not for the other top class ones like the Administrative Service or the Foreign Service. The seven disabled young men and women who qualified in 2001 were relegated to lesser services like the Information Service or the Accounts Service!

Round two of our battle started. I was determined to turn the red-coloured tape into a yellow and blue one. Our Civil Services had to open up. They had to become disabled-friendly, truly disabled-friendly. Round two lasted another three years (2001–4). In fact, our babus became so annoyed by our 'thankless' attitude that they decided to retaliate. As against seven disabled people in 2001, in the next year only three disabled people were taken in. In 2003 and 2004 only four were recruited each year, against a mandated quota of 12 per annum.

It was only in 2005 that we were able to win Round two as well. That year, the full quota of 12 was taken in. It was on that one day in 2005 that I wished I could wheelchair dance!

But wait, the story gets better. In 2006, strictures were passed against the Indian bureaucracy. They were directed by the political masters to ensure that not only was the quota to be fulfilled faithfully each year, but that the backlog, too, was to be cleared. As a result, in 2006, as many as 18 disabled people were recruited against that year's quota of 14. Similarly, in 2007, an exceptional number of 22 disabled people were taken in against that year's quota of 19.

One could say now, with some amount of reasonable satisfaction, that the 'red' tape finally turned yellow and blue.

The results of 2008 are still awaited. However, as of 2007, India has had the privilege of having 70 disabled Civil Servants and, as far as I am concerned, that's phenomenal. In this particular case study, it is not a question of 70 disabled people having obtained jobs. This is the story of the creation of a disabled community who will be our nation's top policy makers and decision makers in some years from now. Also, as the backlog is dealt with and more recruitments take place, this community of disabled bureaucrats will soon be a few hundred people. Thus, imagine India another 10 or 15 years from now!

Concluding comments

So, I have tried to tell you my story and that of my country. I believe that, by and large, the issues are the same across the world: disability, prejudice, stereotypes, self-created barriers, insensitivity, poor leadership, lack of unity among disabled people themselves, and so on. If the issues are the same, then I guess the remedies will also be similar. We have to adopt a rights-based approach and then stick to it. We have to question the basics. The status quo has to be changed.

Social protection can be a safeguard against poverty
Photo: Jenny Matthews/Leonard Cheshire Disability

Chapter 9

Social Protection and Disability

Daniel Mont

Summary

This chapter asks whether people with disabilities are afforded the same protection against poverty as non-disabled people. Starting with a discussion of the concept of social protection, the author outlines different kinds of social protection measures. He goes on to discuss when and how social protection measures should specifically target people with disabilities, and then in the next section discusses how general social protection programmes can be made more inclusive. As an example, he discusses how disability can be incorporated into conditional cash-transfer programmes. The chapter concludes with a set of policy recommendations.[1]

What is social protection?

Social protection programmes serve as a last line of defence against poverty. They consist of a variety of measures that attempt to bolster consumption, as well as safeguard and augment people's ability to generate livelihoods and deal with risk. These measures include targeted income support, insurance programmes, fee waivers, employment programmes, pensions, general subsidies and unemployment benefits (Grosh *et al.*, 2008).

In the past, social protection programmes – particularly safety nets – were seen solely as a way of catching people who fall into poverty and providing them with basic necessities. Recently this conception has broadened. Nowadays these programmes are viewed as mechanisms that allow households to manage risk – that is, to take chances on adopting new farming methods or establishing new enterprises, and when governments adopt economic policies that may pose transitory hardships (Grosh *et al.*, 2008). Higher returns are often associated with risk, so the lack of an insurance policy can keep people mired in activities with lower rates of return.

Social protection programmes encompass a fairly broad set of measures. Some of the key distinctions are discussed below.

Cash versus in-kind benefits

Benefits can be provided in the form of cash, or through payments in kind. Cash transfers are generally taken to be more efficient at combating poverty because they carry lower administrative costs and provide the most flexible benefits for recipients. In other words, individuals can spend that cash on exactly what they consider to be their most important needs. Nevertheless, sometimes in-kind benefits are more popular politically, because they are seen as limiting the possibility for recipients to abuse the programme by directing resources to items generally agreed upon as necessities, such as energy or housing. Also, at times in-kind programmes can use surplus goods – often food – or extra capacity, such as by distributing bus passes on public transportation.

Conditional cash transfer (CCT) programmes are a relatively recent innovation in social assistance programmes. They do not directly affect consumption patterns, as in-kind benefits do, but rather they create incentives for productive activities. Receiving cash benefits is conditional on activities such as children's school attendance or participation in nutrition or health programmes. In this way, CCTs are designed to address short-term poverty while at the same time putting conditions on the receipt of transfers that encourage longer-term investments in human capital. These conditions are designed in the hope of reducing poverty in the future.

Contributory versus non-contributory

Cash benefits fall into two categories: contributory and non-contributory. The former works as an insurance scheme. Workers pay an insurance premium and when they are no longer able to work – usually because of old age or disability – they receive benefits. While the benefit structure for participants is at times progressive, overall the programme does not tend to benefit the poorest of the poor because they are not in a position to take part in it, such as those in informal labour markets. Many developing countries have contributory schemes, but they are not available to most people (Grushka and Demarco, 2003).

Non-contributory programmes are typically means-tested in OECD countries and Eastern Europe, but in other countries they may not be targeted at poverty. Moreover, when they *are* targeted it is generally by using proxy means tests or community-based targeting. Generally speaking, they aim to serve the poorest of the poor. Non-contributory programmes can either be categorical – aimed at people with disabilities, single mothers, or widows – or they can be universal, with eligibility limited solely to income or consumption levels.

Social protection can include the provision of employment
Photo: China Disabled Person's Federation/Leonard Cheshire Disability

Income generation

Another option for social protection programmes is the direct provision of public employment. This directly counteracts the work disincentive of other kinds of programmes and creates a way in which poor people can obtain work experience and contribute to the economy, particularly when there is a shortage of jobs in the private sector. Also included in this category are programmes such as job training, job placement and microcredit programmes.

Increased access to services

Some social protection programmes lower the cost of accessing services like healthcare, education or energy. This can be done through general subsidies or fee waivers. In some countries there is a movement to make some services, such as education, free and universal. In a sense, this is also a social protection idea.

Individual versus community-based eligibility

Eligibility for inclusion in social protection is at times determined at an individual level, either through direct means testing or proxy means testing, which is a mechanism for identifying people based on their observed characteristics (e.g. their assets such as the type of home, water supply, and toilets). In other instances, eligibility is determined at the community level so that all members of a community in a high poverty area are automatically eligible.

Are people with disabilities being served by social protection programmes?

Although approximately 10–12 per cent of the world's population has a disability, little is known about how well social protection programmes serve their needs (Marriott and Gooding, 2007; Mitra, 2005; Mont, 2007). We do not know to what extent barriers in design or implementation are keeping people with disabilities from receiving mainstream social protection benefits. Similarly, we do not know whether benefits designed specifically for people with disabilities are reaching the right people or providing them with the necessary support. Not enough research has been done to provide this information.

The recent broadening of the purpose of social protection programmes makes the inclusion of people with disabilities even more essential. If people with disabilities are excluded from mainstream social protection policies they are not only being deprived of current resources but their long-term ability to raise themselves out of poverty is also undermined. When designing social protection programmes aimed specifically at people with disabilities, the second purpose of social protection policies – i.e., managing risk – must be kept in mind. Too often, programmes targeted at people with disabilities can create work disincentives that act against their capacity to achieve an independent means of generating a livelihood.

At times, disability advocates have been reluctant to discuss social protection for fear that disability policy will be relegated only to those issues. If policy makers approach disability with the model of charity in mind, it hampers any further discussion of inclusive development. This should be avoided, as the UN Convention on the Rights of Persons with Disabilities explains, since all aspects of economic development must incorporate the right of people with disabilities to be fully included in every area of life – from developing their human capital and generating a livelihood, to participating in civic and family life.

Nevertheless, poverty is widespread, and due to their over-representation among the poor, people with disabilities should already be served by existing cash-transfer programmes in countries where they are available (Braithwaite and Mont, 2008; Yeo and Moore, 2003). Existing operational barriers can make it hard, if not impossible, for people with disabilities to access these programmes. Unfortunately, because data on disability status are often not collected, it is difficult to know how well people with disabilities are served compared with non-disabled people of similar economic means. When programmes make a particular effort to reach out to the entire population, we find that a high number of families with a member with disabilities are helped by safety nets. For example, a recent study found that participants in Chile's Solidario programme were twice as likely as non-participants to have at least one family member with a disability (Galasso, 2006). In fact, over 25 per cent of the households of these participants had such a member.

People with disabilities are technically eligible for many existing social protection programmes. The question is, whether they are in fact being served adequately. Are they sometimes excluded? Are their needs being met? And when do people with disabilities require targeted programmes that address particular needs that are not incorporated into general social assistance programmes? The issues involved with inclusive social protection policies are complex, and yet data, policy evaluations and innovative approaches are scarce. This chapter aims to lay out the various options and challenges in incorporating the needs of people with disabilities. It ends with a brief list of policy recommendations.

When and how social protection programmes should specifically target people with disabilities

Starting in the 1990s, there was a policy shift from universal benefits to highly targeted transfers, especially in middle-income or upper-income countries (Mitra, 2005, p. 14).

A fundamental question in designing social protection programmes is, when should they specifically target people with disabilities? The usual answer is when the presence of a disability precludes or at least significantly limits the possibility of working. If a person with a disability is truly incapable of working under any realistic set of circumstances, then they need direct transfers to alleviate their poverty. A disabled person's inability to work, however, often results from barriers to obtaining human capital and then accessing the job market. Therefore, targeting disability benefits could also include vocational and medical rehabilitation, supportive devices like wheelchairs or supported employment. A comprehensive strategy could provide those services, supplemented by cash or in-kind benefits until the person can secure employment.

Table 9.1: Selected Countries with Social Assistance Programs for Persons with Disabilities

Country	Disability Test	Means Test	Benefits
Africa			
Liberia	Inability to work	Yes	N/A
Mauritius	N/A	Yes	N/A
South Africa	Inability to work	Yes	Flat rate
Asia			
Azerbaijan	N/A	Yes	Three flat rates
Georgia	N/A	Yes	Flat rate
Kyrgyzstan	Ability to work, attendance needed and mobility	No	Flat rate (% of minimum wage)
Turkmenistan	Ability to work and attendance needed	Yes	Flat rates (full and partial disability)
Latin America			
Argentina	N/A	Yes	Flat rate
Brazil	Unable to work or unable to live independently	Yes	Flat rate
Costa Rica	N/A	Yes	Flat rate
Dominican Republic	N/A	Yes	Flat rate (% of minimum wage)
Trinidad and Tobago	Age 40 or older if certified as blind and needy	Yes	Flat rate

Source: Mitra, 2005

The most comprehensive approach would make the environment as inclusive as possible – physically, culturally, legally and so on – in order to eliminate the barriers preventing people with disabilities from escaping poverty. Such an inclusive approach to development should be a top priority, but until it has been achieved it is the role of social protection programmes to offer assistance by providing a minimum standard of living and supporting livelihood generation. Even then, there will always be some people whose functioning is so limited that work is impossible (such as, at the extreme, someone who is comatose).

Eligibility

The biggest challenge in crafting disability benefit programmes lies in defining eligibility. The social model of disability states that disability is a societal, not an individual, concept – that is, disability emerges from the interaction between a person's functional status and barriers in the environment. However, a transfer programme is aimed at individuals. Eligibility requirements need to determine which individual characteristics merit inclusion in the programme. Therefore, eligibility criteria gravitate towards a medical, impairment-based approach. Typically these criteria are a combination of particular diagnoses along with some medical assessments aimed at determining functioning.

Mitra (2005) notes that even this approach can be challenging, since some impairments, such as back pain, are invisible, and others are episodic (such as mental illness). Complicating the procedure is the possibility of fraud. Most medical assessments (such as hearing tests) rely on maximal effort from the person being examined, and that person has a financial incentive to underperform.

Efforts have been made to move towards a social model of assessment, like the community assessment scheme in South Africa (Simchowitz, 2004). In that scheme a community panel made an overall determination of a person's ability to participate in the life of the community, taking into account the specific context of the community as well as what they knew of the person's functional status. Unfortunately, it was difficult to implement this procedure in a uniform, rigorous way, so it was viewed as very subjective and open to mistargeting and fraud. Without a medical baseline, it is extremely difficult to fend off fraud and implement eligibility criteria in a fair and uniform fashion. Zeitzer argues that a system should 'start with clearly articulated, objective medical standards to determine who is impaired, but then move on to a more social needs-based assessment to help the individual receive whatever s/he needs to be fully integrated into work and society' (Marriott and Gooding, 2007, p. 49).

For example, the Brazilian Programme for Cash Benefits to Disabled Persons and their Families bases eligibility on a list of impairments, but there are no clear criteria to evaluate the severity of the impairment. So, as often happens in programmes of this nature, the definition of disability varies by doctor. In fact, 45 per cent of medical officers associated with the programme consider the evaluation questionnaires to be less than efficient. Only six per cent approve of them (Medeiros *et al.*, 2006). In some countries – particularly in former Soviet countries – this discretion on the part of doctors has contributed to problems with fraud (Hoopengardner, 2001). This is where adoption of the integrated competency framework can be of use (Australian Institute of Health and Welfare, 2003).

The potential for poor targeting and fraud increases as the functioning threshold required for eligibility is set at lower levels of severity. It is often difficult make a rigorous determination of mild or even moderate disabilities, especially ones that are not clearly visible. Other disabilities, such as an inability to walk, are not difficult to assess.

Work disincentives

A broad body of literature demonstrates that providing cash benefits to people based on their disability status discourages work. Once recipients go on targeted disability cash-benefit programmes they rarely leave them. The outflow rate in most OECD countries – for example, Australia, Canada, Germany, Norway, Portugal, Sweden, and the USA – is generally about one per cent (OECD, 2003). This phenomenon is not particular to people with disabilities. Providing benefits for not working for any reason diminishes the relative returns from work and so discourages the desire to work.

One possible explanation regarding why so few people exit disability benefit programmes is that the eligibility criteria often stipulate that a person must have a disability that is severe enough to preclude returning to work, at least in the current environment. But another important factor is that the programmes have strong work disincentives built into them. The financial rewards for returning to work are simply not large enough. Finding employment could terminate a recipient's benefits, and call into question their disability status. This is especially true in a country like the USA, where health insurance is also provided to people who are eligible for the disability programme but is not guaranteed if they return to work (Mont, 2004).

Around the world, outflow rates are remarkably stable, even in response to programmatic changes and among countries with very different benefit levels. For example, in countries with the smallest outflow rates, the maximum replacement rate for lost earnings due to a disabling condition range from about 35 or 40 per cent in the USA (plus medical insurance) to about 70 per cent in Sweden (OECD, 2003). The unresponsiveness of outflow rates to policy parameters such as replacement rates is troubling and not well understood. Clearly, other barriers to employment dominate people's ability to leave disability programmes.

One possible explanation for the small outflow rates is the risk in taking on employment. If people with disabilities are uncertain about how successful they will be upon returning to work, they may opt to not jeopardise future benefits. Eligibility is based on an inability to work (or, in some countries with partial benefits, a reduced ability to work). This effect is stronger in developing countries where the general unemployment rate is high and where employers might be less willing to make accommodations. It is also stronger in countries with weak general safety net programmes.

Countries have experimented with a variety of reforms aimed at mitigating the risk of leaving a cash benefit programme for entry into the workforce. Some countries allow recipients to put their benefits on hold so that if their attempt to return to work fails, they can restart them without a new application procedure. This on-hold period can be brief – three months in Belgium – or quite extensive – up to three years in the Netherlands, Norway and Sweden. In Canada, benefits are not put on hold but there is a fast-track re-application procedure. Other countries have attempted to increase the financial remuneration for benefits recipients who return to work, by offering temporary wage supplements, tax abatements, or tax credits. The USA has a trial work period where cash benefits continue for at least nine months, after which there is an extended period of eligibility lasting three years. During that time former recipients can immediately start receiving benefits again if their earnings fall below the eligibility limit.

Few people take advantage of these programmes. The reasons for this are not entirely clear, but two hypotheses have been advanced. The first suggests that the problem may lie on the demand side of the equation – that is, either because of the stigma they feel and the discrimination they face, or because of the lack of proper support in the workplace; jobs in which people with disabilities can be successful are hard to come by. Some analysts also blame the effect that cash benefit programmes have on the psyche of people with disabilities. In order to qualify for benefits, they must make the case that they are not capable of working. To return to work, they must repudiate the case they have made. Without a major medical recovery, increased supports or a perceived improvement in the degree to which employers accommodate people with disabilities in the workplace, there is no reason for this self-perception to change.

Furthermore, when people with disabilities are out of the workforce their job skills and self-identification as workers can atrophy. This is especially true for programmes with a waiting period. In some countries, after qualifying on the basis of a disability, people must wait a period of time – without improving their work status – before receiving benefits. In the USA this period is five months (with an additional 24 months for health insurance). In Belgium, Italy and Switzerland the waiting period is a full year.

Even if a disabled person wants to substitute work for cash benefits, structural barriers such as inaccessible transportation and workplaces can impinge on their ability to do so. And in countries with no partial disability benefits, the choice between cash benefits and work can be an all or nothing decision.

How general social protection programmes can be made more inclusive

Even without programmes targeted at people with disabilities, another important issue exists. Simply by being poor, or falling in another targeted category (such as single motherhood), people with disabilities can qualify for social protection benefits. If the architects of mainstream social protection programmes ignore this fact, they undermine the effectiveness of their programmes and, in an important sense, are targeting people with disabilities for exclusion. To make general social protection programmes more inclusive, it is essential to confront barriers to participation.

Barriers

Mitra (2005) points out that people with disabilities face a number of barriers when trying to access mainstream social protection programmes. The first among these is a set of physical barriers. If a service or facility is inaccessible, people with a disability cannot obtain the benefits they deserve. Lack of accessibility could result from the physical structure of a facility itself, or the transportation network that people use to reach it. If benefits can be paid directly into bank accounts, that can lessen part of this problem, but only to the extent that the banks themselves are accessible. When benefits are given in kind, distribution difficulties are greater. One strategy is to allow for proxy recipients, but this introduces the possibility of people with disabilities being robbed of their benefits. It also takes power out of their hands.

Communication poses another barrier, particularly for people with sensory or mental disabilities who may not have access to information about benefit programmes. But this is also an issue for people with physical disabilities who, because of a lack of access to education, are more likely to be illiterate. Programme materials must take these into account in order not to create barriers to participation.

Finally, stigma, discrimination and lack of sensitivity or awareness on the part of programme personnel can impede the ability of a social protection programme to reach people with disabilities. Impatience with people with disabilities, treating them harshly, or even refusing to acknowledge their basic human rights, can all get in the way of effective service delivery.

These barriers create problems in all types of social protection programmes, but the greatest challenge occurs in public employment programmes. In many countries, workplaces are highly inaccessible and people with disabilities often have fewer skills because of their exclusion from education and training. Therefore, jobs created or offered to recipients of social protection are often not suitable for people with disabilities. However, if they were designed with the needs of people with disabilities in mind, public employment programmes could serve as a model to the private sector of how to accommodate people with disabilities in a way that allows them to attain their productive potential.

Benefit levels

The extra costs associated with disability are often neglected in examining social protection benefits for people with disabilities. People with disabilities often face higher costs for carrying out the same life activities as non-disabled people, such as special transportation needs, healthcare, supportive devices, personal assistance and housing requirements. If we are to measure poverty by a capability to maintain a minimum standard of living, then the poverty line for people with disabilities should be adjusted to address the additional costs they face (Braithwaite and Mont, 2008). Without taking into account the differences in costs of various activities (e.g. transportation and medical care), the poverty rates in the UK for people with disabilities and those without are respectively 23.1

An inaccessible school prevented full inclusion
Photo: Leonard Cheshire Disability

and 17.9 per cent.[2] Taking into account the added costs associated with disability – or as Amartya Sen calls it, 'conversion disability' (Sen, 2004) – the poverty rate for people with disabilities is 47.4 per cent (Kuklys, 2005; Sen, 2004).

If the goal of a social protection programme is to bring families up to a certain minimum level of well-being, the income eligibility thresholds and the size of the benefits distributed should take disability into account. The challenge of such an approach lies in administration. How can we operationally assess the poverty threshold of each individual family with a disabled member? And if people with disabilities were given a standard cash premium, would that create an incentive for fraud? Would a uniform cash premium for disability be reasonable, given the wide variance in the nature of disability and the types of support needed?

One way of both minimising fraud and offering the different levels of support needed would be to give in-kind benefits that directly increase the recipients' ability to participate in social and economic activities, rather than cash benefits. An example is supportive devices. These would not be particularly valued by non-disabled people and could be individually tailored to the needs of people with disabilities. The drawback to this

Creating access remains crucial even with cash transfers
Photo: Leonard Cheshire Disability

approach is that directly providing this kind of support would increase the administrative complexity of the programme. Furthermore, in-kind benefits are as a rule less flexible than cash, which is easily fungible and can be put to use more efficiently by families.

A better strategy may be to reimburse approved expenditures for people certified as having a disability. However this, too, has administrative issues as well as other limits. Money for a wheelchair, for example, does not go far in ensuring that children with a mobility disability can obtain an education if their school has no ramps, narrow doorways and inaccessible toilet facilities.

Incorporating disability into CCT programmes

CCT programmes are growing in popularity throughout the world, in part because they show evidence of success. Evaluations of early CCT programmes located in Latin America show increasing school enrolment, decreasing child labour and improved nutrition and immunisation rates. For example, after the establishment of the PROGRESA programme in Mexico, secondary school enrolment rates increased by about eight percentage points for girls and over four per cent for boys.

In Nicaragua the rate of preschool children's enrolment in a nutrition-monitoring programme was over 90 per cent, compared to about 66 per cent for control areas (Rawlings, 2004).

The question of how to benefit people with disabilities in a CCT programme remains. This issue has not yet been addressed. In theory, there are four different strategies that might work:

- treat people with disabilities exactly like non-disabled people under the current system

- exempt people with disabilities from the conditions associated with CCT programmes

- provide additional assistance to people with disabilities to help them comply with CCT requirements

- couple CCT programmes with policies to make service delivery more inclusive.

These options are discussed below.

Treat people with disabilities exactly like non-disabled people under the current system

This is the default approach in most CCT programmes, such as those in Mexico, Colombia and Ecuador. Since low expectations and stigma are often barriers to the participation of people with disabilities in society, CCT programmes could actually provide an incentive for participation that is particularly important for children with disabilities. However, because many people with disabilities have poor access to services, simply making their participation a requirement cannot be effective if they are currently unable to learn about government programmes, enrol, or comply with the conditions placed upon the receipt of benefits. It is therefore likely that this approach excludes some people with disabilities from the benefits provided by CCT programmes. The effect is likely to vary depending on the nature and severity of the disability. Lack of data prevents us from measuring the overall net effect and how these countervailing forces play out in different societies.

Exempt people with disabilities from the conditions associated with CCT programmes

The argument for this is that people with disabilities are not capable of fulfilling the conditions associated with the programme. Children with a disability may face barriers preventing them from attending school or accessing other services. In these cases, exempting people with disabilities would still ensure that their families receive poverty relief even if they were not able to fully comply with the conditions of the CCT programme.

This approach was taken in Jamaica's Programme of Advancement through Health and Education (PATH). Once certified by the National Council for Persons with Disabilities as being permanently disabled to an extent that prevents them from attending school, children do not need to enrol in school to receive benefits. To qualify they do not have to show they are unable to attend school, but they can be perceived as being unable to benefit from school. A deaf child, for example, who could physically attend school, could also be certified as exempt if it is thought he or she would not benefit from instruction in a school setting.

There are problems with this approach. Exempting a category of people from the conditions of a CCT programme goes against its basic philosophy that short-term poverty relief should be coupled with a long-term investment in human capital that mitigates against long-term poverty. Nevertheless, in the short run, if these children are truly unable to attend or benefit from school, this strategy does allow a poor child with a disability to receive benefits. On the other hand, it gives schools a dangerously easy way out of not addressing inclusiveness in the school system. Although the impact of this strategy on the overall inclusivity of the school system is likely to be very small, it still creates a tension between short-run poverty alleviation goals and the promotion of inclusive policies that may be better in the long run. If disabled children were losing benefits because of inaccessible schools, this could create political and moral pressure for reform. In the meanwhile, though, such a programme is not doing its best to achieve the immediate goal of poverty reduction.

The counter-argument, of course, is that making schools more inclusive imposes additional costs. Pressure to reform without the capacity to do so would only serve to deny benefits to poor families with disabled children. Making schools more inclusive, however, often does not involve a large financial outlay (Peters, 2003; Steinfeld, 2005) and can be done in stages. Therefore, this strategy should not be dismissed without a careful examination of what is possible in the local setting.

Provide additional assistance to people with disabilities to help them comply with CCT requirements

Many barriers to service delivery could be overcome with various forms of assistance, such as spectacles, wheelchairs and other supportive devices, sign language interpreters and personal assistants. CCT programmes could provide this assistance to eligible recipients. The downside to this approach is the complex administration of individualised assessment, in addition to the costs of the support recommended by such assessments. In fact, even the second option discussed here requires an administrative structure for disability determination that does not exist in many countries.

On the plus side, however, providing individual support can not only increase the long-term productivity of the disabled person but also the short-term productivity of family members who currently have to care for housebound relatives. In Nicaragua, a family member (generally a woman) spends about ten hours per day caring for relatives with significant disabilities (Braithwaite and Mont, 2008). Once again, though, data do not exist to make sound estimates of how much household labour would be freed up by accommodating children with disabilities, or at what cost.

Couple CCT programmes with policies to make service delivery more inclusive

A common concern with CCT programmes is that their long-term effectiveness is tied to the quality of the health and education services with which they are associated. A benefit of CCT programmes is that they can serve as a mechanism for coordinating services across sectors and as an impetus for improving services. A successful CCT programme is one that links social assistance with existing services that can provide value to recipients. Improving the inclusiveness of health and education systems will strengthen the effectiveness of a CCT programme. As the data from Chile suggest, disability is a common reality of people in these programmes, and available disability prevalence rates in Latin America and the Caribbean suggest this is not a unique situation.

However, it is interesting to note that Jamaica's PATH programme reports fewer recipients with disabilities than projected. According to PATH's estimates, they should be serving about 19,000 people with disabilities. They were only serving 5,000 in 2008 due to the fact that people with disabilities did not join the programme despite intensive promotion efforts. The reasons for this under-representation are unclear, and PATH initiated a study to examine this issue. One possibility is that barriers are preventing people with disabilities from participating in the programme. Another, put forward by programme administrators, is that people with disabilities may be being cared for by their extended family, who are, in essence, providing familial transfers that make the potential recipients ineligible.

In the end, the most efficient way of integrating disability into CCT programmes is the development of cost-effective means of minimising the number of people with disabilities who are not capable of accessing the education and health services as they currently operate. Lessons from inclusive education programmes already under way in countries like Brazil, Panama and Uruguay can be used to leverage the impact of CCT programmes. Inclusiveness does not happen overnight. Often it is a graduated process that emerges in stages – both across different types of disabilities and across different school districts in a country.

In fact, most disabilities among school-aged children are learning disabilities. They are often associated with retention and promotion problems in school but are not as apparent as blindness, deafness, mobility limitations or significant intellectual disabilities. Moreover, many non-disabled children also have similar issues with their learning styles. Thus, inclusive education methods can have a broader impact than the disability prevalence rate would suggest (Peters, 2003).

The acceptance of inclusion as an important element of economic development can vary significantly from one country to another. Only recently has the development community begun searching for best practices. Therefore, while building inclusive services may be the long-term goal, the short-term approach of providing additional assistance to families with disabled members or even exemption of programme conditions for severely disabled people may be in order.

Recommendations

The most important recommendation is that all social protection programmes should be designed inclusively. Everyone – regardless of their disability status, gender, ethnicity, or any other characteristic – should be able to live free of poverty. Since social protection programmes are the final defence against poverty, they should aim to protect everyone.

Doing this effectively requires information. How many people have disabilities? What types of disability do they have? What is the relationship of disability to poverty? What socio-demographic and economic characteristics are associated with disability? What barriers in the community prevent people with disabilities from earning a decent living? What flaws in the design of current social protection programmes are undermining their effectiveness? Without the answers to these questions it will be very difficult to design, implement and monitor effective social protection programmes. Therefore, it is important to include disability and related issues in quantitative and qualitative studies of poverty and social protection.

Other recommendations include the following.

- Promote inclusive development generally. This will diminish the over-representation of people with disabilities in social protection programmes, and at the same time will make those programmes – for example, public employment or CCT programmes – more effective for people with disabilities.

- Address all types of barriers that people with disabilities face in accessing social protection programmes. These include physical, communication-based and social barriers. Examine each component of a social protection programme and identify the barriers that prevent access.

- Include people with disabilities in programme design and oversight. No one understands the barriers they face better than themselves, and no one is more used to devising creative solutions for getting around such barriers.

- Create programmes targeted at people with disabilities only when there are identifiable specific needs. The provision of supportive devices, supported employment, medical rehabilitation and other services can be specific to people with disabilities. In some situations, people with disabilities may face huge barriers to work and may then require special programmes.

- Do not assume that people with disabilities cannot work. Programmes should be designed with support for entering the workforce. Benefits should be structured in a way that creates a bridge to work. Social protection programmes should not contribute to social exclusion.

- Benefit levels should incorporate the extra costs of disability. People with disabilities require more resources to achieve the same standard of living. Social protection programmes should address this.

Acknowledgements

The author would like to thank Jeanine Braithwaite and Margaret Grosh for their comments on an earlier draft of this chapter.

Notes

1. The findings, interpretations, and conclusions expressed here are those of the author, and do not necessarily reflect the views of

the International Bank of Reconstruction and Development, the World Bank and its affiliated organisations, or the executive directors of the World Bank or the governments they represent.

2. Poverty is defined here as 60 per cent of the national median income.

References

Australian Institute of Health and Welfare 2003. *ICF Australian User Guide. Version 1.0. Disability Series. AIHW Cat. No. DIS 33.* Canberra: AIHW.

Braithwaite, J. and Mont, D. 2008. *Disability and Poverty: a Survey of World Bank Poverty Assessments and Implications. SP Discussion Paper No. 0805.* Washington, DC: World Bank.

Galasso, E. 2006. *With Their Effort and One Opportunity: Alleviating Extreme Poverty in Chile. Working paper, Development Research Group.* Washington, DC: World Bank.

Grosh, M., del Ninno, C., Tesliuc, E. and Ouerghi, A., 2008. *For Protection and Promotion: the Design and Implementation of Effective Safety Nets.* Washington DC: World Bank.

Grushka, C.O. and Demarco, G. 2003. *Disability Pensions and Social Security Reform Analysis of the Latin American Experience. World Bank Social Protection Discussion Paper Series No. 0325.* Washington, DC: World Bank.

Hoopengardner, T. 2001. *Disability and Work in Poland. SP Discussion Paper No. 0101.* Washington, DC: World Bank.

Kuklys, W. 2005. *Amartya Sen's Capability Approach: Theoretical Insights and Empirical Applications. Studies in Choice and Welfare.* Berlin, Heidelberg, New York: Springer-Verlag.

Marriott, A. and Gooding, K. 2007. *Social Assistance and Disability in Developing Countries.* Haywards Heath, UK: Sightsavers International.

Medeiros, M., Diniz, D. and Squinca, F. 2006. *Cash Benefits to Disabled Persons and Their Families: an Analysis of the BPC–Continuous Cash Benefit Programme. Working Paper No. 16. International Poverty Centre.* Brazilia: UNDP.

Mitra, S. 2005. *Disability and Social Safety Nets in Developing Countries. SP Discussion Paper No. 0509.* Washington, DC: World Bank.

Mont, D. 2004. *Disability Employment Policy. SP Discussion Paper No. 0413.* Washington, DC: World Bank.

Mont, D. 2007. *Measuring Disability Prevalence. SP Discussion Paper No. 0706.* Washington, DC: World Bank.

OECD 2003. *Transforming Disability into Ability: Policies to Promote Work and Income Security for Disabled People,* Chapter 4. Paris: OECD.

Peters, S.J. 2003. *Inclusive Education: Achieving Education for All by Including Those with Disabilities and Special Education Needs.* Washington, DC: World Bank.

Rawlings, L.B. 2004. *A New Approach to Social Assistance: Latin America's Experience with Conditional Cash Transfer Programmes. SP Discussion Paper No. 0416.* Washington, DC: World Bank.

Sen, A. 2004. *Disability and Justice.* A speech delivered at the World Bank's Second International Conference on Disability, 30 November–1 December. Washington, DC: World Bank.

Simchowitz, B. 2004. *Social Security and HIV/AIDS: Assessing 'Disability' in the Context of ARV Treatment. CSSR Working Paper No. 99.* Cape Town: Centre for Social Science Research, University of Cape Town.

Steinfeld, E. 2005. *Education for All: the Cost of Accessibility. Education Note.* Washington, DC: World Bank.

Yeo, R. and Moore, K. 2003. Including disabled people in poverty reduction work: 'Nothing about us without us'. *World Development,* 31(3), 571–90.

Disabled children in Sierra Leone are among the poorest
Photo: Jenny Matthews/Leonard Cheshire Disability

Chapter 10

Disability and Poverty in Post-conflict Countries

Maria Kett

Summary

There is an ever-expanding literature on the *causes* of conflict – of which poverty, and its resulting inequalities, are seen to be primary factors (Stewart, 2002; Collier *et al.*, 2003; Goodhand, 2003; Cramer, 2003). There is also a growing awareness that poor environments – and poor people – are disproportionately affected by such disasters and emergencies. Furthermore, research now indicates that poverty alone is not the only factor in determining how people fare in times of conflict.

Whereas some people may not be any worse off than others from a monetary point of view, they may be more vulnerable due to additional variables such as illness, unemployment or crop failure – in part because of the lack of protective measures to withstand economic, shocks and social disruptions. There has been considerable debate about the 'conflict trap', in which countries become mired in a cycle of conflict and poverty (Collier *et al.*, 2003). Paul Collier, an economist who has dedicated much of his work to the effects of conflict on development, has noted that despite a global trend in economic growth and development, the gap between the 'bottom billion' and the rest of the developing world is increasing – in large part because of civil conflicts – and it is on this section of the world that global poverty eradication efforts should focus (Collier, 2007).

Violent conflict results in a loss of resources, infrastructure and essential skills and personnel. Social structures and networks are destroyed and there is an increased lack of security. Health systems are also destroyed, and take years to regenerate. The effects of conflict and ensuing poverty are reflected in health indicators such as maternal and child mortality rates, nutrition, infectious diseases (including HIV/AIDS) and mental health problems. Mitigation of conflict encompasses protection from violence, reduction in weapons circulation, empowerment of people through economic security and universal access to basic education and healthcare (Commission on Human Security (CHS), 2003).

Conflict and emergencies therefore drain resources and perpetuate poverty, yet poverty itself is a driving force for war and conflict, and often develops due to scarce or valuable resources or unequal opportunities (perceived or real). Though many countries furthest away from achieving the Millennium Development Goals (MDGs) are affected by violent conflicts, the MDGs make no mention of violence and conflict; it has therefore been argued that without addressing the broad-based issues of violence and conflict, many countries affected by conflict will be unlikely or unable to achieve the MDGs.[1]

Conflict and disability

Despite a plethora of work on the causes and effects of conflict, we still know very little about the effects of conflict on persons with disabilities (Kett and van Ommeron, 2009). Conflict, like disability, is both a *cause* and a *consequence* of poverty. There are, however, a number of assumptions that can be made: persons with disabilities will experience poverty, exclusion (including from post-conflict peace negotiations and recovery and reconciliation programmes), as well as a lack of access to rehabilitation and healthcare services.[2] These programmes and initiatives are frequently couched in a framework that separates ex-combatants (sometimes seen as war heroes) from other persons with disabilities through targeted funding for 'victim assistance'.

However, deciding who is a victim of conflict is, in itself, problematic. For example, a recent article cites a study from Northern Uganda where 99 per cent of the respondents felt they were a victim of conflict (Cevra, 2009).

> ... there are no armed conflicts where *only* individuals are injured. The social fabric in the country is broken, governing system is likely to be oppressive and dysfunctional, and entire communities are victimised by violence. (Cevra, 2009, p. 13, emphasis in original)

Nevertheless, the concept of rights-based victim assistance is relatively recent, and came into being only with the adoption of the Mine Ban Treaty in 1997. This rights-based approach was consolidated in the United Nations Convention on the Rights of Persons with Disabilities (UNCRPD), which came into force in May 2008. Article 11 of the UNCRPD specifically highlights the obligation of states under international law and international human rights law to protect and ensure the safety of persons with disabilities in situations of risk, including armed conflict. However, the Convention is not a panacea, and as the three examples below demonstrate, many challenges lie in its implementation.

The longer-term effects of disasters on affected communities are relatively under-researched, and there is even less information available regarding disability in conflict-affected areas in developing countries. In part this is due to the challenging circumstances of undertaking such research. Therefore much of the data about disability in developing countries, especially in situations of conflict and emergencies, is anecdotal and lacks a strong evidence base. It is important to note, however, that where evidence in this field has been available, it has been utilised effectively and has had a remarkable effect on policy – for example, the International Campaign to Ban Landmines, and the more recent Convention on Cluster Munitions.

While there have been some studies that look at disability prevalence in conflict-affected countries, these have largely been impairment-based, and were mainly undertaken in order to assist donors and government ministries to plan services. One such survey in Rwanda identifies the importance of the estimated rates and causes of muscular skeletal impairment (MSI) to enable the government to plan services effectively. The study gave an overall prevalence rate for MSI of 5.2 per cent across the country. Prevalence of MSI increased with age, but was similar in men and women. Perhaps most significantly in terms of service planning was the fact that 96 per cent of all cases seen required further medical intervention (Atijosan et al., 2008). This can be seen as constituting a considerable burden for an already overstretched healthcare system (Logie et al., 2008).

However, the majority of such studies do not give detailed information on income, access or other key issues that have direct relevance to the daily health and well-being of persons with disabilities in such situations. There are some exceptions to this; for example, one study that does give a broad picture of the conditions for persons with disabilities is the National Disability Survey in Afghanistan (NDSA), which aims to provide an overview of the lived experiences of persons with disabilities in Afghanistan (Bakhshi and Trani, 2006). This survey goes some way towards understanding the links between poverty and conflict, as well as offering some possible suggestions as to how and why certain groups are more vulnerable and in what circumstances. The survey demonstrates that overall, in situations of severe and chronic poverty, disability contributes toward exclusion, discrimination and poverty but is not, in and of itself, the main factor in determining how well persons with disabilities will fare in a conflict area. Significantly, this study also shows that the well-being of persons with disabilities can be tempered by other variables. For example, in Afghanistan, gender was a more significant marker of exclusion; therefore women with disabilities were at higher risk of poverty (Bakhshi and Trani, 2006, p. 59).

These findings have significant implications for post-conflict recovery programmes. They demonstrate that it is not enough to provide welfare support during and immediately after the acute phase, but that there is also a need to think about the longer-term impacts of disability in the post-conflict recovery and development phase:

> ... as households get out of poverty, households that have a disabled member will have to face more difficulties [and] need more resources in order to improve their living conditions. (Bakhshi and Trani, 2006, p. 59)

Disability and vulnerability

Violent conflict increases the overall risk of injuries and impairments to all adults and children: for example, injuries from landmines and other explosive devices; reduced access to preventative healthcare programmes (e.g. vaccinations); lack of access to healthcare services, including maternal and child health and rehabilitation services; under-nutrition and malnutrition. But persons with disabilities may also find their experiences of violent conflict heightened. As social circumstances become harder during conflict, families lose their assets, land or possessions, and people begin to make tough choices. Discriminatory and exclusionary attitudes often (re)surface as people seek to ensure their own survival. This may manifest itself in decisions about which children to continue sending to school, but also in choices about who to leave behind if families have to flee.

Previously existing supportive attitudes and structures may also be lost; for example, in Darfur, the *zakat* system – the giving of alms (one of the five pillars of Islam) – functioned to provide religious-based charity to vulnerable persons in need. This social safety net has been lost because of the conflict.[3]

There are many other challenges along the way. For example, fleeing from danger can be an additional challenge for persons with disabilities – often they are left behind in the chaos of the conflict, and even if they do manage to escape, their journey to safety may take much longer, thus rendering them more vulnerable en route. Following this, often on arrival at a camp persons with disabilities are treated as 'medical problems', requiring specialist intervention. Registration and distribution processes designed to benefit the very vulnerable may in fact (unintentionally) exclude them; for example, if camp leaders do not register all persons with disabilities in camps, as was the case in South-Western Darfur.[4] Many persons with disabilities become separated from their families, and subsequently become less independent. Children and girls with disabilities face further protection issues, as they are at increased risk of abuse (Groce, 2006). Due to their often limited capacity and lack of knowledge or experience of the humanitarian sector, disabled people's organisations (DPOs) are rarely included in planning and coordination meetings, particularly in times of crisis. This results in a perpetual lack of information, poor service coordination, and exclusion. Moreover, humanitarian and emergency organisations also continue to have a lack of understanding about disability within their programmes, despite 'mainstreaming' of information.

Additionally, persons with disabilities are usually either seen as a 'vulnerable group', or as 'war victims'. This can lead to common misunderstandings about needs, in particular around the needs for assistive devices or a focus on support and assistive devices only for those immediately affected by war. The designation of 'war victims' not only raises challenges about access to programmes, but also other issues, such as the right to compensation.

Persons with disabilities face additional challenges in the return and resettlement phase once the conflict has ended. For example, those with mobility impairments may find it difficult or impossible to travel back to areas from which they have fled, or find that they are unable to take advantage of food distribution schemes or distribution of materials to rebuild their houses because they are unable to reach distribution centres.

The challenge for many international non-governmental organisations (INGOs) and UN agencies is to ensure a balance between needs and a rights-based approach to aid and development. This has particular saliency for 'vulnerable groups', as '... the concept of vulnerability is a complex one and cannot be considered simply as a proxy for poverty' (Hemingway and Priestley, 2006, p. 58). Disability is a cross-cutting issue; yet often when disabled people are included, they are seen as a group in need of specialist expertise or a vulnerable group, not as a group entitled to the same programmes and protected by the same rights as all others.

Furthermore, there is much current debate about the effectiveness of targeted versus blanket approaches to aid delivery, and most agencies have a blanket approach to those deemed most vulnerable. However, this identification and targeting of the most vulnerable is a designation often only used for food and emergency non-food item distribution. Many extremely vulnerable people are not included in other arenas, such as immediate assessments, nor in the more general programme implementation, nor in long-term rehabilitation and reconstruction projects. Not only would this inclusion be more equitable, and more cost-effective in the long run, it is also in line with the recent UNCRPD.

In order to deliver aid effectively, there is a need to reduce vulnerability. However, it is often the case that it is easier to treat groups identified as specifically vulnerable – women, children, older adults, persons with disabilities, persons living with HIV/AIDS – with a blanket approach, rather than address the *situation* that is making people particularly vulnerable. There are other confounding factors that decrease vulnerability and enhance capacity, including: support of an extended family; social status; gender; access to other NGO programmes; government support (e.g. for war heroes). Nevertheless, this does not mean that the basic needs in the immediate post-disaster phase are not the same for everyone (e.g. shelter, food, sanitation and so forth). However, it is how these resources are provided that makes the difference; for example, making toilet facilities accessible to everyone, ensuring equitable and equal access to information and so forth. Complicating this is the question of whether targeting specific groups further exacerbates tensions and inequalities and, in fact, increases vulnerability.

It should also be acknowledged that the particular challenges that have arisen from war and conflict have also offered some unexpected opportunities. These have included raising the profile of DPOs in many countries so that they have become stronger and more active as a result of war, for example in Sierra Leone (dos Santos-Zingale and McColl, 2006).

Nevertheless, as the following three examples demonstrate, persons with disabilities continue to face ongoing challenges in the post-conflict phase.[5] The three examples illustrate examples of how persons with disabilities fare in three areas at different stages of post-conflict recovery: Darfur, still an active conflict; Sri Lanka, in the very early stages of recovery; and Sierra Leone, in the process of making the transition to post-conflict. It should also be noted that the particular challenges of implementing the UNCRPD vary according to where a country is in terms of conflict recovery: in many instances, rights-based approaches, inclusive programming, targeted aid and development may well be more readily available in the immediate post-conflict phase, when many UN agencies, multidonor trust funds, international financial institutions and a plethora of other NGOs and actors are in the field. This is substantially reduced as the country recovers from the conflict and global attention moves elsewhere. As the media glare dies down, so too can the attention to human rights, equity and justice, unless strong national and international partners have taken this on board.

Darfur, Sudan

Sudan is the largest country in Africa, with an ethnically and culturally diverse population of over 40 million.[6] The seat of government (Government of National Unity) is located in Khartoum. Sudan shares borders with nine different countries, as well as a coastline with the Red Sea. It is rich in oil and minerals, and these have been a source of considerable tensions between groups – in particular, between the dominant northern peoples and those in the south and, more recently, the west, in particular Darfur.

The history of Sudan and its conflict is complicated and protracted and there is not sufficient space to elaborate on it here. But after over two decades of civil war, the Comprehensive Peace Agreement (CPA) was signed in 2005, creating a semi-autonomous region of Southern Sudan, with substantial powers through its own government (Government of Southern Sudan), oil-wealth sharing protocols and an elected leader. There is to be a referendum in the south in 2011, to decide whether to progress to full independence or to remain a semi-autonomous region.

Donor money to finance reconstruction and development activities is channelled through two multidonor trust funds (MDTFs), one for Southern Sudan, and one for other areas of the country affected by the conflict. However, continuing conflict in the Darfur region, and sporadic outbreaks elsewhere, continue to threaten the stability and development of the entire country.

Development indicators reflect the size of the challenge ahead, as simply providing the minimum services and relief to this population is a major undertaking. Sudan was ranked number 147 (out of 179) worldwide in terms of human development in 2008.[7] Its position reflects the gross inequalities across different regions and the low status of women: maternal mortality rates are high and literacy rates are among the lowest in the world, with pronounced gender disparities. These are particularly stark in the Darfur region.

There has been ongoing conflict in Darfur since 2003, despite numerous UN Security Council Resolutions to enforce stability in the region; these have led to little improvement for the security of the civilian population. It is estimated that 200–400,000 people have been killed by government-backed armed militias known as the *Janjaweed* since the start of the conflict, and as many as 2½ million people (of whom 75–85 per cent are women and children) have been displaced by the violent campaign that deliberately targeted Fur, Zaghawa, Massalit, and other ethnic groups who were perceived to be associated with the two main rebel groups: the Sudan Liberation Army/Movement (SLA/M) and the Justice and Equality Movement (JEM).[8]

The UN International Commission of Inquiry in January 2005 concluded that rape and sexual violence were used by government forces and *Janjaweed* militias as a 'deliberate strategy'.[9] Multiple patterns of violence persist and the conflict has caused a general breakdown of law and order and led to an upsurge in looting and banditry by rebels and opportunists alike. Weapons continue to flow into Darfur in violation of a UN arms embargo. Internally displaced persons (IDP) camps have become more insecure. Armed groups have targeted UN agencies, the African Union peacekeepers, and international and local humanitarian workers. Currently there is only a small force of African Union and United Nations (UNAMID) peacekeepers in the region to protect the civilian population.

The decision by the International Criminal Court (ICC) in March 2009 to issue an arrest warrant for the Sudanese president on charges of war crimes and crimes against humanity arising out of the war in Darfur led to the immediate expulsion of ten international NGOs from Sudan, with a further three being expelled in the following days. It is argued that between them, these ten NGOs were responsible for delivering up to 70 per cent or more of the food aid to the region. Many observers and aid agencies fear that this expulsion and the subsequent vacuum will lead to a significant worsening of the humanitarian crisis (Flint and de Waal, 2009).

Given the ongoing conflict and humanitarian protection crisis in Darfur, the situation for most of the adults and children with disabilities in the region is especially challenging. Overall, attitudes by non-disabled Darfurians to adults and children with disabilities is that of charity, based on (Islamic) religious beliefs. Prior to the conflict, adults and children with disabilities were frequently beneficiaries of *zakat*, the Islamic system of charity for those seen as most in need.

However, since the conflict and a large influx of humanitarian aid, the *zakat* system has been disbanded, and most people are in a vulnerable and precarious situation. In order to assist those seen as especially in need, many agencies follow the UN High Commission for Refugees (UNHCR) categorisation of 'extremely vulnerable individuals' (EVIs) to provide blanket assistance with food and non-food items and preference in programme delivery. This group includes: orphans and unaccompanied children; female-headed households; older adults; people with disabilities; and people with mental health problems.

As noted above, in situations of chronic poverty and insecurity other factors compound vulnerability, including gender and geographical location. Therefore a blanket approach, rather than the targeting of specific individuals, means it is likely that many of the poorest of the poor will continue to miss out if they are excluded from methods to determine and assess who should be seen as an EVI (methods such as identification and registration by local Sheiks and/or identification through DPOs, if available).

Official registration can benefit persons with disabilities in a number of ways, including access to additional humanitarian aid, a reduction in healthcare bills, and free schooling. However, it is debatable to what extent these benefits are actually realised in the current context, and whether persons with disabilities perceive registration to be beneficial. In theory, the process of registration eventually links to the Ministry of Social Welfare, and is primarily undertaken by local DPOs in the field.

It is also questionable to what extent ministries actually take any responsibility for the welfare of persons with disabilities; most services are provided by organisations such as the International Committee of the Red Cross (ICRC) and Red Crescent. DPOs have limited capacity for advocacy or awareness-raising campaigns, and overall receive little external assistance as much of their previous support came from disability and development agencies that no longer operate in the region. Most support now is in kind, such as the provision of assistive devices (i.e. wheelchairs, crutches and so forth).

For most of the displaced persons with disabilities, there is a desperate need for livelihoods, food and welfare support. There are limited opportunities for income-generating activities in general within the region, and poverty is endemic. For many persons with disabilities, their main source of income comes from begging in the local marketplace. The presence of a person with disabilities within the household can put extra strain not only on finances, but also on a family's coping strategies. In some cases, families are separated during flight to a place of safety – sometimes by accident, but often because a decision is made that for the welfare of all other members of the family, who must flee quickly and survive in the unknown surroundings of a refugee camp, the person with a disability must be left behind. Some families choose to send their children to stay with relatives or friends, or leave them in orphanages.

Other protective mechanisms, such as education, are also severely curtailed. According to UNICEF, primary school enrolment in Darfur has increased from 516,000 children in 2006 to more than 976,000 in 2008, though this information is not disaggregated by gender or disability.[10] However, classes are overcrowded and there is a lack of trained teachers, materials and other resources. According to one very experienced teacher at a school in a semi-settled nomad camp, there are very few children with disabilities attending schools in the region because of parent and teacher attitudes – including common misunderstandings about disability, lack of access and assistive devices, and overall lack of support.

Though schooling is ostensibly free, there are often extra costs associated with sending children to school. Sudan has legislated free education for children with disabilities, though the extent to which such legislation is implemented in Darfur is unclear.

Access to school for a child with disabilities therefore depends on a number of factors: parent attitudes, proximity, physical access and likelihood of acceptance in class. Moreover, it seems from discussions held with teachers in the region that even if there are children with disabilities registered in school, they often do not attend school regularly; and the absence of good governance structures means that such cases are rarely followed up.

There are other non-formal education structures for children in the region, including child-friendly spaces or children's clubs, though there are few children with disabilities attending these clubs and no specific provisions made for them – for example, there are no sign interpreters for deaf children.[11] Most of the assistants at these clubs, when interviewed, thought the lack of children with disabilities was due to shame on the part of their families (in particular regarding physical disabilities) and the reactions of other children (e.g. teasing them). Few had thought about ways that children with disabilities could specifically be included in these children's clubs.

Sri Lanka

Sri Lanka is defined as a middle-income country, and is 102nd out of 182 countries in the latest Human Development Index.[12] As with Sudan, the long-running and brutal civil war between the government and the Liberation Tigers of the Tamil Eelam (LTTE) has caused uneven growth and development in the country, and is a major cause of poverty in Sri Lanka, in particular in the north and east of the country.[13] However, following an intense period of fighting between the Sri Lankan Army (SLA) and the LTTE in 2009 (in which tens of thousands of civilians were trapped in a small area that was meant to be a safe zone), the war is now officially over.

The fighting left many civilians injured or dead, and there was international condemnation as well as allegations of human rights abuses, such as the deliberate targeting of civilians and the use of civilians as human shields by both factions. The UN Human Rights Council investigated the allegations, but no action was taken.[14] On 16 May 2009, the President, Mahinda Rajapaksa, declared victory over the LTTE. On 19 May the Sri Lankan government announced the death of the LTTE leader Prabhakaran. Many countries congratulated Sri Lanka on their victory against terrorism, including India and Pakistan, and there were celebrations in the capital, Colombo.

Civil conflict in Sri Lanka increased disability
Photo: Leonard Cheshire Disability

According to various media and UN sources, because of the intense and contained nature of the fighting in the two weeks leading up to the events of 19 May, there were large numbers of casualties, mainly as a result of wounds sustained from shelling and shrapnel.[15] Many people were unable to access medical attention during the fighting, and their wounds developed secondary complications. UN staff also reported other impairments, including hearing loss and visual impairments, as a result of the continued shelling. To compound this situation, many of the civilians were malnourished due to lack of food and water in the time leading up to their arrival at the camps set up by the SLA, where the majority remained, and there were many landmine injuries as the area in which these civilian groups were trapped was heavily mined.

The actual number of casualty figures and war crimes may never be known, but the UN estimated there were thousands of civilians with injuries such as fractures, spinal cord injuries and amputations (particularly from landmines and other exploding devices), in addition to an unknown number of ex-combatants with injuries.[16] Such large numbers put a strain on the ability of hospitals and other healthcare providers to offer immediate (life-saving) medical care, but they also call into question the availability of long-term planning for post-operative care, physiotherapy and other rehabilitation needs, or for psychosocial rehabilitation.

There were already a number of INGOs working in the region due to the conflict; whilst many of these have stayed, the political situation between the international community and the Sri Lankan government has restricted both movement of aid workers to the region and the money available to carry out programmes. There are also a number of local NGOs that have been active in the region for several years, though it was unclear how much access they had to the camps at the time of writing. Additionally, there are a number of local DPOs in the region who have been active for many years but, again, their current priorities and capacity are unknown.

In distributions of non-food items (e.g. plastic sheeting, cooking utensils, etc.) in the IDP camps, extra supplies have been given to families identified as having a person with special needs.[17] The UN Office for the Coordination of Humanitarian Affairs (OCHA) reported that a vulnerable group feeding programme for economically affected beneficiaries has been redesigned as a food-for-work programme.[18]

What this information does not tell us is who is identified as a person having special needs, or as being particularly vulnerable. It also raises the question of how some programmes unintentionally exclude the very people they are designed to protect; for example, how – or if – the food-for-work scheme ensures inclusion of all marginalised and vulnerable groups. We do know that conditions of poverty, discrimination and social exclusion are more pronounced among persons with disabilities, and that situations of conflict and emergency exacerbate this (Kett and Twigg, 2007). It is certainly a matter of grave concern that only a small number of persons with disabilities and their families seem to have been reached thus far – it can be anticipated, for example, that far more than the families identified as having a person with special needs in them could benefit from extra supplies.

Even prior to the final incursions, the conflict in the north and east had left more than 350,000 people displaced from their homes. Many were, and are, still accommodated in government-run welfare centres.[19] In common with many countries, IDPs in Sri Lanka are among the poorest sections of the population, often living on less than US$1 per day, with limited access to employment, housing and education. Those IDPs who had made the decision to return to villages in the north and east often suffered dire circumstances before they fled, as there had been little investment into rehabilitation and reconstruction of conflict-affected areas. Even if the political issue of the current IDP situation is resolved, resettlement will be a long and drawn-out process, with the need for reconstructed and secure housing, hospitals and many other essential services, as well as the need to de-mine large areas.

Sierra Leone

An example of the consequences of the shift in media (and donor) attention noted above can be found in Sierra Leone, now considered a post-conflict transitional country by the World Bank. In the immediate period following the civil war (1991–2002), aid increased fourfold by 2001; however, by 2003 it had fallen by 50 per cent. Such unpredictable levels of funding make it difficult to plan and implement services, an activity particularly important in the post-conflict reconstruction and development phase (Rockhold and McDonald, 2008).

Despite some good initial progress after the war, economic growth has slowed, and Sierra Leone remains at the bottom of the United Nations Development Programme (UNDP) Human Development Index (179th), with some of the worst health indicators in the world.[20] According to the World Bank, poverty is particularly concentrated in the rural areas and semi-urban areas outside the capital, Freetown. Transportation and transport networks have been slow to improve; unemployment across the country remains high and there remains limited access to public utilities, in particular electricity.[21]

How do persons with disabilities and their families fare in these circumstances, given the strong linkages between poverty and disability? Persons with physical and psychological disabilities were noted as being among the poorest segment of the population in participatory poverty assessments conducted by the World Bank as part of the Sierra Leone Poverty Reduction Strategy Papers process, including the Country Assistance Strategy (World Bank, 2005, p. 3). According to a recent study by the

World Bank that synthesised all currently available data and information about adults and children with disabilities in Sierra Leone, persons with disabilities are discriminated against on the basis of gender and impairment throughout the workforce. For example, only 38 per cent of persons with disabilities are employed or self-employed; this drops to 31 per cent for females with disabilities, to 26 per cent for persons with mental disabilities, and drops right down to only 8 per cent of people with hearing/speech disabilities being employed. By comparison, it is calculated that 46 per cent of the general population (between 10 and 65 years old) are employed or self-employed. Furthermore, average earnings are likely to be lower for persons with disabilities compared to persons without disabilities of the same age. High rates of unemployment, as well as the conflict, have led to a significant number of adults and children with disabilities becoming street beggars, especially in Freetown (Zampaglione and Ovadiya, 2009).

In focus group discussions with persons with disabilities across Sierra Leone, most of the issues they felt strongly about – availability of food, water, utilities; lack of transport; infrastructure; and children's education – were common problems for the whole community, but are intensified for persons with disabilities.[22] Most assistance is still provided by NGOs and UN agencies, though much of this is in the process of being phased out. Moreover, Zampaglione and Ovadiya report that because of the high levels of poverty and recent conflict, disability prevalence rates should be estimated at least at four per cent of the total population, rather than the comparatively low estimates of persons with disabilities from the 2004 Census – which gave a prevalence rate of 2.4 per cent of the total population. There is also a slightly higher ratio of men to women. These authors also estimate that five per cent of households have one or more person with disabilities living in them – while reporting that information on the social and economic impact of disability at the household level in Sierra Leone is currently limited. It should also be noted that neighbouring Liberia, which also underwent conflict, has an estimated disability prevalence rate of 17 per cent (Zampaglione and Ovadiya, 2009).

As part of the government's initiative toward Education for All and achieving the MDGs, primary education is free in Sierra Leone; however, parents have to pay for materials, uniforms and other supplementary costs such as exam fees. This effectively excludes children from very poor families and children with disabilities. There are draft plans to improve access to education for children with mobility issues and to increase the number of vulnerable and disadvantaged children enrolling and staying in school through a number of initiatives, including increased accessibility, teacher training, social worker input and skills training. Most of the support for these education services is currently provided by NGOs (Zampaglione and Ovadiya, 2009).

Many persons with disabilities also legally qualify for free primary healthcare services; however, this right is not backed up by allocation of resources to support its provision. Again, access is not consistent and many services, such as rehabilitation services, are provided by INGOs. However, INGO input was largely premised on a charity, rather than rights-based, model and has led to increased aid dependency.

This problem is neither unique to Sierra Leone, nor to persons with disabilities, but is heightened by the particular mechanisms for support. In the immediate aftermath of the conflict there was a considerable focus by INGOs on the very visible war wounded and amputee groups. INGOs often moved 'colonies' of war wounded and amputees to supported camps outside of urban areas. This was because many of the camps were built on land donated by the government, often some distance from urban centres, thereby reducing opportunities for integration, schooling, shopping and employment, with subsequent problems of sustainability.

This has led to a segregation that is being reflected amongst other impairment groups in a bid to get recognition and support (see also dos Santos-Zingale and McColl, 2006). The INGOs offered rehabilitation services, prosthetics and skills training, and even built resettlement camps for the war wounded and amputees. However, little provision was made for families, and most of the support for these camps has now ceased. Some residents engage in small-scale agriculture on

All disabled people in a post-conflict country need services
Photo: Jenny Matthews/Leonard Cheshire Disability

surrounding land; others, if lucky, run small businesses, but most resort to begging. Many of the younger residents move in and out of the camps according to the season on a temporary or permanent basis, leaving behind the older adults or single female-headed households.

There is a sense that these people have been abandoned with little social support, unusable prostheses, few skills and no money. Many would like to move nearer to areas where they could find work and not be so isolated. There are also many examples of the amputees and other persons with disabilities begging in the streets of Freetown. Many of these are the youth — in Sierra Leone, young men and women with disabilities face double discrimination. They are unemployed, alienated — especially those deemed as ex-combatants — disempowered and disrespected. Young people are seen as potentially destabilising forces within society, but discriminatory and exclusionary policies and practices toward disabled youth will not make the situation any less fragile.

Another issue is that there has been limited implementation of the specific recommendations toward war victims by the Sierra Leone Truth and Reconciliation Commission (2004). A 'war victim' typically is understood as someone maimed or impaired as a result of the conflict, so only those directly affected by conflict will be eligible if the government ever provides compensation. For most persons with disabilities, social welfare and support remains limited, and is constrained by resources.

There are a number of reasons why the recommendations have not yet been carried out: these include the large welfare burden such payments would place on the state and ongoing challenges to access services — in particular, education and healthcare. But a bigger factor is the ongoing lack of any national disability legislation in Sierra Leone, despite its being a signatory to the UNCRPD.

Nevertheless, on a more positive note, whilst there has been a great deal of focus on the war wounded and amputees in the immediate post-conflict period, an unexpected outcome of the conflict has been the development of a vibrant DPO movement in Sierra Leone. Initially set up to provide emergency relief and support to disabled people during the war, often as self-help groups, many have formalised into DPOs, some of which provide livelihoods (e.g. through tailoring, blacksmithing, etc.); and some also undertake advocacy and campaigning on disability issues. The Sierra Leone Union of Disability Issues (SLUDI) is an umbrella organisation of DPOs and is actively involved in promulgating reform and the creation of disability legislation that would give disabled people more rights within society. These DPOs are specifically for adults with disabilities – children with disabilities, and their parents, are as yet an under-represented group.

DPOs have been active in campaigning to get the government to sign and ratify the UNCRPD. The current government, elected in 2007, signed the Convention and ratified it in July 2009. The government is also in the process of approving a National Disability Act; however, there has been much discussion about this and progress remains slow, hindered by parliamentary debates on the passage of the bill. Concerns also remain as to how the bill will be enforced if and when it comes into existence. The implementation and monitoring of the draft legislation is to be undertaken by a National Council for Persons with Disabilities, though many observers have raised concerns as to the efficacy of such a body (Zampaglione and Ovadiya, 2009).

Conclusions

The three examples cited above demonstrate different points along the continuum of conflict: Darfur is still an active conflict, Sri Lanka is at the very early stages of recovery and Sierra Leone is in the process of making the transition to a post-conflict country. But they all demonstrate a strikingly similar pattern: immediate health and other needs that are a challenge for UN agencies, INGOs, governments and donors to fulfil; a lack of inclusion in major areas of decision making that will affect the lives of persons with disabilities; a *blanket* approach rather than a *targeted* approach; separation of victim assistance from broader disability issues; and lack of a long-term perspective.

Zampaglione and Ovadiya's comprehensive report (2009) identifies a number of key challenges for Sierra Leone. These are listed below, and I have expanded upon them a little to show how these can be extrapolated to most immediate and longer-term situations of conflict.

1. **A lack of dedicated funding makes comprehensive long-term programming difficult.** It is also important to note that, as yet, there is no effective mechanism to assess how much donor money is allocated to disability-specific areas within mainstream humanitarian programmes.

2. **Lack of dedicated technical capacity, and over-reliance on donors and INGOs.** Again, I would add to this that there is an over-reliance on specialist NGOs and under-utilisation of DPOs, rather than mainstreaming disability across humanitarian programmes.

3. **The need for a governmental decision regarding inclusion, and what it means for policy and services.** This can be extended to most areas of mainstreaming across policies, which are often at odds with targeted approaches.

4. **Lack of political will to address disability beyond a policy framework and to execute such a framework.** In the humanitarian context, this may also highlight the issues of rights versus needs.

5. **There is a need for the government to capitalise on lessons learned through various NGO programmes and to coherently implement disability strategy based on these according to priorities identified by persons with disabilities.** Again, this can be extended to incorporate inclusion in post-conflict recovery programmes and other strategies to enhance poverty alleviation.

6. **Need to increase capacity and involvement of local advocacy and civil society organisations in the design and implementation of programmes.** This is particularly the case in humanitarian and emergency situations, where there is often mutual incomprehension.

7. **Ability to monitor government policies in line with the Convention and other legislation.** Again, this could be extended to include monitoring and evaluation of inclusion in all humanitarian aid and development programmes. However, this will require more work to develop standards and indicators.

Ways forward

It is still too early to assess the impact of the UNCRPD and, in particular, any effects Article 11 will have on the ground. Nevertheless, the Convention has drawn much greater attention to disability within the UN, especially at the level of implementing agencies, and there have been a number of UN initiatives to consolidate this, including within the humanitarian sector.[23] Disability is included as a specific cross-cutting issue in the revised *Sphere Handbook*, a key text for humanitarian practitioners.[24] Better training on the use of projects like the *Sphere Handbook* for both humanitarian staff and DPOs in conflict-affected countries will increase awareness and understanding, as well as capacity to address disability.

To break the cycle of disability and poverty within any country, a number of practical issues also have to be addressed, such as the necessity for many children of disabled parents to work in order to bring money into the household. These include difficult questions, such as how a child can attend school if their labour is the only source of income for the household; conversely, how can a parent attend a training programme if they are the sole carer for a member of the family with a disability? What are the gender implications of access to work for women with disabilities, or women related to a man with a disability (wives, daughters, sisters, etc.)?

There is research being done to examine these kinds of questions, including that done by the Leonard Cheshire Disability and Inclusion Development Centre, University College London. However, as yet there are limited means to evaluate the degree and success of such inclusion. In part this is because more research is needed on the causal links between disability and poverty, particularly in countries affected by conflict. For instance, where are the specific areas of discrimination? Are they in relationships, access to healthcare, decision-making processes or in all of these?

It should also be acknowledged that in the immediate emergency phase, targeting specific groups is challenging, and takes considerable time and effort. To deliver effective humanitarian aid, approaches that target such specific groups are needed. A combination of mainstreaming disability and specific targeting (what the Department for International Development calls 'twin-tracking'; DFID, 2000) within humanitarian and post-conflict work can lead to greater inclusion and long-term benefits for the whole community, including equality and integration. This may, in turn, even contribute to the pro-motion of security, reconciliation and reintegration in conflict-affected countries. It is vital to build on this throughout the transitional period. It is also important to build on opportunities that can emerge, including the strengthening of civil society networks and organisations to support the full and effective inclusion of persons with disabilities.

Notes

1. http://www.undp.org/cpr/we_do/conflict_prevention.shtml [Accessed 18 March 2010].

2. See, for example, Kett and Twigg, 2007; Rockhold and McDonald, 2008.

3. Trani, J. and Kett, M. *Study on Affected and Excluded Vulnerable Children in South Western Darfur. Working Paper.* London: Leonard Cheshire Disability and Inclusive Development Centre, UCL. Available online at http://www.ucl.ac.uk/lc-ccr/centrepublications/ workingpapers/WP13_Affected_and_excluded_vulnerable_children_ in_Southern_West_Darfur.pdf [Accessed 12 July 2010].

4. See note 3.

5. Data for these three countries is drawn from published resources as well as fieldwork undertaken by the author in each of these countries.

6. See note 3.

7. http://hdr.undp.org/en/statistics/ [Accessed 18 March 2010].

8. Human Rights Watch April 2008. Available online at http:// sofawarrior.blog.com/2008/02/14/human-rights-watch-calls-for- protection-of-civilians-in-darfur-conflict/ [Accessed 18 March 2010].

9. http://www.un.org/News/dh/sudan/com_inq_darfur.pdf [Accessed 18 March 2010].

10. http://www.unicef.org/infobycountry/sudan_darfuraction.html [Accessed 18 March 2010].

11. Many of these children use 'home signs' rather than formal sign language.

12. http://hdrstats.undp.org/en/countries/country_fact_sheets/cty_fs_ LKA.html [Accessed 18 March 2010].

13. http://www.worldbank.lk/WBSITE/EXTERNAL/COUNTRIES/ SOUTHASIAEXT/SRILANKAEXTN/0,,contentMDK:20133668~menuP K:287038~pagePK:141137~piPK:141127~theSitePK:233047,00.html [Accessed 18 March 2010].

14. http://ochaonline.un.org/tabid/5362/language/en-US/Default. aspx [Accessed 18 March 2010].

15. The Guardian (2009) 'The fight for survival goes on in Sri Lanka amid reports of 15,000 killed'. Available online at http://www. guardian.co.uk/world/2009/may/19/sri-lankan-war [Accessed 18 March 2010].
Amnesty International 'More civilians killed in Sri Lanka fighting'. Available online at http://www.amnesty.org/en/news-and-updates/ news/more-civilians-killed-sri-lanka-fighting-20090210 [Accessed 18 March 2010].

16. http://www.guardian.co.uk/world/2009/may/24/sri-lanka-children-civilian-casualties [Accessed 18 March 2010].

17. OCHA Situation Report: Joint Humanitarian Update – Jaffna, Kilinochchi, Mullaitivu, Mannar, Vavuniya, Trincomalee and Batticaloa Districts Report No 9, 15–30 June 2009. Available online at http://ochaonline.un.org/Default.aspx?alias=ochaonline.un.org/ srilanka [Accessed 18 March 2010].

18. See note 17.

19. Global IDP Project. Available online at http://www.internal-displacement.org/8025708F004CE90B/(httpCountries)/0BB9CBD9 90450F5F802570A7004C148F?opendocument [Accessed 18 March 2010].

20. http://hdr.undp.org/en/statistics/ [Accessed 18 March 2010].

21. World Bank Country Brief: Sierra Leone. Available online at http://web.worldbank.org/WBSITE/EXTERNAL/COUNTRIES/ AFRICAEXT/SIERRALEONEEXTN/0,,menuPK:367833~pagePK:141132 ~piPK:141107~theSitePK:367809,00.html [Accessed 18 March 2010].

22. Focus group interviews undertaken by the author over a period of time in Sierra Leone are part of the qualitative data included in a Leonard Cheshire Disability report *Disability In and Around Urban Areas of Sierra Leone* (2010). Available online at http://www.lcint. org/?lid=5136 [Accessed 12 July 2010].

23. For example, Handicap International seconded a disability focal point to UNHCR in 2008.

24. http://www.sphereproject.org/ [Accessed 18 March 2010].

References

Atijosan, O., Rischewski, D., Simms, V., Kuper, H., Linganwa, B., Nuhi, A., Foster, A. and Lavy, C. 2008. A national survey of musculoskeletal impairment in Rwanda: prevalence, causes and service implications. *Public Library of Science (PLoS)*, 3(7), 1–7. Available online at http://ukpmc.ac.uk/picrender. cgi?artid=1610910&blobtype=pdf [Accessed 18 March 2010].

Bakhshi, P. and Trani, J. 2006. *Understanding the vulnerability of Afghans with disability: livelihoods, employment, income.* In the *National Disability Survey in Afghanistan.* Lyon, France: Handicap International.

Cevra, N. 2009. Connecting the dots: victim assistance and transitional justice. *Journal for Disability and International Development,* 1, 4–11.

Commission on Human Security (CHS) 2003. *Human Security Now.* New York: UN Commission on Human Security. Available online at http://www.humansecurity-chs.org/finalreport/English/FinalReport. pdf [Accessed 18 March 2010].

Collier, P. 2007. *The Bottom Billion: Why the Poorest Countries Are Failing and What Can Be Done About It.* New York: Oxford University Press.

Collier, P., Elliott, L., Hegre, H., Hoeffler, A., Reynal-Querol, M. and Sambanis, N. 2003. *Breaking the Conflict Trap: Civil War and Development Policy.* Washington, DC: World Bank/Oxford University Press.

Cramer, C. 2003. Does inequality cause conflict? *Journal of International Development,* 15(4), 397–412.

DFID 2000. *Disability, Poverty and Development. Issue Paper.* London: DFID. Available online at http://www.dfid.gov.uk/ Documents/publications/disabilitypovertydevelopment.pdf [Accessed 18 March 2010].

dos Santos-Zingale, M. and McColl, M.A. 2006. Disability and participation in post-conflict situations: the case of Sierra Leone. *Disability & Society,* 21(3), 243–57. Available online at http://dx.doi. org/10.1080/09687590600617428 [Accessed 18 March 2010].

Flint, J. and de Waal, A. 2009. To put justice before peace spells disaster for Sudan. *The Guardian,* Friday 6 March 2009. Available online at http://www.guardian.co.uk/commentisfree/2009/mar/06/ sudan-war-crimes [Accessed 31 March 2010].

Goodhand, J. 2003. Enduring disorder and persistent poverty: a review of the linkages between war and chronic poverty. *World Development,* 31(3), 629–46.

Groce, N. 2006. *Violence Against Disabled Children.* Report for UNICEF and United Nations Secretary General's Office. Background Report for UN Secretary General's Report: Violence Against Children. New York: UNICEF/UN Secretariat.

Hemingway, L. and Priestley, M. 2006. Natural hazards, human vulnerability and disabling societies: a disaster for disabled people? *Review of Disability Studies,* 2(3), 57-67.

Kett, M. and Twigg, J. 2007. Disability and disasters: towards an inclusive approach. In *World Disaster Report.* Geneva: International Federation of the Red Cross and Red Crescent.

Kett, M. and van Ommeron, M. 2009. Disability, conflict and emergencies. *The Lancet,* 374(9704), 1801–3.

Logie, D., Rowson, M. and Ndagijie, F. 2008. Innovation in Rwanda's health system: looking to the future. *The Lancet,* 372(9634), 256–61.

Rockhold, P. and McDonald, L. 2008. The World Bank's work on mental and psychosocial health in the context of conflict affected countries: the IASC Guidelines on Mental Health and Psychosocial Support in Emergency Settings. *Intervention,* 6(3–4), 314–22.

Sierra Leone Truth and Reconciliation Commission (2004). *Final Report.* Available online at http://www.sierra-leone.org/ TRCDocuments.html [Accessed 18 March 2010].

Stewart, F. 2002. Root causes of violent conflict in developing countries. *BMJ,* 324, 342–5.

Zampaglione, G. and Ovadiya, M. 2009. *Escaping Stigma and Neglect: People with Disabilities in Sierra Leone, Africa Human Development 2.* Washington, DC: World Bank. Available online at http://siteresources.worldbank.org/DISABILITY/Resources/News- --Events/463933-1184017167861/3975400-1229373211417/ SL_PWD_Policy_Note_Jan7.pdf [Accessed 18 March 2010].

World Bank 2005. *Country Assistance Strategy for the Republic Of Sierra Leone for the Period FY 2006–2009.* Washington, DC: World Bank. Available online at http://www-wds.worldbank.org/external/ default/main?pagePK=64193027&piPK=64187937&theSitePK=52367 9&menuPK=64187510&searchMenuPK=64187283&theSitePK=52367 9&entityID=000090341_20050526085619&searchMenuPK=641872 83&theSitePK=523679 [Accessed 18 March 2010].

Further Resources and Reading

General

American Red Cross. *Preparing for Disaster for People with Disabilities and Other Special Needs* (A4497). Available online at http://www.redcross.org/www-files/Documents/Preparing/A4497. pdf [Accessed 18 March 2010].

Handicap International 2008. *Training Manual on Mainstreaming Disability in Community Based Disaster Risk Reduction along with the Facilitator's Guide.* London: Handicap International.

Rockhold, P. and McDonald, L. 2009. The hidden issue in international development aid: health and disability in conflict-affected settings in Sub-Saharan Africa. *Journal for Disability and International Development,* 1, 4–11.

Women's Commission for Refugees 2008. *Disabilities among Refugees and Conflict-affected Populations.* New York: Women's Commission for Refugees. Available online at http://www. womenscommission.org/docs/disab_fulll_report.pdf [Accessed 18 March 2010].

The report is accompanied by a resource kit for agency staff and fieldworkers. Available online at http://www.womenscommission.org/ docs/disab_res_kit.pdf [Accessed 18 March 2010].

Water, Sanitation and Hygiene

Jones, H. and Reed, B. 2005. *Water and Sanitation for Disabled People and Other Vulnerable Groups: Designing Services to Improve Accessibility.* Loughborough, UK: WEDC, Loughborough University.

A complete list of Loughborough University's Water, Engineering and Development Centre research projects is available online at http:// wedc.lboro.ac.uk/research/rsch_projects_list.html [Accessed 18 March 2010].

Education

Interagency Network for Education in Emergencies (INEE). *Including Everyone: INEE Pocket Guide to Inclusive Education in Emergencies.* Available online at http://www.ineesite.org/uploads/documents/store/INEE_pocket_guide_Final.pdf [Accessed 18 March 2010].

Websites

Harvard Project on Disability (humanitarian resources): http://www.hpod.org/resources/humanitarian-relief [Accessed 18 March 2010].

Global Campaign on Disability and Disasters: http://www.smrcorissa.org/ [Accessed 18 March 2010].

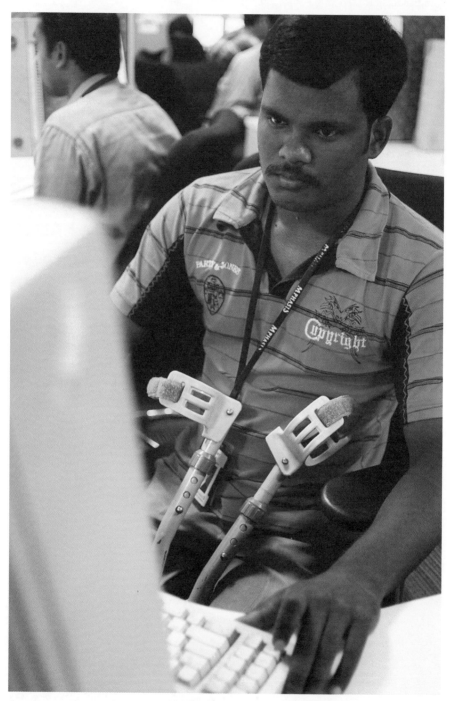

An impairment need not create disability
Photo: Gideon Mendel/Leonard Cheshire Disability

Chapter 11

Inclusive Development: Paving the Way as We Walk

Rosangela Berman-Bieler

Summary

This chapter proposes that disability is an experience that we all undergo at one time or another during the course of our life. After discussing the relationship between disability, poverty and exclusion, the author presents an inclusive concept of development. At the core of this is an understanding of the relationship between impairment and the social and economic environment that is responsible for disability. The first section describes how demographic changes impact on the issue. This is followed by a sketch of the steps needed to initiate inclusive design and to implement policies and changes to the built environment. The next section describes the research and data collection needed for improving the quality of life of people with disability, after which the author explains why planning for all is possible and how an inclusive approach to disability will enhance the lives and security of all. This is followed by articulation of the author's vision that an inclusive approach to disability will enhance general human experience and reduce poverty.

Introduction: an inclusive model of disability

The worldwide disability community says loud and proud, 'Nothing about us, without us'. By this we mean that, now an international Convention on the Rights of Persons with Disability (CRPD) has been agreed, we are ready to become central actors in implementing and monitoring it. The CRPD introduced a model that is still under construction: a social and human rights model of disability, or a proposal for a new model of society based on inclusion. The concepts and terms it employs have been used in the disability community for decades, but many of them are not equally well known or well understood in various different cultures and countries, or even by different leaders in our own disability community. As we work towards putting the CRPD into practice, we have the opportunity to renew and apply afresh these old concepts through our concrete actions. We need to build up a body of evidence as we transform theories into practice, test new approaches, adapt lessons learned in the past to the new challenges that face us, and reinvent our own roles as advocates, professionals and citizens in a society that must change to incorporate our revolutionary concepts and terms. However, it is not only society that must change in this process. We, the disability community, must also review and expand our central role in building a new society for all. To be an effective, well-coordinated force, we need to act and speak in harmony with others and aim for coherence among ourselves, agreeing on our goals and practising what we preach in promoting inclusion and equal opportunities for all.

As the CRPD notes, international cooperation can play a role in defending human rights and including persons with disability by promoting inclusive development practices. As in current practices and safeguards in areas such as gender, all programmes, projects, activities and materials generated and implemented with funding from international cooperation or financial development institutions should be inclusive and accessible to people with disability. This measure alone would initiate a virtuous cycle in favour of the construction of a society for all.

This chapter examines the inclusive development concept and approach, not only from the perspective of the disability rights movement, but from the perspective of persons living with disability, in poverty, condemned to exclusion and with no representative voice. They do not show up in meetings or statistics. They usually do not even have identity cards in societies where such things are a social and political necessity. They must be reached, helped and included in all the benefits that society has to offer.

Conceptual framework

Until now, the various models of development on offer have failed to ensure the global community's well-being and some groups have been systematically and persistently excluded from full participation in society and from enjoying the benefits of development. They include indigenous peoples, women, the elderly, people with disability, migrants or refugees, orphans or street children and those with other specific characteristics or needs, such as ethnic, racial, religious and sexual needs, and social minorities in general. These groups are known to be in situations of vulnerability.

To solve the specific problems of each of these groups, international agreements – such as human rights treaties – have been created, 'achievable' development goals have been established, advocacy groups have developed monitoring mechanisms and socio-economic indexes have been kept in different countries. The international agreements focus on only one aspect of social life at a time – such as childhood, gender, race, disability – and they have been effective in pointing to the concerns of each group when developing ways of addressing them. The most recent mechanism of this kind is the CRPD, the first Human Rights Treaty of the third millennium, which came into force in May 2008. But if society has built all these mechanisms, and if they can be effective in promoting the rights of people, why are poverty, discrimination and exclusion still so prevalent? If international law and agreements protect us from violations of our right to live in equality and diversity, why do we still have to raise awareness about inequality? In part the answer lies in the multiple roles each individual plays and thus the inherent weaknesses in single-issue approaches to realising the equal rights of diverse and complex human beings.

The time has come to reach beyond this narrow, compartmentalised approach to our different social needs. By recognising their common ground they can strengthen each other. This thought leads to proposing a global agenda based on the concept of inclusive development to provide a broad, over-arching strategy to meet multidimensional human needs. In order to improve the efficacy of development policies and for them to reach all people, they must be designed to take into account all the diverse aspects of human beings, living and functioning in society, throughout the life cycle. Universal inclusion and access are not just human rights issues and principles of equity. They must be put into practice so that human capacities and differences can be fully developed and utilised to their best potential.

The disability community can make a substantial contribution to this approach as it has always promoted concepts such as diversity, inclusion, equal opportunities, personal autonomy and solidarity. We have used our understanding in these areas to fight against our own exclusion. But it is clear that our situation will not change until the living conditions of the general population also improve. It is now time for us to use our knowledge to contribute to the building of a better society for all.

If our claim for social inclusion is the basis of our discourse, to be consistent we too must be open to an agenda that promotes more than improved conditions for people with disabilities. Our own inclusive approach to development cannot propose specific and isolated responses. It must offer comprehensive responses that encompass human diversity at the broadest dimension – from the most privileged to the most excluded – in a cross-cutting way that reaches all areas of society. This strategy, which we call inclusive development, is still being built. It takes into account the contributions and experiences of the widest possible range of social sectors and actors. In this chapter I outline some of the ways in which development can put in place a truly inclusive society. I describe and analyse this concept from the disability perspective, expanding it to embrace various segments in society, especially groups in situations of vulnerability. I especially dedicate this article to those whose poverty and exclusion has rendered them invisible, but who we know are out there, everywhere.

If human rights are our main instrument for making people aware of others' suffering and mobilising them into action, it is the development agenda that moves these rights from simple words on paper into actions that impact on the lives of persons: when they wake up, have their breakfast, lunch and dinner, go to school or to work, form their families, participate in the community, go to a football game and kiss their children goodnight. The concept of citizenship implies a law plus an actor. In this article I show how we can build our concept of citizenship.

Poverty and disability in Latin America and the Caribbean (LAC)

Much has been said about the vicious circle of poverty and disability. Conservative estimates indicate that there are more than 650 million people living with a disability, of whom around 400 million live in the global South. This number is expected to increase by 120 per cent in the next 30 years in developing countries and by 40 per cent in developed countries. Poverty is correlated with about 80 per cent of disabilities (UN Enable, n.d.; World Bank, 2007).

In LAC about 90 million people live in poverty (OAS – Organization of the American States, 2006). Nearly 82 per cent of those with disabilities in Latin America are poor and in most of these cases, poverty also affects their families The *PENDIS Disability Study* (Republic of Panama, 2006) in Panama indicates that 11.3 per cent of Panamanians have disabilities, a figure that rises to 13.5 per cent among indigenous people and in rural areas. One in three households (33.6 per cent) contains a person with a disability and of these 90,730 households are poor. The 2000 Census in Brazil estimates the prevalence of disability in the country is 14.5 per cent. Of the nearly 25 million Brazilians with a disability, 27 per cent live in situations of extreme poverty and 53 per cent are poor. The *ENDIS Disability Study* (INEC, 2003) in Nicaragua records that in households with one or more members with a disability, the caregiver is generally a female family member (mother, child or grandmother) and caregiving takes up to 10 hours a day, preventing the caregiver from engaging or remaining in the workforce or having a personal life. In Uruguay, a recent study of 500 people living below the poverty line who are direct beneficiaries of the Poverty Emergency Plan[1] revealed that 25 per cent of the households have at least one person with a disability and, in many cases, there are two or more. In Honduras, people with disabilities have an illiteracy rate of 51 per cent compared to 19 per cent for the general population (Pizzolitto, 2006). In countries for which data are available, less than 20 per cent of disabled people receive insurance benefits. In Ecuador, for instance, 84 per cent of disabled people have no insurance benefits. In Argentina the unemployment rate of disabled people is estimated to be close to 91 per cent (Inter-American Development Bank, 2006).

Poverty and social exclusion affect millions of people worldwide, preventing human development and a decent quality of life. In countries of the South this situation affects over half the population. Exclusion and poverty, together with inequality, diseases, insecurity, environmental pollution and degradation, and inappropriate housing design are public hazards affecting many people directly and threatening everyone indirectly. To sustain and promote well-being and socio-economic growth under a rights approach, the concept of human functioning and inclusiveness must be incorporated into development programmes.

A conceptual basis for inclusive development

Inclusive development involves designing and implementing actions and policies for socio-economic and human development that promote personal autonomy and dignity for all, regardless of their social status, gender, age, physical or intellectual condition, race, religion or sexual orientation, in harmony with their environment. Inclusive development includes and empowers the rights and capacities of all dimensions of human life (economic, social, political and cultural) in all their diversity and specificity, based on the search for and guarantee of universal access, equalisation of opportunities and equity.

The approach does not discriminate against difference: it promotes and celebrates diversity and transforms it into an advantage, a value, an opportunity and a right. In fact, inclusive development approaches the struggle against poverty by aiming to give visibility to groups in situations of vulnerability, placing them within the scenario of public programmes and policies in general.

Disability is a social condition

According to the CRPD,

Persons with disabilities include those who have long-term physical, mental, intellectual or sensory impairments which in interaction with various barriers may hinder their full and effective participation in society on an equal basis with others (UN, 2006).

Like most other recent documents and instruments in this area, this definition is rooted in a social model of disability. It affirms that disability results from the interaction between people and their physical, cultural and social environment. The different conditions that limit aspects of human functioning thus become a disability only if people face barriers in accessing their physical surroundings or social goods. Thus, having a disability depends less on our individual characteristics and more on the way in which our society organises services to the general population.

Functioning depends on the limitations of the environment

The following equation illustrates the environment's impact on the relationship between disability and functional diversity/limitation from a mathematical perspective (Medeiros, 2005):

> Functional limitation x environment = disability

If an environment without barriers is given a value of zero, the result of this equation will always be zero, whatever weight we give to disability.

> Functional limitation 1 x environment 0 = 0 disability
> Functional limitation 5 x environment 0 = 0 disability

However, if the environment has a value higher than zero the functional impact of disability on the person's life increases in proportion.

> Functional limitation 1 x environment 1 = 1 disability
> Functional limitation 5 x environment 5 = 25 disability

Anyone in the world can acquire any type of disability. It may be present from birth or it may develop during a lifetime, through malnutrition or disease, accident, violence or abuse, or environmental conditions. As people's life expectancy increases, so too does their probability of acquiring a disability. The number of people living with disability is growing, but their quality of life varies greatly, depending on the respect given to human rights in their country and its socio-economic development. In most developing countries statistics are scarce and incomplete. Reliable information is needed on the prevalence of disability in the population for public surveillance and action to promote equal opportunities and rights to be put in place.

The World Health Organization estimates that in countries of the South, health, education, social protection and other such services reach only two to three per cent of the people with disabilities who need them. Those who can obtain these services are found in specialised institutions and are centralised in the main urban areas. As general public services are commonly not available to them, the invisible 97–8 per cent of people with disabilities and their families are systematically excluded and condemned to poverty.

Disability is part of the life cycle

If we understand disability to be the result of interactions between people with different levels of functioning and the failure of societies to take these differences into account, we see that disability is an integral part of each individual's life cycle. Looking beyond the typical areas of disability (motor, hearing, visual and mental/intellectual), we see that people in general face disabling conditions at one time or another in societies that do not appreciate and respond to human diversity. Here are some examples:

- a baby that needs to be carried in someone's arms or pushed by someone in a pram

- a child who cannot reach the top button in the lift

- someone who has had an accident and is trying to climb stairs

- a woman in late pregnancy trying to catch a bus

- an illiterate citizen who needs information from the internet

- a foreigner who doesn't speak the local language trying to ask the way

- someone who can't read the small print instructions on his medication

- an elderly woman with arthritis who cannot turn and open a round doorknob.

Any of these situations could have happened or could happen in the future to any one of us. In such a situation we have a disability.

The impact of demographic and epidemiological changes

Recent worldwide demographic and epidemiological changes are creating new population profiles. People live longer than before. Although advances in science and technology have a big impact on the prevention and treatment of disease, chronic, non-communicable diseases are increasing. Inadequate maternal and child care, especially in developing countries, leads to high levels of death or permanent disability. Death and chronic conditions are caused by accidents and urban and domestic violence, especially in economically active populations. Old and new forms of diseases, including HIV/AIDS, especially when associated with poor living conditions, generate permanent illnesses that lead to increased poverty and social exclusion.

Ageing is related to disability

The latest demographic surveys reveal that the most disabilities are concentrated in people aged 70 years and over, when people may start to experience some kind of progressive or permanent functional limitation. This increase in life expectancy does not prolong youth: it prolongs ageing and its natural consequences. Worldwide, at least among populations less affected by poverty, the third age – and its consequent tendency to disabilities – is expected to last for 20 years or more. The demographic ageing of populations is a new and irreversible phenomenon in human history. It is becoming increasingly widespread in both developed and developing societies. The growing awareness of the significance of an ageing population and its implications has led governments to start addressing its impacts, particularly on social security, the cost of health and the provision of social support services for the elderly and their families.

The result of population ageing is that disability lies at the core of the life cycle, not only for those of us who will live longer than the previous generation, but also for the current cohort of older adults who make up nearly one third of the population in some countries. For sustainable national economic and social development, the rights of the growing population of older persons to an autonomous, decent quality of life must be met.

The effect of non-communicable diseases on disability

The current health profile of the world's population shows that non-communicable diseases (NCDs) like heart diseases and asthma are on the increase. Most NCDs lead to functional limitations and disability, particularly among those living in poverty who may lack the knowledge and the money to access medical services. From conception to implementation, public health programmes need to be inclusive, offering universal coverage with equitable and sustainable access. This includes the needs of groups that currently fall beneath the radar of health services, those marginalised by their poverty or lack of access to the system as a whole and those who live in social exclusion. Prominent among these are older adults and persons with disability of all ages, who are especially vulnerable to NCDs.

Ageing and the need for personal assistance and care

The deteriorating health that accompanies ageing leads to increasing numbers of persons living with a disability. This has a major impact on their families, which have a key role in communicating with, caring for and providing services to older adults. For ageing individuals, the family becomes the main – and sometimes the only – focus of their social relations, especially when their health deteriorates and their loss of functional capacities leads to permanent disabilities. While most people whose autonomy is limited depend on the family in order to live, families worldwide have been shrinking for some time, meaning that there are fewer children to care for more parents (Goicoechea, 2004).

Various public health policies in different countries are incorporating an improved quality of life in their programmes for older adults (Kalache, n.d.), an approach based on quality, accessibility and equity, in working towards a model of comprehensive care and of strengthening primary health care. Others intending to follow this example should focus on this population group's multidimensional needs.

Sexual and reproductive health, sexually transmitted diseases and HIV/AIDS

People with disability have often been and remain excluded from information, education and communication programmes on sexual and reproductive health and have poor access to service networks, including those on HIV prevention as well as AIDS care efforts, because it is presumed they are not sexually active and are thus at no risk of infection. The truth is that the chances of men and women with disabilities becoming victims of sexual violence are higher compared to the non-disabled population. Also, due to medical advances, people living with AIDS have a higher survival rate; as a consequence of this, there are an increasing number of disabilities secondary to the disease itself or its pharmacology treatment (World Bank, 2007).

Mainstreaming disability in programmes and policies

If society is composed of people with diverse ways of functioning; if disability is part of everyone's life cycle and can appear at any moment during life; if we tend to acquire functional limitations as we age and the world population is ageing more and more; if many causes of disability are a result of poverty and exclusion; if people with a disability tend to be invisible to or excluded from the system; then we should ask who and where these people are, so that specific public policies can be designed to address their needs.

The answer is that they are everyone and everywhere. But whoever we are, where we live and how we function, we are all equal citizens with equal rights and responsibilities under the law.

Developing special services to address the specific needs of each social group is much more expensive and less cost-effective than having general public policies and programmes designed and implemented for everyone. Only an inclusive approach to development can adequately address this issue.

Box 11.1 The cost of special services

A rural mother takes her 10-year-old daughter with Down's syndrome to her local health clinic, because the child has flu and a fever. The doctor says he cannot help them because he cannot treat disabled people, and she must take the child to an institution in the capital that specialises in children with disabilities. This is an example from Panama of what happens when priority is given to centralised specialised services, instead of bringing knowledge and services to the primary healthcare level. This could happen in any country, in any part of the world, even in the North.

There are many more people with low and moderate disability than those with severe disability. In most cases they can receive primary care attention at the community level with simple and cheap interventions. The World Health Organization has developed a community-based rehabilitation matrix[2] for good practice, which offers excellent advice that can be used in any health clinic primary care programme throughout the world. Without receiving the necessary attention, a small functional limitation can become a severe disability, and generate social and economic exclusion.

The universal design principle and strategy

The Rio Charter[3] states that the purpose of universal design is to meet the needs of the widest possible range of users. The world needs successful policies for social participation and access to goods and services to minimise the marginalisation of excluded groups such as people living in poverty, those belonging to certain cultural, racial, or ethnic groups, people living with different types of disability, very obese, tall or short people, pregnant women, children, and those who are also excluded for other reasons.

By putting in place universal or inclusive design, we will develop environments, services, programmes, policies and technologies that appreciate the diversity of human functioning, aim to promote individual autonomy, are equitable and accessible to all and can be used safely – to the greatest extent possible – without having to be specifically adapted or readapted.

The seven original principles of universal design (UD) were first compiled by its advocates in 1997: the principles are copyrighted to the Center for Universal Design, School of Design, State University of North Carolina at Raleigh, USA. They are as follows.

- Equitable Use: The design does not disadvantage or stigmatise any group of users.

- Flexibility in Use: The design accommodates a wide range of individual preferences and abilities.

- Simple, Intuitive Use: Use of the design is easy to understand, regardless of the user's experience, knowledge, language skills or current concentration level.

- Perceptible Information: The design communicates necessary information effectively to the user, regardless of ambient conditions or the user's sensory abilities.

- Tolerance for Error: The design minimises hazards and the adverse consequences of accidental or unintended actions.

- Low Physical Effort: The design can be used efficiently and comfortably, and with a minimum of fatigue.

- Size and Space for Approach and Use: Appropriate size and space is provided for approach, reach, manipulation and use, regardless of the user's body size, posture or mobility.

Redefining universal design

As a new development in the field, Edward Steinfeld, Researcher and Professor at the Center for Inclusive Design and Environmental Access (IDEA Center), School of Architecture and Planning, University at Buffalo, one of the authors of the concept of universal design, jointly with Gary Scott Danford, PhD, of the same university, proposed a redefinition of the principles of UD, based on an evolutionary approach, recognising differences in context and resources and taking into consideration the *International Classification of Functioning, Disability and Health (ICF)*[4].

The new approach was introduced in their paper presented at the 'Living in Our Environment, the Promise of ICF' Conference (Steinfeld and Scott Danford, 2006) and has been strongly supported by stakeholders. In the new definition, it is proposed that the principle should not only support function, but also social participation and social identity, social roles and cultural fit, as an evolutionary approach of the ideals of UD. The proposed redefinition of UD does not exclude the prior concept or principle, but expands them towards the new understanding of human functioning.

Under this new approach to UD, the proposed concept is:

> Universal Design of products, environments and systems is 'a process of continual improvement to improve function, activity and participation for all users, and to extend those benefits to an ever broader population within the context of resources available'.

The redefined seven principles that guide the new UD perspective are:

- Body Fit: Accommodate people with the widest range of body sizes, postures and movement abilities.

- Comfort: Ensure that the physical demands for safe and effective use are within the comfort range of the widest range of people.

Paved rural roads improve access for everyone
Photo: Jenny Matthews/Leonard Cheshire Disability

- Awareness: Make information needed for safe and effective use readily available in all necessary forms.

- Understanding: Ensure that the methods of operation and use are easily understood by all users.

- Identity: Support the construction of positive self-image and social status for the end users.

- Social Integration: Support effective participation by all and reduce barriers between user groups.

- Cultural Appropriateness: Ensure that differences in cultural values and attitudes are respected.

The poverty and exclusion that affect millions of persons worldwide prevent human development and a decent quality of life for all. They affect more than half the world's population and threaten everyone. From this perspective, universal design strategies can help to reduce poverty and usher in a future world that is more inclusive and sustainable for everyone.

Inclusion is vital in all health programmes
Photo: Upul Wasantha Liyanage/Leonard Cheshire Disability

Inclusion: from design to implementation

As the principles for universal design are user-centred, persons with disabilities and other users or beneficiaries must be involved in decision making and consulted during all steps of the development process, from the planning and design stage to implementing, monitoring and evaluating the final service or product. When programmes, services and infrastructure are inappropriately designed, inaccessibility and exclusion are perpetuated. It is unacceptable for public funds to be used to design and construct programmes incorporating barriers. This approach is explained and recommended by the CRPD.

Furthermore, sustainable inclusive development must be incorporated in the overall policies of each country in fields such as health, education, work, housing, childhood and youth, infrastructure and social protection. It is only in this way that each country's development strategies and policies will cover the needs of all of its inhabitants. For example, instead of addressing disability with separate measures added on to a system that is already hugely complex, it can be integrated into existing programmes and projects, improving their design and overall service quality and thus enhancing the likelihood of their subsequent success.

389

- Any new STD or AIDS education programme should be designed so that that the information is available to everyone, including those who are deaf, blind or have intellectual disabilities, to name only some of the socially invisible groups in situations of risk.

- The curriculum of any new teacher training programme should address the whole potential student population and comprise different learning styles in order to meet the needs of all.

- Any new item of built infrastructure should be accessible to people with limited mobility, such as the elderly, pregnant women and wheelchair users, and it should include specific signing for – among others – the blind and deaf.

- Any investment in information and communication technologies should ensure that these tools are completely and widely accessible (to people who are blind, visually impaired, deaf, have communication difficulties and so on) so that no one is excluded from the opportunities generated by the development of knowledge-based economies.[5] (For most people, technology makes life easier. For people with disability, it makes life possible.)

As it is more cost-effective, the inclusive approach holds out greater prospects of sustainability for public services and makes for higher and more equitable levels of social and economic development.

It is important to remember that mainstreaming strategies do not imply the dismantling of existing special or disability-specific services, policies and programmes. The main focus should be on expanding the attention and bringing into general settings the valuable expertise that currently is mainly concentrated in specialised institutions and services. As in every other area, there are situations where special attention is required, and the social safety nets for disability are still very scarce where they are most needed. But the effort to expand access and outreach to the majority of persons living in poverty and with a disability must be by investing in new approaches at the community level, through general existing and new services.

Research, monitoring and evaluation for social inclusion

To improve proposals and action for social inclusion in public policies, a scientific evidence base is urgently needed. Existing indicators of social inclusion in research programmes and initiatives, as well as overall public policy monitoring and evaluation mechanisms and instruments, can be used to do this. Programmes and policies can be monitored for their inclusivity using equity indicators (whether they serve groups and situations where vulnerability is greater), and qualitative and quantitative indicators. The former examine the improved quality of interventions, the latter their greater coverage of groups that are typically excluded.

During a presentation entitled *Poverty and Disability*, at a World Bank Workshop held in Nicaragua in 2005,[6] economist and sociologist Marcelo Medeiros, former Director of the UNDP International Poverty Centre in Brazil, pointed out that:

> Our efforts to research disability generally relate to examining the characteristics of individuals. The information we gain from population censuses, for example, have to do with the numbers of individuals with certain attributes. We use these attributes to measure disability and to relate it to other characteristics of individuals, such as education, age, etc. However, it is increasingly clear that disability is not an attribute of the individual, but rather the outcome of individuals and the surroundings they live in. The characteristics of individuals can tell only part of the story; the other part has to do with the characteristics of the environments where individuals live. Therefore, we need to start studying environments and learning about the real impact they generate on social participation.

> Medeiros goes on to say:

> We do not know much about how processes of discrimination occur in schools, about the barriers to access in transport systems, about how workplaces are able to absorb people with different

characteristics, etc. Gathering this type of information is crucial to how we can offer better recommendations for designing effective public policies. Just as in populations censuses, we are beginning to include questions on disability alongside the traditional questions on age and sex, so we need to create a culture of bringing in questions about inclusion in health services, in the same way as we ask about installations, numbers of doctors and nurses, etc. (Medeiros, 2005)

Following this line of reasoning, all data collection, analysis, monitoring and evaluation of public projects and actions should incorporate indicators of people with disability and other groups in situations of vulnerability. To assess the level of inclusion that a service achieves, the conditions of access to the physical environment must be measured, as well as the characteristics of the individuals and the services. Thus, the infrastructure consisting of the surroundings and transport, information and communication, need to be taken into account.

Planning for all

To begin creating inclusive practices, all public and private organisations should ensure that accessibility and universal design are built into the following.

- Every physical structure, from the design through to final construction and maintenance.

- Every public service.

- All print, audio-visual and digital materials used for information, education and communication.

- All requests of application, offers of employment and public tenders (explicitly mentioning equal opportunities for contractors with disabilities and specifying the requirement of accessibility aspect to be met in the services being contracted).

- All instruments for monitoring and evaluation of public projects, programmes and actions, through the adoption of disability-related indicators.

- Outreach approaches to communities, households and individuals where, as a result of poverty or other conditions leading to exclusion, the service is not available.

- All budget allocation.

Not only must health, education and social protection services and facilities be accessible. People with disabilities have daily needs that are not necessarily related to their disability, such as:

- going to a bank to pay their bills

- taking their children to school or for vaccinations at the local health centre

- voting, working, eating, going to the movies, taking vacations, socialising

- participating as full citizens in their own community, like everybody else – because they *are* everybody else!

How to meet the costs of social inclusion

Governments and development agencies making financial decisions must allocate funds for accessibility, universal design and inclusion aspects in their regular budgets. The costs should be accounted for in each item of the budget, not sourced from a special fund set aside explicitly for this purpose. To mainstream social inclusions, it must be integrated from the design all the way through to implementation. Funds must be allocated for this purpose in the same way as for other areas. The additional costs of providing universal access to infrastructure, for example, are estimated to be less than one per cent at the design and planning stage. The cost of renovation or retrofitting is much higher. Most countries have the know-how and technical standards as well as the capacity to implement solutions to social exclusion. All that is needed is to take them into account in public policies.

Incorporating a social inclusion approach across sectors

To succeed in incorporating a social inclusion approach into government programmes and actions, the isolation and invisibility of sectors such as disability, mental health, older adults and others affected by poverty and exclusion must be broken. This can be achieved only when steps are taken to incorporate inclusion into public policies. In this way universal inclusion is transformed from an issue only related to human rights into an operating approach, so that the capacities and diversities of our species can be used to produce better quality of life and dignity for all.

Key points to be considered

Other key components for social inclusion of people with disability, recommended by the UN Commission for Social Development's Secretariat Report, *Mainstreaming disability in the development agenda* (Commission for Social Development, 2007), are as follows.

- Disability mainstreaming requires efforts to broaden the equitable participation of persons with disabilities at all levels of decision making.

- The involvement of civil society, including organisations of people with disabilities, in national and international mechanisms is an essential ingredient in effectively guiding this development agenda.

These strategies can be adopted immediately:

- taking advantage of the existing opportunities

- proposing inclusive strategies in the programmes and projects that are being implemented

- developing capacity among the different actors and stakeholders to include wider inclusive projects and programmes

- establishing mechanisms for people with disability and their families to participate and collaborate in implementing, monitoring and evaluating these programmes.

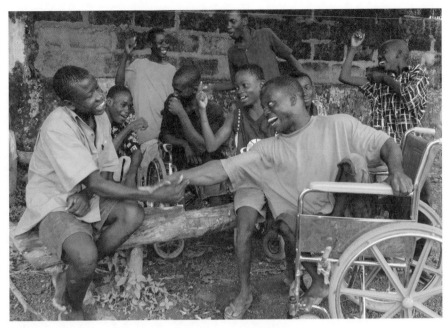

Universal inclusion develops everyone's capability
Photo: Jenny Matthews/Leonard Cheshire Disability

Alliances for the generation of an inclusive culture

When we understand that the only way of solving disability issues is by solving the issues of all excluded groups jointly; when social justice becomes a reality for each and for all, we will begin to construct a truly inclusive society, outside the ghetto and in alliance with those who have similar vision and goals to ours. That is when social transformation will really begin to be felt.

The Convention guarantees rights to people with disability that fit in with the definition adopted to determine its beneficiaries. Besides protecting individuals, this binding instrument is starting to generate a positive wave of interest and actions that may to some degree neutralise the current vicious circle of poverty and disability. This will also influence public opinion and open new opportunities for rethinking and assessing existing programmes and policies, improving their quality and outreach, and benefit society as a whole.

Conclusion

We need to recover the impetus, the leadership and the knowledge that the disability community worldwide has generated over the past 30 years, which culminated in the CRPD, and invest in new alliances to implement the rights of persons with disabilities in an inclusive development approach. As in any other area, knowledge exists in institutions and special services that should now become reference centres. It can also be gathered from communities and families that have been able to care for their members without being handed any recipe or supplementary means, instead using their own creativity and a commitment to finding solutions to their problems.

We must not be intimidated by not having all the answers, the evidence and the data; nor that enough best practices have not been demonstrated, evaluated and selected for scaling up. This is not to say that we do not need them: on the contrary, we have to work hard and fast to build up this kind of information. However, to do it, we need to be given the opportunity to take risks, experience the new, and put our theories into practice. When people have a vision, they find a way of making it a reality. Humankind got to the Moon before creating the internet, and we will get much further if we have a clear vision that will help us build a better way forward. What we cannot afford is to keep investing in old paradigms. We must focus on the new, even if it seems Utopian at present. By establishing the right alliances and focusing on inclusion as our main vision and goal, we can accept the provocative challenge and, at the same time, offer our most generous gift to society: 'Nothing about us, without us'.

Notes

1. Plan de Emergencia Nacional, Republic of Uruguay, 2005.

2. *Community Based Rehabilitation* available online at http://www.icdr.utoronto.ca/Files/PDF/5e8bd08c35c67dd.pdf [Accessed 22 March 2010].

3. *Rio Charter* available online at http://siteresources.worldbank.org/ DISABILITY/Resources/280658-1172672474385/RioCharterUnivEng. doc [Accessed 22 March 2010].

4. *International Classification of Functioning, Disability and Health (ICF)* available online at http://www3.who.int/icf/icftemplate.cfm [Accessed 22 March 2010].

5. The model of digital inclusion should provide for the just and democratic distribution of information society resources and make a clear option for groups currently excluded. That means youth policies with gender equity, respect for the disabled and for the issues of race and ethnicity (adapted from Selaimen and Lima, 2003).

6. World Bank Workshop: *Alliances for Inclusive Development,* Managua, Nicaragua, 2005.

References

Commission for Social Development 2007. *Secretariat Report, Mainstreaming Disability in the Development Agenda.* Geneva: UN Commission for Social Development.

Disabled Peoples' International. Available online at http://v1.dpi.org/ lang-en/index.php? [Accessed 26 February 2010].

Goicoechea, L.M. 2004. *Banco de Datos de Discapacitados: Informe de avances.* Montevideo, Uruguay: INE.

INEC 2003. *Encuesta Nicaraguense de Discapacidad (ENDIS).* Nicaragua: Instituto Nacional de Estadisticas y Censos.

Inter-American Development Bank 2006. *Country Reports on Disability Statistics.* Available online at http://www.iadb.org/sds/soc/ publication/gen_6191_4114_e.htm [Accessed 19 March 2010].

Kalache, A. n.d. *The Global Age-friendly Cities Project.* Geneva: WHO. Kalache is the WHO Senior Advisor on Global Ageing. Available online at http://www.who.int/ageing/publications/Age_ friendly_brochure_English.pdf [Accessed 19 March 2010].

Medeiros, M. 2005. *Poverty, Development, and Disability.* Paper read at the Workshop on Alliances for Inclusive Development. Nicaragua: World Bank.

OAS 2006. *Declaration of the 'Decade of the Americas for the Rights and Dignity of Persons with Disabilities (2006-2016)'*, adopted in Santo Domingo, Dominican Republic, on June 6.

Pizzolitto, G.V. 2006. *Informe sobre personas con discapacidad en Nicaragua.* Available online at http://www.iadb.org/sds/doc/soc-NicaraguaInformeDiscapacidad-s.pdf [Accessed 26 February 2010].

Republic of Panama 2006. *Presentation of the Results of the Study about Prevalence and Characterization of the Disability.* [*Encuesta Nacional de Discapacidad* (PENDIS).] Panama: National Secretary for the Social Integration of Persons with Disability.

Selaimen, G. and Lima, P. 2003. Infoinclusão e os novos horizontes da inclusão social. *Revista do Terceiro Setor*, 15 July 2003.

Steinfeld, E. and Scott Danford, G. 2006. *Universal Design and the ICF*, presented at the Living in Our Environment, the Promise of ICF Conference in Vancouver, June 4–5. Available online at http://futureofud.wikispaces.com/UD+and+the+ICF [Accessed 19 March 2010].

UN 2006. *UN Convention on the Rights of Persons with Disabilities.* New York: UN.

UNDP and the Government of Brazil. *International Poverty Centre.* Available online at http://www.undp-povertycentre.org [Accessed 26 February 2010].

UN Enable/CRPD. Home page. Available online at: http://www.un.org/disabilities/default.asp?id=33 [Accessed 19 March 2010].

World Bank 2007. *Social Analysis and Disability: A Guidance Note.* Washington, DC: World Bank, March.

Further Reading

Websites on UN Convention: http://www.un.org/disabilities/ convention/ [Accessed 26 February 2010].

Astorga-Gatjens, L.F. 2004. *Incluyendo a las personas con discapacidad en las Políticas de Desarrollo.* Washington, DC: Inter-American Development Bank.

Astorga-Gatjens, L.F. 2008. *Módulos de Capacitación sobre Derechos Humanos y Discapacidad, Desarrollo Inclusivo e Incidencia política, Proyecto Hacia una Centroamérica Inclusiva para las Personas con Discapacidad.* (Training Modules on Human Rights and Disability, Inclusive Development and political advocacy, Project: Towards an Inclusive Central America for Persons with Disability). Joint initiative, Inter-American Institute on Disability and Inclusive Development and Handicap International. Sponsor: PAIRCA-FLACSO-Costa Rica.

Astorga-Gatjens, L.F. and Laitamo, S. 2007. *Manual básico sobre desarrollo inclusivo* (Basic manual on inclusive development), joint publication, 1st ed. Managua, Nicaragua: Inter-American Institute on Disability and Inclusive Development/Handicap International. .

Astorga-Gatjens, L.F. and Laitamo, S. 2008. *Por un mundo accesible e inclusivo: Guía básica para comprender y utilizar mejor la Convención sobre los derechos de las personas con discapacidad* (For an accessible and inclusive world: Practical Guidelines for a better understanding and utilisation of the Convention on the Rights of Persons with Disability), joint publication, 1st ed. San José, Costa Rica: Inter-American Institute on Disability and Inclusive Development/ Handicap International.

Berman-Bieler, R. 2000. Inclusion and Universal Cooperation, *Disability World*, Issue 2, April-May. Available online at http:// www.disabilityworld.org/April-May2000/IntntalNews/Inclusion.htm [Accessed 26 February 2010].

Berman-Bieler, R. 2001. *Including Disability Issues on the Poverty Reduction and Social Development Agenda: Raising awareness and defining a role for development agencies working in Latin America and the Caribbean.* Inter-American Development Bank (TC-00-08-02-8-RG), October.

Berman-Bieler, R. 2002. Including Disability in the Development Policy Agenda. In *Building an Inclusive Development Community: A Manual on Including People with Disabilities in International Development Programs.* Eugene, OR: MIUSA/USAID.

Berman-Bieler, R. 2003. *El Movimiento de Vida Independiente en Latinoamerica.* (published in English and Spanish). Madrid, Spain: Movimiento de Vida Independiente: Experiencias Internacionales, Fundación Luis Vives.

Berman-Bieler, R. 2004. In Hershey, L. *Survival Strategies for Going Abroad: A Guide for People with Disabilities.* Eugene, OR: MIUSA.

Berman-Bieler, R. 2005. 'Desarrollo Inclusivo: Un Aporte Universal desde la Discapacidad'. In *Foro Montevideo-Diversidad.* Montevideo, Uruguay: UNESCO, p. 26.

Berman-Bieler, R. 2006. *Cómo utilizar a la Convención Internacional sobre Derechos de las Personas con Discapacidad como instrumento para el desarrollo inclusivo?* Paper Project South, UN ad hoc Committee, International Disability Convention, New York, August.

Berman-Bieler, R. 2007. *The Independent Living Movement in Latin-America: From Human Rights to Inclusive Development. Lessons Learned from the Brazilian IL Experience.* UN DESA Expert Group Meeting: Ensuring Access through the Convention on the Rights of Persons with Disabilities, New York, February.

Gil, M. and Meresman, S. 2006. *Signs of Health for All: HIV/ AIDS and People with Disabilities.* Washington, DC: World Bank. Available online at http://siteresources.worldbank.org/ EXTLACREGTOPHIVAIDS/Resources/AIDSMGSM.doc [Accessed 26 February 2010].

Handicap International and the Christoffel-Blindenmission (CBM) 2008. *Making PRSP Inclusive*. Washington, DC: World Bank. Available online at http://www.making-prsp-inclusive.org [Accessed 26 February 2010].

International Disability Rights Monitor (IDRM) 2004. Available online at http://www.ideanet.org/cir/uploads/File/IDRM_Americas_2004.pdf [Accessed 26 February 2010].

Medeiros, M., Diniz, D. and Squinca, F. 2006. *Cash Benefits to Disabled Persons in Brazil: An Analysis of the Continuous Cash Benefit Programme. Working Paper*. Brazilia: World Bank, UNDP/International Poverty Center – Brazil.

Meresman, S. 2006. *Inclusive Education: An Experience in Uruguay*. Washington, DC: World Bank.

Meresman, S. and Gil, M. 2006. SIDA y personas con discapacidad: el lenguaje de la prevención. *Revista El Cisne, Argentina*, January. Available online at http://www.aidsportugal.com/article.php?sid=5954 [Accessed 26 February 2010].

Meresman, S., Siede, M.A., Gil, M., Astorga-Gatjens, L.F., Berman-Bieler, R. and Devandas-Aguilar, C. 2005 *Alianzas para un Desarrollo Inclusivo: el rol de las organizaciones de personas con discapacidad en el proceso de Metas del Milenio* (in Spanish and English). Washington, DC: Health and Human Development Department, World Bank.

Meresman, S., Siede, M.A., Gil, M., Astorga-Gatjens, L.F., Berman-Bieler, R. and Devandas-Aguilar, C. 2006. *Plataforma del Desarrollo Inclusivo* (Inclusive Development Platform). Washington, DC: World Bank. CD Rom, CNOTINFOR Portugal. Available online at http://www.cnotinfor.pt/pdi/ [Accessed 26 February 2010].

Ministry of Health, Brazil. *National STD and AIDS programme*. Available online at http://www.aids.gov.br/main.asp?LangID=en [Accessed 26 February 2010].

Mont, D. 2006. *Disability in Conditional Cash Transfer Programs: Drawing on Experience in LAC.* Washington, DC: World Bank.

Siede, M.A. and Tamargo, M.dC. 2005. *La política social en la emergencia: reflexión crítica sobre los programas de ingreso y la noción de contraprestación de salud desde la mirada de las mujeres beneficiarias.* Available online at http://iniciativasyestrategias.org/experiencias.html [Accessed 11 March 2010]

UN Convention available online at http://www.un.org/disabilities/convention/ [Accessed 22 March 2010].

UN Economic and Social Council 2007. *Report: Mainstreaming Disability in the Development Agenda.* UN Economic and Social Council, E/CN.5/2008/6, 23 November. New York: ECOSOC.

UN Enable. *Rights and dignity of persons with disabilities.* Available online at http://www.un.org/disabilities/ [Accessed 26 February 2010].

World Bank 2007. *Social analysis and disability – a guidance note.* Washington, DC: World Bank. Available online at http://siteresources.worldbank.org/DISABILITY/Resources/280658-1172606907476/SAnalysisDis.pdf [Accessed 26 February 2010].

World Bank. *HIV/AIDS in Latin America and the Caribbean.* Available online at www.worldbank.org/lacaids [Accessed 26 February 2010].

World Health Organization. *About the Community-based Rehabilitation (CBR) Matrix.* Geneva: Disability and Rehabilitation Team, WHO. Available online at http://www.who.int/disabilities/cbr/matrix/en/ [Accessed 26 February 2010].

Index